10/28/97

DATE			

map pages missing- CL 8/22/19

Tales of Giant Snakes:
A Historical Natural History of Anacondas and Pythons

John C. Murphy and Robert W. Henderson

Krieger Publishing Company
Malabar, Florida
1997

Original Edition 1997

Printed and Published by
KRIEGER PUBLISHING COMPANY
KRIEGER DRIVE
MALABAR, FLORIDA 32950

Copyright © 1997 by Krieger Publishing Company

Library of Congress Cataloging-In-Publication Data

Murphy, John C., 1947–
    Tales of giant snakes : a historical natural history of anacondas and pythons / John C. Murphy and Robert W. Henderson.
      p. cm.
    Includes bibliographical references and index.
    ISBN 0-89464-995-7 (hc : alk. paper)
    1. Anaconda. 2. Indian python. 3. Reticulated python. 4. African rock python. I. Henderson, Robert W., 1945– . II. Title.
QL666.063M87 1997   96-54033
597.96—dc21   CIP

10 9 8 7 6 5 4 3 2

DEDICATION

J. C. M.

To the following individuals who,
knowingly or not,
inspired, encouraged, and/or provided direction
to my interest in herpetology

RONALD A. BRANDON
RAYMOND L. DITMARS
ROBERT F. INGER
CARL F. KAUFFELD
LAURENCE M. KLAUBER
SHERMAN A. MINTON
RAY PAWLEY
NORMAN RICHARD
HAROLD K. VORIS

R. W. H.

To the following individuals who,
knowingly or not,
inspired, encouraged, and/or provided direction
to my career in herpetology

ROSS ALLEN
RAYMOND L. DITMARS
WILLIAM E. DUELLMAN
HENRY S. FITCH
CARL F. KAUFFELD
LAURENCE M. KLAUBER
MAX A. NICKERSON
ALBERT SCHWARTZ

CONTENTS

LIST OF ILLUSTRATIONS

FIGURES

MAPS

ACKNOWLEDGMENTS

Sherman A. Minton reviewed an earlier version of the manuscript in its entirety, offered constructive criticisms, and provided additional sources of information. We are grateful for the time he devoted to the manuscript. Don Wheeler provided original artwork for this project, and to him goes our sincerest appreciation. For comments on various sections of the manuscript we are grateful to Bea Bourgeois, Robert W. Bourgeois, Rose M. Henderson, Ky Henderson, William F. Holmstrom, Joan Jass, James Kranz, Kirsten Kranz, Kathy Murphy, Robert Oestreich, Ray Pawley, George Ulrich, and Don Wheeler. For assistance with interlibrary loans we are appreciative of the efforts of Gerry Boe (Plainfield High School) and Susan Otto (Milwaukee Public Museum). Joanne Peterson (Milwaukee Public Museum) provided additional assistance in matters photographic. Carter Lupton (Milwaukee Public Museum) and Char Samarawera provided French translations; Judith Hirt translated Kopstein's article. For sharing their important and enlightening firsthand experiences with us, we extend an enthusiastic thank you to William W. Lamar and María del C. Muñoz. For information on the diet of *Python reticulata* we are most grateful to Richard Shine. The maps and graphs are due to the competent and generous efforts of John S. Parmerlee, Jr. and Robert Powell. William F. Holmstrom, Laurie J. Vitt, and Mark O'Shea kindly allowed us to use their photographs, and O'Shea sent prepublication python accounts from his book on the snakes of Papua New Guinea. William Branch provided photos and accounts of a man killed by an African python. Brian Groombridge was kind enough to furnish a manuscript copy of his 1991 book with R. Luxmoore. Marty Appel of the Topps Co., Inc., gave permission to reproduce the Frank Buck bubble gum cards. We are grateful to the IUCN for providing information on exports of giant snakes and to the Society for the Study of Amphibians and Reptiles for permission to reprint a large portion of Branch and Haacke (1980). At the Field Museum, Alan Resetar provided a variety of assistance and suggestions, and Michelle Calhoun and Benjamin Williams assissted with locating literature, photocopying, and photography; Nina Cummings and Margarie Pannell provided photographic and line art permissions. Henderson is grateful to Bill Holmstrom, María Muñoz, Jesús Rivas, and John Thorbjarnarson for introducing him to the world of *Eunectes murinus*.

Finally, we thank Elaine Harland and Elaine Rudd of Krieger for their conscientious proofreading and copyediting. Their patient, painstaking efforts with a difficult text caught many errors that we missed; naturally, any mistakes that remain are our responsibility only.

CHAPTER 1

INTRODUCTION

> We all . . . stared ahead at a large dark object, resting on a moon-lit sand bar
> not far from us . . . An indescribable feeling of awe seized me. I knew now that I
> was to face the awful master of the swamps, the great silent monster of the river,
> of which so much had been said, and which so few ever meet in its lair . . .
>
> The snake was coiled, forming an enormous pile of round, scaly monstrosity,
> large enough to crush us all to death at once . . . I felt as if I were spellbound, un-
> able to move a step farther or even to think or act on my own initiative.

So wrote Algot Lange (1912:226–229), describing his encounter with a common
anaconda (*Eunectes murinus*) in Brazil. The anaconda is one of at least four snake
species that often attains a length in excess of 20 feet (6.1 meters), and to which the
term "giant" has been subjectively applied. Lange's account is only one of many
highly descriptive encounters humans have had with giant snakes and which they felt
were worthy of sharing. While not all accounts are so colorful as this, it is, conversely, remarkably tempered in comparison to many others. What it does illustrate
is common attitudes toward snakes in general and, perhaps, giant snakes in particular. Here is an organism capable of (1) arousing great curiosity and almost reverence in humans ("the great silent monster"); (2) repulsing the people looking at it
("scaly monstrosity"); (3) killing a group of men simultaneously ("crush us all to
death at once"); and (4) apparently casting a spell, leaving the writer immobile ("unable . . . to think or act on my own . . ."").

But Lange is not alone. Despite the fear and repugnance many people feel toward
snakes, most will, albeit grudgingly, admit to an uneasy curiosity about them. The
"reptile house" is often the most popular building at zoos. Visitors apparently are
drawn to snakes as long as they know they can view them safely, that there is no risk
involved despite the potentially dangerous nature of some snakes, and that there will
be no contact with them.

Although snakes are usually considered of little economic importance in most human economies, people in some cultures use their hides and meat, and some traditional medicines are derived from them. However, snakes have played a much more
subtle role in many cultures, where they are viewed as symbols of life, death, and
magic; they are sources of aesthetic inspiration and stimulate curiosity about nature.
No matter how repulsed a person may say they are by snakes, curiosity can overcome the learned feelings of revulsion.

This book focuses primarily on what is known about four species of snakes reported to exceed 20 feet in length and which we collectively refer to as "giant" snakes:

Common (or Green) Anaconda (*Eunectes murinus*)

African (or Rock) Python (*Python sebae*)

Indian (including Burmese) Python (*Python molurus*)

Reticulated Python (*Python reticulata*)

Four other python species, the Papuan python (*Apodora papuanus*), the scrub python (*Morelia amethistina*), the Oenpelli python, (*Morelia oenpelliensis*), and the olive python (*Liasis olivaceus*), from the Australasian region, may reach or exceed 20 feet in length, but so little is known about them and, consequently, so little has been written about them, that we refer to them only occasionally. We do not consider the common boa constrictor (*Boa constrictor*) of Mexico, Central, and South America, one of the most famous snake species in the world, a giant snake. The previously accepted record length for this species was 18.5 feet, but it has now been demonstrated that this record was based upon a specimen of the common anaconda (Chapter 3), and the actual record size for the boa constrictor is probably somewhere in the neighborhood of 16 feet (about 5 meters) or less.

Our objectives in writing this book were threefold: (1) to review the historical, usually anecdotal, literature that discusses giant snakes and present this literature in an informative yet entertaining manner; (2) to use the same literature as a resource of information that, when used carefully and objectively, will shed new light on the lives of the giants (especially when employed in concert with the scientific literature); and (3) to increase the reader's appreciation for snakes in general and the giants in particular.

Methods

Our approach to locating literature for inclusion in this book was a combination of the haphazard and the systematic. The scientific literature can be quite methodically searched by way of publications such as *The Zoological Record* and *Wildlife Review,* and, more recently, by computerized databases. Other sources (books intended for mass consumption) were located by a hit-or-miss method with a beneficial snowballing factor. That is, over a period of about 10 years, Murphy routinely examined books that might conceivably contain reference to giant snakes. This was done at the Field Museum of Natural History and at public and school libraries in the Chicago area. More recently, Henderson used the same approach at the Milwaukee Public Museum and the Central Public Library in Milwaukee. Interlibrary loans through the Milwaukee Public Museum also expedited our search for additional information. Often one source made reference to another source, thereby increasing the size of our database. Colleagues, aware of this project, also made suggestions for additional sources of information. Originally, our source material comprised 500–600 references. Once we began sifting through it and made our initial outline for this book, we started to eliminate sources that were redundant or that we felt contributed nothing to our knowledge of the giants, or were completely devoid of any entertainment value. We were eventually left with more than 300 references and they comprise the basis for what follows.

Some outrageous and amusing stories are presented here, although they were not meant to be so by those who wrote them. Others are clearly fictionalized to a point where they could not be taken seriously by anyone with a working knowledge of basic snake biology. Exaggerated stories are repeated here for entertainment value and to point out the unreasonable fear of snakes lingering in the minds of many, and also to demonstrate how writers have used snake stories to enliven rather routine accounts of their experiences in tropical countries.

Nevertheless, there is much here to take seriously, too. If read with a critical eye, many of the stories do provide some insight into the biology of giant snakes, especially when examined as a whole rather than each individually (e.g., attacks on humans by giant snakes in nature are rare, but when death and ingestion occurs, it is almost invariably a child who is the victim; adults appear more formidable, are rarely attacked, and are too large to swallow). It is important to consider the context in which the events occurred and also who is telling the story: an "adventurer" hoping to create a *macho* image and sell some books, or a trained biologist who is more interested in providing an objective account of an event for its scientific value.

Tall tales should not be confused with the folklore and myths of tribal peoples who use stories to pass cultural ideals from one generation to another. Unfortunately, the myths of various cultures have sometimes been translated into tall tales and sorting them out is not always possible. Where mythological stories involving giant snakes are available we have included them, but it is often difficult to distinguish between the role of real giant snakes in the stories, and mythical animals that exist only in the minds of the people who created them. Thus, while this book is about giant snakes, it is also about human attitudes toward animals and nature.

The natural history (ecology and behavior) of giant snakes is, in general, poorly known, and this book will raise more questions than it will answer about giant snake biology and life history. Information on basic snake biology is used to hypothesize about the unanswered questions, and provide the reader, unfamiliar with snakes, a perspective on snake natural history. However, giant snakes are well-known as captive animals, and a surprising number of people keep them as pets. Therefore, their feeding behavior and reproduction in captivity are relatively well documented.

Extinction due to human greed is a problem faced by many organisms as we approach the 21st century and giant snakes are no exception. Although the African python is probably not overexploited, the common anaconda, Indian python, and the reticulated python may very well be. A staggering number of snakes are turned into leather products each year (Chapter 8) and it is entirely possible that they are doomed to an early extinction at the hands of humans. Habitat loss is probably a more serious problem, however. As forests are cut, swamps are drained, and grasslands are plowed into fields for agriculture, the habitat for many species disappears. Although several of the giants do well in ecologically disturbed habitats (e.g., cultivated areas which often have high densities of rodents, an excellent food source for many snake species), their proximity to humans and the customary response by humans toward snakes in general does not bode well for the future.

Snakes are no less important in nature's scheme than any other animals. Despite their lack of fur or feathers (the usual requisite criteria for gaining public support when the future of an animal species is threatened), we feel that snakes in general, and the giants in particular, are every bit as spectacular and worthy of awe (but not the same kind of awe expressed by our quotable friend Lange) and admiration as are giant pandas, bald eagles, or mountain gorillas.

A Note on Taxonomy

The scientific names given to animals are in a perpetual state of flux, and the giant snakes are not exceptions to this sometimes confusing name game. Despite the frustration that may accompany this flux, scientific names are, in reality, extremely useful. Among other things, they provide people with a common language when discussing a particular organism. That is, the scientific name of the common anaconda is *Eunectes murinus* regardless of whether you live in Chicago, Caracas, or Calcutta. On the other hand, a single species of snake may be known by a dozen or more common (vernacular) names (e.g., anaconda, reticulated python) from throughout its range. Even people who share a common language may not know that they are talking about the same species because they are using different vernacular names. The common names that we are using for the giant snakes in this book would probably be meaningless to most people who live in the countries in which the giants live.

In the chapters that follow, we have adopted the taxonomy used by Kluge (1991, 1993). For the most part, we do not try to differentiate populations at the subspecies level with the exception of, in some instances, the African python. Following is the taxonomy used for giant (or in some cases, potential giant) species discussed in the chapters that follow, and the rationale for our decisions.

Boidae: Boinae

Eunectes murinus. Two subspecies are sometimes recognized (*E. m. murinus* and *E. m. gigas*), but the diagnostic characters distinguishing the two taxa are suspect. We do not designate subspecies in the anaconda accounts.

Boidae: Pythoninae

Apodora papuanus. No subspecies are recognized.
Liasis olivaceus. Two subspecies (*L. o. olivaceus* and *L. o. barroni*) are recognized, and *L. o. barroni* apparently attains a much greater size than the nominate subspecies (Barker and Barker, 1994:35). Our few references to this species do not designate subspecies.
Morelia amethistina. Two subspecies are occasionally recognized (*M. a. amethistina* and *M. a. kinghorni*), but the characteristics used to distinguish them are not diagnostic, and most authorities do not recognize subspecies.
Python molurus. Two subspecies are recognized, *P. m. molurus* (West Pakistan, through India to Nepal and south to Sri Lanka) and *P. m. bivittatus* (Burma and southern China, south into Indochina; Hainan; Borneo, Celebes, Java, Sumbawa); we have made no attempt to distinguish the two subspecies in the accounts of *P. molurus*.
Python reticulata. No subspecies are recognized.
Python sebae. Two subspecies are recognized (*P. s. sebae* and *P. s. natalensis*); based on their parapatric distribution and the definition of the categorical rank species (Frost and Hillis, 1990), Kluge (1993:8) suggested they might be considered separate species. We have opted to treat them as a single species, but have referred to them by their subspecific names whenever possible in order to provide potential evidence for future workers investigating their status.

Conversions For Weights and Measures

Because we have quoted material from hundreds of sources, and because those sources were not uniform in whether they used the metric or U.S. system of weights and measures, we here present a few conversions for those who wish to make them.

To Convert	Into	Multiply By
centimeters	inches	0.3937
feet	meters	0.3048
hectares	acres	2.471
inches	centimeters	2.540
kilograms	pounds	2.205
kilometers	miles	0.6214
meters	feet	3.281
miles	kilometers	1.609
pounds	kilograms	0.4536

We made no attempt to verify or correct the spelling of place names that appear in quotes.

Brazilian Amazon is accurate and nicely phrased. Giant snakes are restricted to the land masses between about 33° north latitude and 32° south latitude (Map 1) in areas where conditions are favorable for hunting, assimilating prey, and reproducing. Snakes living at low elevations at or near the equator can maintain a relatively constant body temperature day and night throughout the year because air and water temperatures do not fluctuate greatly. Moving to higher latitudes, or to higher elevations, wider daily and annual temperature fluctuations make it more difficult for giant snakes to maintain the body temperature needed for optimal maintenance. Habitats for big snakes range from semidesert, grasslands, and temperate forests to tropical rain forest, and all show a preference for proximity to water.

The Common Anaconda, *Eunectes murinus* (Map 2)

The common anaconda, *Eunectes murinus*, inhabits many river systems in tropical South America. It is known from Colombia, Venezuela, Guyana, Suriname, French Guiana, Ecuador, Peru, Brazil, and Bolivia. It also occurs on the island of Trinidad which lies just north of the mouth of the Río Orinoco, off the coast of Venezuela. The distribution of this giant occurs between approximately 10° north latitude and 26° south latitude (Henderson et al., 1995).

Anacondas are usually closely associated with rivers and lakes; they are undoubtedly the most specialized giant snakes in their habitat preference. During the exploration of the Venezuelan llanos, a seasonally inundated, tropical savanna, Alexander von Humbolt (1885, 2:312) wrote,

> Enormous water-snakes, in shape resembling the boas, are unfortunately very common, and are dangerous to Indians who bathe. We saw them almost from the first day we embarked, swimming by the side of our canoe; they were at most twelve or fourteen feet long.

Famed tropical naturalist and writer William Beebe (1946:20) described his encounters with anacondas in Venezuela where they were found in jungle but never very far from the river, and often coiled on a branch over the water or on the sandy shoreline.

R. R. Mole (1924:237), a Trinidad journalist and naturalist, described their habitats on the island:

Map 1. The world distribution of snakes known to exceed 20 feet or 6.1 meters.

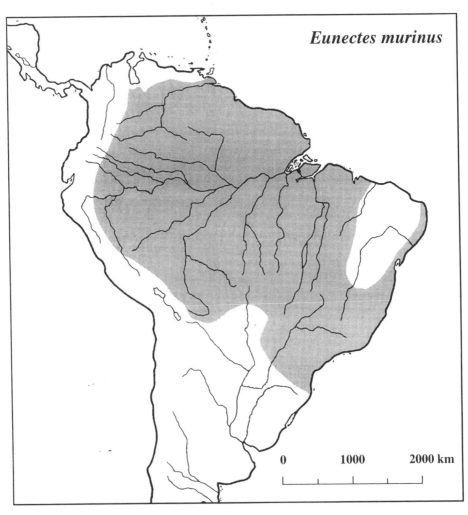

Eunectes murinus

0   1000   2000 km

Map 2. The distribution of the anaconda, *Eunectes murinus*.

The adult anaconda lives in pools and sluggish rivers. One lived in such a locality in the village of Guaico and was frequently to be seen on the bank basking in
the afternoon sun, and the school children used to stone it from the opposite
bank. It would disappear for quite long intervals, and then be unexpectedly found
in its old haunt. Occasionally the young ones may be seen in bushes or on the
branches of small trees in the vicinity of water.

Bacon (1978:293) reported that Trinidad anacondas have adapted to human-
modified environments, and it has become common in abandoned gravel pits which
are rich in waterfowl, frogs, and fish.

Quelch (1898:298) described the habitat of *Eunectes murinus* in Guyana:

> These snakes are aquatic, and frequent especially the grassy and sheltered
> banks in the still reaches of the streams and the wide open water savannahs. They
> are widely distributed in all such places over the colony, and are abundant in all
> the coast districts, more especially in the sheltered waterways close to settlements
> in the country where poultry is reared. Small specimens up to about 10 feet in
> length are very frequently caught in such shallow waters, and larger specimens
> are met with occasionally lying on the grass or tree-stumps by the waterside . . .

Thorbjarnarson (1995) described the habitat of anacondas in an area of the
Venezuelan llanos that is almost treeless except along rivers, and which exhibits dramatic seasonal changes in precipitation, from a wet season landscape that is nearly
inundated to one that is parched and dotted with shallow muddy pools in the dry season. During the dry season anacondas are encountered in the drying pools, along the
banks of streams and rivers, and in holes and burrows along stream and river banks.
Like many widespread snake species, they also exploit human modifications of the
habitat: They occasionally seek shelter under large slabs of concrete in culverts. The
anacondas tend to be very localized in the dry season, but according to Thorbjarnarson
(1995: 45), once the rains begin "the snakes spread out into the newly flooded
savannas." Researchers working at the site described by Thorbjarnarson found that
the anacondas had "well-defined" home (or activity) ranges, and that "The snakes
would move around these home ranges, with certain areas being preferred during
certain times of the year, mostly depending on water level."

In summary, we quote Strimple (1993:27):

> *Eunectes murinus* is seldom found far from water and inhabits a large variety of
> aquatic environs including rivers, large and small streams, lakes, ponds, swamps,
> ditches, temporary pools, and flooded forests. In addition, they can be found in ar-
> eas such as dry forests and the llanos, primarily because of the abundance of surface
> water in these areas for 6–8 months of the year during the wet season . . .

The Indian Python, *Python molurus* (Map 3)

The Indian subcontinent (Pakistan, India, and Sri Lanka) as well as parts of southeastern Asia (southern China to Thailand, Java, and possibly Borneo and Sulawesi)
are home to the Indian python, *Python molurus*. The western limit of its distribution appears to be the Indus Valley. Minton (1966:118) wrote,

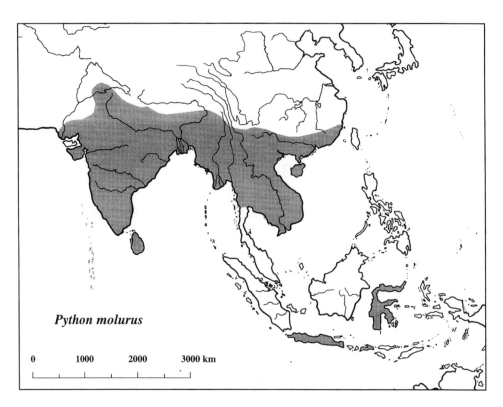

Map 3. The distribution of the Indian python, *Python molurus.*

In West Pakistan, according to information from professional snake hunters and natives, pythons are found at scattered localities throughout the Indus delta and the lower valley, mostly east of the river northward at least to Nawabshah District. I also have reports from Haleji Lake and from near Dureji in the upper Hab Valley.

Swan and Leviton (1962:139) reported it from central Nepal, the western Himalayas, Sikkim-Darjeeling and the plains of northern India adjacent to Nepal; and expect it to occur in eastern Nepal. They describe the species' distribution as Panoriental. And a recent reference (Deyang, 1986) suggests it occurs as far north as Qingchuan County of Sichuan Province, China.

Its apparent absence from the Malayan Peninsula is somewhat of a puzzle. Cox (1991:107) noted that it occurs in all the provinces of Thailand, except those found south of Chumphon; this region is at the base of the Malayan Peninsula. The species occurs on Java and, while there is some evidence of its occurrence on Borneo, its presence there is highly questionable; however, Zhao and Adler (1993) included Borneo in its range. There are also reports of it from Sulawesi. Humans may play a role in the distribution of this snake: Flower (1899:655) wrote,

> In recording localities of animals, such as this python, which form part of the usual stock-in-trade of itinerant native jugglers, it behoves [sic] collectors to be very careful and to make all possible enquiries regarding them: for instance, when in Bangkok I once was brought a live *Python molurus,* but found by questioning that it had been brought there by an Indian conjurer from Bombay.

Pope (1961:29) proposed that the hiatus in its distribution may result from humans carrying it to islands beyond its natural distribution, and the subsequent establishment of feral populations. Minton and Minton (1973:199) concurred.

Wall (1912:474) gave the upper altitudinal range of *Python molurus* as about 6000 feet in the Himalayas and other Indian ranges. This places it on the border between the middle and upper monsoon forests.

Python molurus is tolerant of a wide range of environments. For example, Whitaker (1978:8) wrote about this species in India:

> Pythons are found in estuarine mangrove forests, arid scrub jungle and the cool dense rain forests up to 2000 m above sea level . . .
> . . . Though able to adapt to many types of environment, pythons require large undisturbed areas to hunt and hide in. They live in rocky clefts and caves, abandoned mammals burrows, hollow trees, dense water reed and mangrove thickets, usually near permanent water source.

He later (Whitaker, 1993:88) reported that in the urbanized districts of Burdwan and Hoogly, *P. molurus* is absent, but that it survives in the marshlands adjoining Calcutta. They sometimes live in large drains; and in January 1992, a 3 m *P. molurus* was collected in the city and presented to the Calcutta Zoo. He concluded that for a snake as large as *P. molurus* to survive in a country of a billion people, it must adapt to changing habitats. And, fortunately, *P. molurus* adapts. Where not disturbed by humans, it is found from sea level to over 2500 m in rain forests, mangrove swamps, savanna, scrub forests and semideserts.

Dhungel (1983:7–8) described *Python molurus* habitat in Nepal's Chitwan National Park:

> Their preferred habitat is tall grasslands of Kans and Dhadi where the sloth bear digs a lot of holes in search of food like roots and tubers of many plants and thus makes a nice place for the pythons to shelter. These holes are up to four feet deep and slant in at an angle. Grasses and dhadies surround the hole and provide a natural camouflage. During the monsoon season these pythons prefer to live under dead trees or logs.

Minton (1966:117) described its habitat in Pakistan:

> These big snakes inhabit marshes, gallery forests, and rocky ledges if near to marshes or streams. Their refuges are burrows near the edge of water, dense clumps of vegetation, large rotted logs, caves, and ruins. . . . Although slow on land, they swim rapidly and apparently spend considerable time in the water. I saw a large one that had been gaffed by fishermen in the Nara Canal.

Python molurus habitat on Sri Lanka was described by Deraniyagala (1955:7).

> It inhabits swamps and remains submerged in the water with only its head exposed and will spend intervals of ten minutes under water without any provocation. It frequently drifts out to sea upon forest trees swept down by rivers and specimens have been taken on the small islands off Trincomalee.

Pope (1935:73–74) summarized what is known about this giant's distribution in China:

> Mell . . . found this snake only in the lower, coastal region of Kwangtung, but the specimen killed near Yenping was discovered in the mountains above that city at perhaps an altitude of 1000 feet, and it is therefore probable that *molurus* inhabits the lower mountains of southeastern China and is not confined to the immediate coastal region. The altitude of Yuankiang is 1500 feet, so *bivittatus* reaches at least that altitude in southern Yunnan. . . .
>
> Mell . . . mentions the preference of *bivittatus* in Kwangtung for the vicinity of water, while I observed that Hainan specimens climbed even large trees with great agility. . . .

In Hong Kong, Reitinger (1978:51) noted its presence in the jungle of hilly areas near water, and reported one captured in Hong Kong harbor after it had dived and surfaced several times.

Wall has two widely quoted accounts of this snake, one published in 1912, the other in 1921. The two accounts are almost identical. Wall (1912:453) stated,

> For the most part the Indian python is a jungle inhabitant. It may be met with in the interior of the densest forest tracts, or in sparser forest growth such as that which clothes the rocky slopes of many low hills. Where jungle is not available it most usually attaches itself to rivers and jheels, especially the former. In jungle areas it is frequently observed in trees and at times at some considerable elevation aloft. It climbs stealthily but well, and having established itself in the branches secrets itself. . . .

Microhabitats and how they are used are poorly known for most of the giants, *Python molurus* is the exception. Floodplains of the Indus Valley are studded with rocky knolls topped with stone tombs or watch towers. Pythons use these for hibernation between late October and February, and Minton and Minton (1973:200) report four snakes being dug out of these kinds of situations during dormancy. Drainage pipes also apparently serve as an attraction to these snakes; Minton and Minton (1973: 200) and Whitaker (1993:88) describe this species taking refuge in these structures. Two papers by Indian researchers provide more detail on the microhabitat of *Python molurus*. Bhupathy and Haque (1985:449–450) and Bhupathy and Vuayan (1989:384) describe the den ecology of pythons in north-central India's Keoladeo National Park, Bharatpur, Rajastan. On 30 November 1985 they observed four pythons entering a porcupine hole. Observations throughout the night revealed that this microhabitat was also used by about 50 bicolored leafnosed bats, *Hipposideros fulvus*, and they observed porcupines and pythons passing in the night without any aggression or apparent interest in each other. Porcupines occasionally become python prey, but the limited space within the burrows they share may restrict predation by the snake. The whitebreasted kingfisher, *Halocyon smyrnensis*, was also seen nesting successfully at the entrance to python holes; and a jackal, *Canis aureus*, entered a python hole three times in January 1986, possibly looking for a place to give birth. Tracks and droppings of the striped hyena, *Hyena hyena*, were observed at the entrance of several python holes.

Forty-six python points, or dens, were identified inside the Park; 41 of these were on land and 5 were in aquatic situations. The distribution of python dens on land was dependent upon the availability of freshwater, abandoned porcupine burrows, and saline patches. However, in marshy areas the snakes preferred hollow trees and termite mounds. Saline patches with abundant porcupine burrows were preferred by the pythons. Eighty-three percent of the burrows were situated in slightly elevated areas. Perhaps because such sites have comparatively loose soil making excavation by the porcupine easy, and elevated sites protect burrows from flooding during the monsoon. Vegetation surrounding the python dens consisted mainly of scrub bushes, and the snakes were seldom seen in woodland or open grassland. Maximum cover was provided by *Salvadora* spp. At 39 den sites studied, *S. persica* was seen in 29, and it offered more than 50% of cover at 28 dens. The preference for *Salvadora* spp. may be due to its dense foliage, which shades the burrows during the hot summer.

Additionally, Goodyear (1994:71–72) radio-tracked a single, 2.7 meter (total length) *Python molurus* at Shui Hau, Lantau Island, Hong Kong, for 24 days. During that time, the snake's (which was displaced 170 meters from the point of capture) "home range" was 12.3 hectares with a maximum linear dimension of 550 meters (based on the minimum convex polygon method). On 2 days it was partially or completely submerged in abandoned rice paddies, and on three occasions daytime retreats were inside large rock piles or in vegetation near rock walls of cultivated orchards. The snake spent the majority of tracking days near the beach in a dense *Pandanus* thicket. Virtually all of the area that the snake occupied was under some kind of cultivation.

The Reticulated Python, *Python reticulata* (Map 4)

This is a snake of Southeast Asia. On the western perimeter of its distribution it occurs in the Nicobar Islands, and is found in Burma, down the Malayan Peninsula and across Indochina (Thailand, Cambodia and Vietnam); it occurs in the Philippines, throughout the Indonesian Archipelago, Borneo, Sulawesi, and eastward to Ceram and Timor. It apparently does not enter China, even though accounts at the turn of the century reported that it occurs in southern China. Pope (1935:72) believed Chinese records were based upon captive specimens transported into China by humans. Similarly, Wall (1926:90) suggested that this species is a frequent stowaway on ships.

> This python has at times been transported in ships from port to port. One . . . was found in Rangoon in a cargo ship. One was discovered in the cargo of a ship in Bombay that had arrived from Moulmein. Another was found in the hold of a ship in the Albert Docks, London, in 1907, and transferred alive to Regent's Park [London Zoo].

Because of this snake's popularity in circuses and sideshows it may be transported out of its normal range. O'Shea (personal communication) reported an 18-foot specimen abandoned by a US/Guam circus owner in Papua New Guinea (Figure 2–1).

Considering the number of islands they have colonized, reticulated pythons are apparently experts at dispersal. Occasionally firsthand observation is possible to confirm an animal's ability to colonize new environments, and such was the case following the volcanic eruption of Krakatau in 1883. The island's forest was completely obliterated, all life was exterminated, and science was presented with the opportunity to see how long it would take life to return to the island and reestablish itself. Dammerman (1948:348–349) provided the following narrative:

> Jacobson recorded no snakes from Krakatau and made the statement that they were not observed during his stay on the island in May 1908. However,

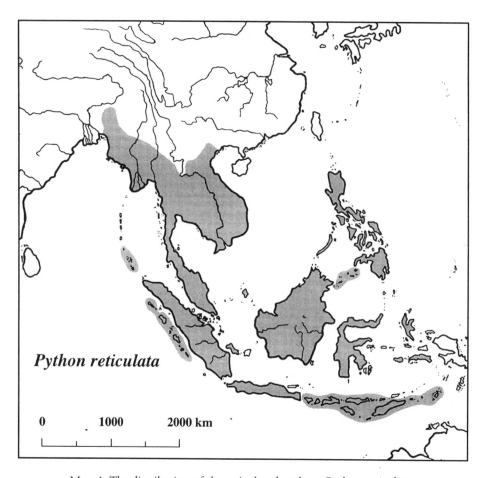

Map 4. The distribution of the reticulated python, *Python reticulata*.

shortly afterwards they must have arrived as Brun, who visited Krakatau in September 1908, in his work of 1911 published a plate showing a ravine with the explanation that at the end of the ravine a big boa constrictor was found. By 'boa' nothing else could be meant than our common python. During our visits we came upon these giant snakes on several occasions and they are present on all three islands of the group. . . . According to staff members of the Volcanological Survey pythons are also to be found on Lang Island and should occur in the cave at the southern end of the island which is only accessible from the sea-side. At our visit in December 1933, however, no snakes were to be seen there.

The reticulated python uses a variety of habitats, including those that have been dramatically altered by humans. Stanley S. Flower (1899:654–655), a British military officer and herpetologist stationed in Asia at the end of the 19th century, related the following:

This python is very numerous in the city and suburbs of Bangkok; in almost every compound of which I know the occupants, either private houses or offices, one or more pythons have been found within the last few years. Strange to say, it is not in the quiet jungle-forest that the python seems to prefer to live, but in the

Figure 2–1. An 18-foot reticulated python, *Python reticulata,* abandoned by a Guam/USA circus in Papua New Guinea. This species does not naturally inhabit New Guinea. *Mark O'Shea.*

busiest spots along the Menam, where steamers and junks are loading and un-loading, steam-launches whistling, steam-saws buzzing, rice-mill chimneys filling the air with smoke, and hundreds of noisy coolies passing to and fro; here he se-lects some hole or crevice in building, timber-stack, or bank to spend the day in, and at night makes an easy living, devouring fowls, ducks, cats, dogs, and, it is said pigs (which, together with countless pariah-dogs, vultures, kites, and crows, are the regular scavengers of Bangkok). . . .

In May 1897, a python, 2820 mm, (or 9 ft 3 in) in length, was found in the Wang Luang (King's Palace) . . . In January 1898 another, 2438 mm (or 8 ft.) in length, was caught alive in the Wang Na (2nd King's Palace).

British physician and herpetologist Malcom Smith also reported reticulated pythons in the urban landscape of Bangkok. In an early paper (1914:9) he noted that during the day they often seek an elevated position, often lying in the most exposed situations. Later (1943:110) he wrote.

When I went to live there [Bangkok] a few years later it was quite common, and for many years after, until the city became much larger and more crowded, I could usually catch two or three every year in my compound, which was within 100 yards of the main thoroughfare. Like the Indian Python the Reticulated Python is a great lover of water and is seldom found far from it.

Today, Bangkok is a bustling, overpopulated Asian city with well-documented air pollution problems. Nevertheless, Cox (1991:109) has observed that large speci-mens of *Python reticulata* are still caught within the city limits.

Despite the fact that the three previously quoted authors found the reticulated python sharing environments with humans, Wall (1926:84–85) described it from more pristine environments.

> In Burma this python is only met with in the densest jungles, places unknown to Europeans with the exception of a few forest officers, and an occasional sportsman. In the Malay States and in Siam it is a fairly frequent intruder into habitations. . . .

Reitinger (1978:52) described the habitat in Hong Kong as jungle areas, but noted several were caught near houses and farm buildings and the snake seems to prefer areas near water and readily enters the water.

Tweedie (1957:32) described *Python reticulata* in Malaya as fond of water and seldom found far away from it. Campden-Main (1970:10) described it as common throughout South Vietnam; always near water; and collected it near Bien Hoa, often under bridges over rapidly flowing streams.

In Cambodia, Saint Girons (1972:41–42) described *Python molurus* as occurring in the same biotopes as *P. reticulata,* but notes that it must not share the same ecological niche as that species. He commented that it would be interesting to determine the differences in their respective ecologies in areas of overlap.

The African Python, *Python sebae*
(Map 5)

The African python is widespread through sub-Saharan Africa, avoiding only the extremely dry deserts and high, cool, elevations of mountains. Two races of *Python sebae* are recognized. The northern African python's, *Python sebae sebae,* distribution is described by Broadley (1983:362) as Africa south of the Sahara, from Senegal east to Ethiopia and Somalia, extending southwards into northern Angola (as far south as Ambriz on the coast), the Shaba Province of Zaire, interdigitating and in some areas intergrading with *P. s. natalensis* in Kenya and northern Tanzania. The distribution of the southern race, *Python sebae natalensis,* is described by Broadley (1983:364) as southern Angola, southeastern and eastern Zaire, Zambia, Burundi, and southern Tanzania, south to northern Namibia, Botswana and the northeastern parts of South Africa and he notes that it was formerly found in the eastern parts of the Cape Province, but is now extinct.

Another large python from Mwingi, Kenya was recently described by Miller and Smith (1979:70) and named *Python saxuloides.* Broadley (1983:365–366) reviewed the situation and concluded that the specimens of *P. saxuloides* are from an area where the two races of *P. sebae* are parapatric (adjacent but non-overlapping) and that the "new" species is best regarded as a slightly aberrant, peripheral population of *P. s. natalensis.*

Two authors have commented on the upper limits of the elevational distribution of *Python sebae.* Laurent (1956:85) reported the northern race from 1350 m in Rwanda and the southern race from 1750 m in Zaire. Pitman (1974:68) recorded it throughout tropical and southern Africa at altitudes not exceeding 7500 feet.

The northern race's habitat is evergreen forest and moist savanna; in drier savanna areas it is restricted to riparian habitats. While the southern race inhabits mostly savanna, attaining the greatest abundance in areas of permanent water (Broadley, 1983:362).

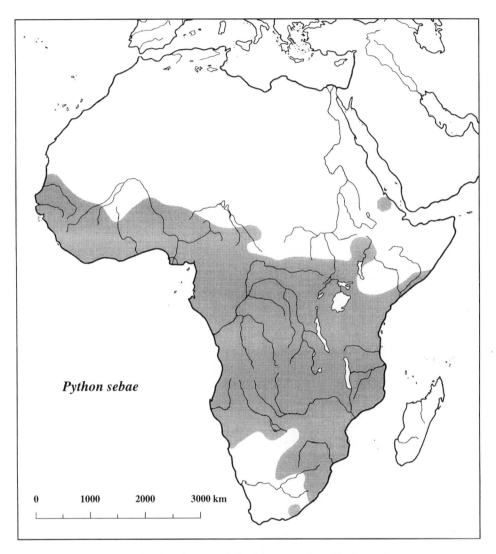

Map 5. The distribution of the African python, *Python sebae*.

Python sebae's close association with water was commented upon by Sweeney (1961:44) who found it throughout Nyasaland but common only in the vicinity of the lakes, rivers and marshes. Pitman (1974:68), writing about this snake in Uganda, states that except at higher altitudes and in arid eastern regions the python is ubiquitous, and that the presence of surface water combined with humid tropical heat make for ideal conditions. He found it locally common, particularly on Victoria Nyanza islands where it swims freely between the islands and mainland. Writing about West African populations of this species Cansdale (1961:17) reported:

> A number of pythons which I collected in Ghana had been found by fishermen in fishtraps set underwater. . . . They can survive for several hours under water without breathing: there is obviously a limit to the time they can stay submerged,

but I did not hear of many being found dead. Perhaps the fishermen just threw them away and did not bother to inform me.

South African populations also show a liking for aquatic environs, and F. W. FitzSimons (1930:21–22) found that,

> Pythons prefer bush-covered, rocky valleys and hillsides, or bush-veld and the scrub-covered margins of streams. As they love to submerge in water they are invariable found in its vicinity. . . .
> Another reason for their partiality to well-watered localities is that the birds and animals which are their natural food are more abundant in these localities than in the open, dry, rocky and sandy hill-sides, gorges, and veld so common in the central and western parts of South Africa.

Hay and Martin (1966:151) provided the following description of African python habitat in the Toro Game Reserve in Uganda's Semliki Valley.

> The area consists largely of dry savannah with a large area of marsh marginal to Lake Albert and also contains two fair sized rivers. The Wasa river flows the full length of the reserve; it is a permanent stream with seasonal swamps and backwaters bordering it.

And one last reference to illustrate the African python's aquatic tendencies. Haagner (1991:23–24) and members of the Hoedspruit Diving Club investigated a large, 9-meter-deep hippo pool on the Blyde River. While scuba diving at a depth of 6 or 7 meters they observed a 2.1 meter, male python. He wrote,

> The snake was observed from a distance and left alone and the diving group continued downstream. Due to a series of rapids the group had to return 25 minutes later, and found the snake still slowly "crawling" among the rocky bottom. The snake was captured, photographed and returned to the water. Although the aquatic habits of pythons are well known, it is nevertheless interesting to note the depth and duration of the snake's "dive."

African pythons also show some ability to enter xeric habitats, but when they do so they may stay near the usually dry river beds, the area with the maximum amount of available moisture. Haacke and Jacobsen (1990:56) described finding a specimen in Botswana's Kgalagadi District:

> . . . 33 km NW of Werda along track in dry river bed, 6 km before track turns W on cutline leading to Mpathutlwa Pan in Mbua Sehuba Game Reserve. . . . A young male python, about 2.3 m in length was tracked on 17 April 1987 in the late afternoon while moving among *Acacia, Grewia* and *Rhigozum* and smaller shrubs on red sand, having emerged from a hole in the clay soil of the river valley. . . . it is worth recording as it extends the known range . . . by more than two degrees (about 230 km) westwards into . . . the southern Kalahari. . . .

The Abuko Nature Reserve, in the small West African country of The Gambia, was the study site of Starin and Burghardt (1992:51–54). While doing a long-term study of Temminck's red colobus monkey they collected observations on pythons. Their description of the microhabitat use by *Python sebae* reports these snakes almost always on the ground, although one snake was seen 4.5 meters up in a raphia palm. Climbing abilities of pythons were, however, evident because the snakes scaled wire fences and climbed trees to enter a small zoo and feed on the caged animals. One was found in a photographic hide mounted in a tree. Three snakes were seen entering holes in the ground, and the authors postulated that they share these holes with monitor lizards. While it was impossible to observe them underground or in the water, had the snakes been using the trees they would have been observed more frequently because these researchers were watching the crowns of trees for monkeys. Most of the python observations were made in clearings, the next most frequent location was tree and shrub savanna, and the fewest sightings were made in woodland savanna. When they adjusted the data for the relative area of habitat, the clearing made up only 1% of the habitat, yet it accounted for 40% of the pythons observed. Furthermore, the authors suggested that the clearing had low visibility because grasses were present year-round. A gallery forest had the best ground visibility, but few pythons were seen there. A swamp also made up less than 1% of the total habitat, yet it accounted for 13.5% of all python sightings. Thus, this population of African pythons frequently used open clearings with grass cover and swamp habitats.

Stevenson-Hamilton (1947:319) described the African python using underground retreats; it appears very similar to the Indian python in habitat use:

> Pythons usually rest underground, making use of old ant-bear and porcupine holes for the purpose. Sometimes they lie coiled up asleep in thick bush or among long grass, and I once unwittingly took my midday siesta . . . within three feet of a large one. . . .

The Near Giants

O'Shea (1996) described the scrub python (*Morelia amethistina*) (Map 6) as occurring in a wide variety of habitats in Papua New Guinea, from savanna to rain forest and up to 1600 meters above sea level. It was frequently encountered along river banks, around out-buildings or crossing roads at night; by day it was secretive. Similarly, according to O'Shea (1996), large individuals of the Papuan python (*Apodora papuana*) (Map 7) are frequently encountered on roads at night and 3–4 m road killed specimens are not uncommon (Figure 2–2). The western olive python (*Liasis olivaceus barroni*) (Map 8) is associated with water courses in the arid Pilbara region of Western Australia and the islands of the nearby Dampier Archipelago (Barker and Barker, 1994:35). The Oenpelli python (*Morelia oenpelliensis*) (Map 8) inhabits the monsoon forests surrounding sandstone rock outcroppings of the Arnhem Land escarpment, Northern Territory, Australia (Gow, 1989:65–66).

Summary

The habitat used by giant snakes is variable, exhibits considerable ecological versatility, and none seems to show a preference for a highly specific microhabitat. The anaconda demonstrates the strongest preference for aquatic habitats, but all four species use water to a greater or lesser degree. The Indian and African pythons show some preferences for mammal burrows with nearby bodies of water.

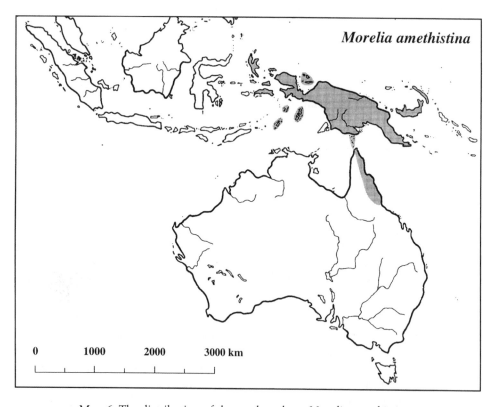

Map 6. The distribution of the scrub python, *Morelia amethistina*.

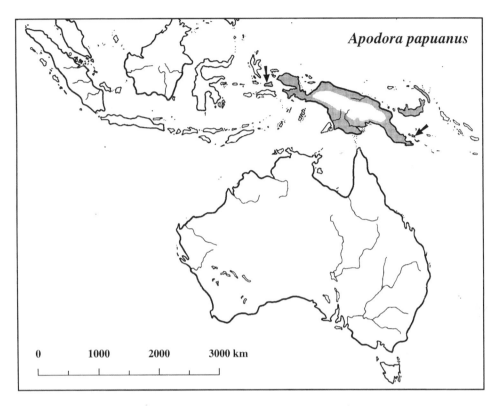

Map 7. The distribution of the Papuan python, *Apodora papuanus*.

Figure 2–2. A road-killed Papuan python, *Apodora papuanus,* near Lae, Morobe Province, Papua New Guinea. This specimen was almost 15 feet in length. *Mark O'Shea*.

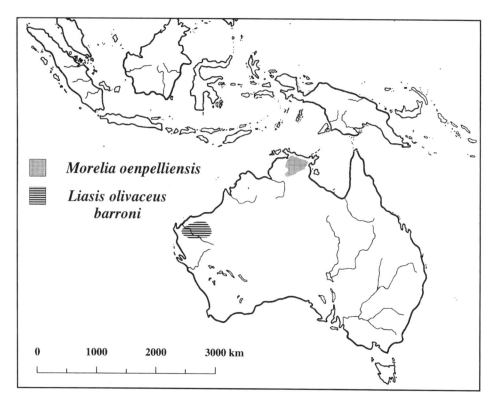

Map 8. The distributions of the Oenpelli python, *Morelia oenpelliensis,* and the western olive python, *Liasis olivaceus barroni.*

The frequent use of habitats associated with water by giant snakes suggests several potential advantages: (1) It supports their great mass and makes movement less energy demanding. (2) Water has a high specific heat, thus its temperature fluctuates much less than air temperatures. Snakes can use aquatic environments to stay warm when the air temperature drops, and they can use it to lower their body temperature when high air temperatures threaten to overload their body with heat. (3) Aquatic environments provide concealment from terrestrial predators. (4) Aquatic habitats harbor and attract many prey species as well as provide concealment for hunting from ambush. None of the giant snakes ranges into latitudes or elevations with extended periods of cold weather. *Python molurus* ranges farthest north, and it may have some adaptations to surviving cooler temperatures than the other giants.

CHAPTER 3

HOW BIG DO GIANT SNAKES GET?

The python was measured and found to be 130 feet long but alas! I have not the skin to prove it. It is an exceedingly old creature and was known locally—I found one man whose grandfather knew it in his time. A special pool was reserved for it and all people warned not to touch this water. Usually only very local people were told about it because its home is along the Bwamba escarpment road (i.e. few people about) but since the advent of the Bwamba working there they were told of this creature and his pool. Local people used to take it offerings of ugoli, beer, etc. and dump these offerings near this pool (a pocket amongst rocks); they affirm that occasionally the python ate these offerings. On the 22nd January the creature was observed crossing the road and a hue and cry was raised by the Bwamba porters. They attacked the animal (which broke three spears) and eventually dispatched it with pangas. The Bwamba wished to eat the animal but the headman and one or two others forbade this (chiefly I think on account of religious superstition) stating that anyone who did so would be sure to die, as they would also if they drank from its pool. He therefore had a pit dug and the python buried. During the night however, three Bwamba went and dug it up and consumed the creature. All were ill the next day and one died the following day. The other two have recovered. I have been out to try and save any bones or pieces, but they made such a good meal that practically nothing was left. I have however managed to obtain the mouth with teeth and two pieces of its vertebrae and I am having these dispatched in due course to the Game Warden. In regard to length, I have no reason to disbelieve what the headman says: he is a reliable man and he measured it with a linear tape measure (which he has for his road work). I had this tape measure drawn out to its full extent and every single soul who was present when the snake was measured states that it much exceeded the tape measure. I was shown the place where they stretched it out and the limits of the head and the tail: this was certainly approximately 130 feet as stated by the headman.

This straight-forward, matter-of-fact account was reported to Captain Charles Pitman and quoted in his (1938:60) book on Ugandan snakes. Pitman's correspondent was obviously serious about this super-sized python, but for lack of evidence it is unlikely that any professional herpetologist or zoologist alive in 1938, or today, would take this story as an accurate account of a real giant snake. Let's keep in mind that a snake 130 feet long would weigh many hundreds, even thousands, of pounds. For the three men to have eaten the entire animal in one sitting would require that each had to eat several hundred pounds of snake carcass. No matter how hungry they were, we think that is unlikely. Uganda is, however, home to several tribes that worship pythons, and it seems probable that the anonymous letter writer may have confused a mythical rainbow snake with a real snake. Rainbow snakes are known as guardians of important resources in many tribal cultures and will be discussed further in Chapter 8.

There is often more than one approach to solving a particular problem, and determining the size attained by giant snakes is no exception. In our opinion, however, there is only one accurate method to determining a snake's length, and that is direct measurement. Unfortunately, this is not always possible with large, live snakes in the wild, and explorers often give estimates and measurements made using questionable techniques. This has resulted in accounts of snake sizes that are undoubtedly inaccurate. When the exaggeration factor is added, some of the accounts of sizes attained by snakes read more like fiction than fact, as in the letter reported by Pitman.

Clifford Pope (1961:152–153), the author of the only other book devoted entirely to giant snakes, notes three approaches to determining maximum size of snakes.

> The first is strictly scientific, which demands concrete proof and therefore may err on the conservative side by waiting for evidence in the flesh. This approach rejects virtually all field measurements. The next level attempts to weigh varied evidence and come to a balanced, sensible conclusion; field measurements by experienced explorers are not rejected, and even reports of a less scientific nature are duly evaluated. The third level leans on a belief that a lot of smoke means some fire.

Pope also observed that previous authors had used these different approaches. James Oliver (1958), a New York Zoological Society herpetologist has taken the second approach, while Bernard Heuvelmans (1958), the father of cryptozoology, has taken the third approach. We adhere to the first.

Reports of exceptionally large snakes containing elements consistent with currently accepted scientific paradigms of snakes are much more likely to be acceptable than stories which contain outlandish claims. Tales of giant snakes with luminescent eyes, swimming at high speed, or with psychic powers over humans lack credibility because they do not match the paradigms of what is known about snakes. Although these outlandish claims do not necessarily discredit the entire story, they do send a signal that the reporters' ability to make accurate observations, as well as their intellectual honesty and good judgment, are suspect. What evidence a person will accept is personal preference, but clearly for the more discriminating, direct measurement is the most acceptable, particularly when accompanied by a skull, skeleton, or live animal.

Are Snake Skins Useful Artifacts to Determine Size?

Snake skins are not acceptable as proof of a giant snake's size because they are easily stretched. Harvard zoologist Arthur Loveridge (1931:12) used an African python, *Python sebae*, to illustrate the problem. He wrote,

> With a view to obtaining data which might prove of assistance in estimating the actual length of a snake whose dried skin only is available, I measured one of these snakes in the flesh and found it to be 2180 mm., while its dried, and not unduly stretched, skin measured no less than 2650 mm. That is to say an increase of at least .21 of the total length should be allowed for, or in other words a dried skin is nearly a quarter as long again as was the living reptile from which it was taken. The skull of this same snake measured 84 mm. in its greatest length so that it may be assumed that a python is about twenty-six times longer than its skull, though this proportion varies with age for the larger snake measured 4330 mm. in the flesh with a skull length of only 128 mm. or a thirty-third of its total length.

Ralph Blomberg (1956:93) also commented that skins are not acceptable evidence of snake size in life.

One reason there are exaggerated ideas about the size of snakes is that it is no trick at all to stretch a skin as much as 20 per cent. In this manner, an unscrupulous person is able to manufacture a much larger snake than ever existed. In fact, it is difficult to skin a snake without stretching the hide appreciably.

In opposition to these comments is Clark (1953:282), who suggested that skins *shrink* after being removed from the snake. Anyone who has skinned a snake will realize Clark is in error, and it is important to note he offers no observations or data to back up his statement.

After gazing at the 320 monstrous skins in their warehouse, I had to reconsider; these skins were from three to four feet wide, so that the snake was easily a foot in diameter! They said the skins were mostly of the mottled black peculiar to the middle Morona, though some were a beautiful brownish gold. Eighteen anaconda skins exceeding twenty feet were shown us, one which I measured at 26 feet 81/2 inches. In a fresh state they would have been longer, for these were dried and shrunken. . . .

Frank Wall (1921:67) also described a case of the skin from an Indian python, *Python molurus*, shrinking; but in this instance it results from an inflated original estimate.

Dr. J. R. Henderson showed me the skin of a python in the Madras Museum in 1917, which measured after death 16 feet, though during life its length had been estimated at 26 feet. I very much suspect that this was the specimen alluded to by Ambercromby as 27 feet in length.

Perhaps the most telltale evidence incriminating snake skins as valid records of length comes from William W. Lamar (personal communication to RWH), a respected herpetologist with years of experience in South America. Bill was forced to kill a huge anaconda in Colombia (see Chapter 7) in 1978. He carefully measured the snake's intact carcass and found it to be 24 feet 7 inches in total length. Already aware that snake skins were susceptible to stretching, Bill was extremely careful as he skinned the snake in order that stretching be kept to a minimum. It took several hours to complete the tedious chore due to Bill's meticulous effort to not distort the hide. Upon measuring the skin, Lamar found that it now had a total length of 34 feet 7 inches. Despite every effort to avoid unnecessary stretching, the skin gained an additional 10 feet!

Dickey (1932:222) recounted a story about a man who dealt in snake skins.

. . . My Brazilian friend never sold a snake skin less than twenty feet in length, and I would be willing to wager that he never killed a snake that measured more than twelve.

I wonder how many of this man's product's are decorating the walls of their proud possessors in the United States to-day, pointing tales of dread encounters with these perilous denizens of the deep forests of the southern jungle land.

To let you into a secret, my friend had a process for stretching the skins of snakes to incredible lengths. And it was a simple process. By it he could add at least fifty percent to the length of any serpent ever seen.

Dickey went on to explain how the man used the fat of the manatee (or sea cow). He

. . . anointed a snake skin, before it was dry, with quantities of manatee fat, leaving the skin thus anointed in the sun throughout one entire day. The next morning, one end of the snake was attached to an upright of the man's house, the other end was pulled upon by two men until the desired length was achieved.

My friend did a considerable, very lucrative, tourist trade with his snake skins . . .

Field Estimates as Reliable Measures

An explanation for how estimating snake size in the field can be overdone is provided by Savage-Landor (1913:141–142). The incident occurred on the Arinos River, where he observed a large anaconda, estimated its length while it basked, killed the snake, and then took an exact measurement; the results are telling. He wrote:

> We were going along fairly gaily when I saw a huge snake, another sucuriú, floating upon the water among the foliage and branches of a fallen tree. The section of the body which I could perceive measured fully two and one-half feet in diameter, and I must say that for one moment - we were only about twenty feet away from it - I was somewhat surprised, as my quickly calculating mind constructed in my imagination a snake at least 100 feet long . . . they [Savage-Landor's men] opened a fusillade until a bullet actually struck the snake and it wriggled about. . . . The snake was dead. When they had made quite sure that life was extinct, my men returned and pulled the snake out of the water. Although the section we had seen floating was so big, the rest of the body was not more than four inches in diameter. The snake had eaten an entire veado (deer), and that was the cause of the great swelling of the central part of the body. The shape of the devoured animal could be seen plainly inside it. . . . the snake, which after all was only eighteen feet five inches long. . . . I have seen it stated, in some books which have been published about South America, that snakes of incredible length are believed to exist on that continent. Undoubtedly the notion has been suggested by the fact that inexperienced travellers have seen immensely broad traces of snakes on the soft ground near rivers. Measuring the diameter of those trails they came to the conclusion that the snake was 80 to 100 feet long, and without taking further trouble to ascertain they had actually seen a snake of that length. Whereas, as a matter fact, as in the case I have described, the immense diameter of the snake was merely in the section which enclosed some big animal which had been swallowed.

Hyatt Verrill (1937; in Heuvelmans, 1958:288) also demonstrated how easily the size of a snake can be overestimated by providing a very similar prediction to the one made above by Savage-Landor. Verrill observed an anaconda coiled on a rock ledge along a Guyana river, and asked each of his companions to estimate its length. Here are the results.

> The camera man, who had never before been in the jungle, said sixty feet. The missionary who had spent seven years in the interior and had seen scores of big snakes was more conservative and said thirty feet. The Indians' estimates varied from twenty to forty feet; my camp boy, who had accompanied a party of snake collectors a few years earlier, said thirty feet, while the grizzled old 'captain' remarked, "Takin all de fac's of da case in consiation, I don't can state positively, chief, but Ah knows for de truf tha camudi (anaconda) is jus too long."
>
> A twenty-two rifle bullet through the head brought an end to the big ana-

conda's career and when he was straightened out and measured he proved to be exactly nineteen feet and six inches in length. But what a monster! About his middle he measured thirty-three inches and a fraction and he weighed over 360 pounds and was a heavy load for five Indians. So huge were his proportions that even after we had measured the creature it was difficult to believe that he was so 'small.'

Thus we are left with the issue of direct measurement versus field estimate. Acceptance of huge snakes, those exceeding 30 feet, are left to the personal discretion of the reader. There are stories of snakes of truly gigantic proportions and before we deal with the more mundane issue of how big snakes actually get we need to examine the supersnake stories similar to that of the Ugandan python related by Pitman at the beginning of this chapter.

The Supersnake Hypothesis

The issue of how large snakes get has been clouded by authors suggesting that the supersnakes (snakes reported to be in the 50–150-foot range) are species not currently known to science, but instead represent undescribed species. Perry (1970:86–100) devoted an entire chapter to *Sucuriji Gigante,* a supersnake of the Amazon apparently distinct from the common anaconda. In a similar vein, Dinardo (1993:275) wrote:

> Perhaps another (undescribed and truly huge) species of anaconda was responsible for the early reports—a Pleistocene relict already on the way to extinction. It is conceivable that the early South American explorers were viewing an already rare and disappearing species.

We should point out that supersnake stories are ancient, qualifying them for true legendary status. Supersnake stories are also present in the Eastern Hemisphere, and an anonymous author (1903:149) stated that stories about reticulated pythons in the Philippines often mention snakes 50 feet long, with eyes like saucers, and heads as big as demijohns. The opening quote of this chapter by Pitman suggests supersnakes occur in Africa, and the following comment by Goodrich (1870:404) suggests the same:

> Livy, the ancient historian of Rome, tells us of a serpent one hundred and twenty feet long, which was met with by the Roman army under Regulus, on the banks of the river Bagrada, in Africa, near Utica, and which devoured many of the soldiers. It was finally slain by military engines, which hurled heavy stones upon it. Its carcass was so enormous, that when it decayed, it tainted the whole atmosphere, and compelled the army to remove its encampment to a distance. The story is told with so much particularity that we cannot reject it. Another account is furnished of a serpent sixty-two feet in length which not many years since attacked a sailor in a boat on the coast of the Bay of Bengal, and was killed by the crew.

To a great degree this simply deflects the question of how large do serpents grow from one species to another, but assume for the moment that the supersnake is a viable hypothesis.

A snake 50 to 150 feet long has far fewer hiding places than a 25-foot snake and the huge size would make it more vulnerable to discovery. Supersnakes must reproduce, their offspring must be born small and grow, and, since the number of offspring or eggs a female snake produces is related to body size in large boids, consider what the clutch size of a 130-foot female super snake would be (a 20–30 foot anaconda or python produces 70–100 offspring or eggs). With such huge litters the probability of a smaller one being captured would or should increase. Also, supersnakes are likely to be at a serious biomechanical disadvantage since their great mass is subject to the forces of gravity (which poses some serious problems to normal-sized snakes). Distributing blood to the head and tail simultaneously in a normal-sized snake that climbs results in blood pooling at the back end of the snake. Snakes that climb tend to have the heart closer to the head, which allows them to maintain blood pressure in the head region. Aquatic snakes tend to have the heart at mid-body, while ground dwelling snakes tend to have the heart slightly forward of the mid-body, but not as far forward as arboreal species. Real giant snakes use all three of these habitats. But, for sake of argument, we will assume that the supersnakes are more aquatic, like the anaconda, and have solved the problem of blood pooling at the tail-end of the serpent when they climb or raise their body out of the water (Lillywhite, 1988:92–98).

Lorenz Hagenbeck (in Heuvelmans, 1958:296), son of Carl Hagenbeck the animal collector and one-time director of the Hamburg Zoo, examined reports of supersnakes and speculated that *sucuriji gigante* was a real snake attaining 130 feet in length, 2.5 feet in diameter and a mass of 5 tons; its color was dark chestnut, its belly was spotted with off white; its eyes were very large, and they were phosphorescent blue at night! Hagenbeck's acceptance of supersnakes was fueled by a missionary, Father Victor Heinz, who collected stories dealing with these legendary beasts.

Victor Heinz (in Heuvelmans, 1958:294) described events which are completely beyond belief based upon what is known about snake biology. One can only wonder at the gullibility (and visual acuity) of Father Heinz considering the following story in which he mistakes a supersnake for a steamship!

> My second encounter with a giant water-snake took place on 29 October 1929. To escape the great heat I had decided to go down the river at about 7 p.m. in the direction of Alemquer. About midnight, we found ourselves above the mouth of the Piaba when my crew, seized with a sudden fear, began to row hard towards the shore. . . .
>
> At the same moment I heard the water move as if a steamboat had passed. I immediately noticed several feet above the surface of the water two bluish-green lights like the navigation lights on the bridge of a river boat, and shouted:
>
> "No, look, it's the steamer! Row to the side so that it doesn't upset us."
>
> "*Que vapor que nada,*" they replied. "*Una cobra grande!*"
>
> Petrified, we all watched the monster approach; it avoided us and recrossed the river in less than a minute, a crossing which would have taken us in calm water ten to fifteen times as long. On the safety of dry land we took courage and shouted to attract attention to the snake. At this very moment a human figure began to wave an oil-lamp on the other shore, thinking no doubt, that someone was in danger. Almost at once the snake rose on the surface and we were able to appreciate clearly the difference between the light of the lamp and the phosphorescent light of the monster's eyes. Later, on my return, the inhabitants of this place assured me that above the mouth of the Piaba there dwelt a *sucuriju gigante*.

So Heinz's supersnake has phosphorescent eyes, a trait unknown in any other species of serpent and as highly improbable as high speed locomotion in a snake. A Portuguese merchant named Reymondo Zima, well known to Father Heinz, lived for 9 years opposite the town of Faro on the Rio Jamundá; his story is suspiciously similar to that of Father Heinz and it was published by a newspaper in Rio de Janeiro (Heuvelmans, 1958:295).

> On 6 July 1930 I was going up the Jamunda in company with my wife and the boy who looks after my motor-boat. Night was falling when we saw a light on the right bank. In the belief that it was the house I was looking for I steered towards the light and switched on my searchlight. But then suddenly we noticed that the light was charging towards us at an incredible rate of speed. A huge wave lifted the bow of the boat and almost made it capsize. My wife screamed in terror. At the same moment we made out the shape of a giant snake rising out of the water and performing a St. Vitus's dance around the boat. After which the monster crossed this tributary of the Amazon about half a mile wide at fabulous speed, leaving a huge wake, larger than any of the steamboats make at full speed. The waves hit our 43 foot boat with such force that at every moment we were in danger of capsizing. I opened my motor flat out and made for dry land. Owing to the understandable excitement at the time it was not possible for me to reckon the monster's length. I presume that as a result of a wound the animal lost one eye, since I saw only one light. I think the giant snake must have mistaken our searchlight for the eye of one of his fellow-snakes.

Heinz described the strength of a supersnake in a story that supposedly took place on 27 September 1930, in a channel connecting Lake Maruricaña and the Rio Iguarapé. A Brazilian named João Penha was clearing vegetation from the bank to make it easier for the turtles to come up and lay their eggs (probably so he could collect the turtle eggs for food). Beyond a floating island of plants, tree trunks and tangled branches, he observed two green lights (Heuvelmans, 1958:295–296).

> Penha thought at first that it was some fisherman who was looking for eggs. But suddenly the whole barrier shook for 100 yards. He had to retreat hurriedly for a foaming wave 6 feet high struck the bank. Then he called his two sons, and all three of them saw a snake rising out of the water pushing the barrier in front of it for a distance of some 300 yards until the narrow arm of water was finally freed of it.
> During all this time they could observe at leisure its phosphorescent eyes and the huge teeth of the lower jaw.

Penha's story adds some previously unknown characteristics to the hypothesized supersnake. Its ability to push a floating island of vegetation in order to clear a path for itself makes it quite unique among snakes, which will otherwise crawl over, or around objects which are in their way. Following the margin of a barrier is a behavioral trait of snakes that herpetologists exploit to trap snakes with a drift fence and funnel traps. Additionally, the huge teeth in the lower jaw, no doubt visible because of the phosphorescent light emitted by the eyes, are not present in any of the snakes with which we are familiar. In fact, the mouth is normally kept closed except when feeding, striking, or stretching the jaws, and the bottom teeth are usually not larger than the upper teeth.

All of these characteristics suggest that the animals Heinz, Zima, and Penha reported seeing were not snakes at all. We don't pretend to know what these men actually did see, but we are confident they were not snakes.

In a very dramatic, manhood-enhancing account, Lange (1912:229–238) described killing and measuring a 56-foot supersnake which also had glowing eyes. Unlike that of snakes, its skin does shrink after being removed, but only slightly—1 foot, 4 inches, or 2.3% of the live length, according to Lange.

> The snake still made no move, but in the clear moonlight I could see its body expand and contract in breathing; its yellow eyes seeming to radiate a phosphorescent light. I felt no fear, nor any inclination to retreat, yet I was now facing a beast that few men had ever succeeded in seeing. Thus we stood looking at each other, scarcely moving an eyelid, while the great silent monster looked at us. I slid my right hand down to the holster of my automatic pistol, the 9 mm Luger, and slowly removed the safety lock, at the same time staring into the faces of the men. In this manner I was less under the spell of the mesmerism of the snake, and could to some extent think and act. I wheeled around while I still held control of my faculties, and, perceiving a slight movement of the snake's coils, I fired point-blank at the head, letting go the entire chamber of soft nose bullets. Instantly the other men woke up from their trance and in their turn fired, emptying their Winchesters into the huge head, which by this time was raised to a great height above us, loudly hissing in agony.

The next morning, Lange and the other men rose early to measure and skin the snake.

> It was a most astonishing sight, that giant snake lying there full length, while around it gathered six Amazon Indians and the one solitary New Yorker, here in the woods about as far from civilization as it is possible to get. I proceeded to take measurements and used the span between my thumb and little finger tips as a unit, knowing that this was exactly eight inches.
>
> Beginning at the mouth of the snake, I continued to the end and found that this unit was contained eighty-four times. Thus 84 times 8 divided by 12 gives exactly 56 feet as the total length. In circumference, the unit, the "palma," was contained 8 times and a fraction, around the thickest part of the body. From this I derived the diameter 2 feet 1 inch.
>
> These measurements are the result of very careful work. I went from the tail to the nose over again so as to eliminate any error, and then asked the men with me also to take careful measurements in their own manner, which only confirmed the figures given above. . . .
>
> The snake had been laid on its belly and it was split open, following the spinal column throughout its length, the ventral part being far too hard and unyielding. About two o'clock in the afternoon we had the work finished and the carcass was thrown into the river, where it was instantly set upon by the vigilant piranhas and alligators.
>
> Standing in front of this immense skin I could not withhold my elation. . . .
>
> We brought the skin to headquarters, where I prepared it with arsenical soap and boxed it for later shipment to New York. The skin measured, when dried 54 feet 8 inches, with a width of 5 feet 1 inch.

Colonel Percy Fawcett's (1953:92–93) report of a 62-foot supersnake is widely quoted (Heuvelmans, 1958; Perry, 1970; Greenwell, 1993), but the story is questionable not only because of the extreme size, but also because of his comment about its bad breath. This incident happened in January of 1907 on the Rio Abuna, in Brazil, near the Peruvian-Bolivian border while Fawcett, at the request of The Royal Geographical Society, was mediating a border dispute between the three countries in an attempt to halt an escalating risk of war.

> We were drifting easily along in the sluggish current not far below the confluence of the Rio Negro when almost under the bow of the *igarité* there appeared a triangular head and several feet of undulating body. It was a giant anaconda. I sprang for my rifle as the creature began to make its way up the bank, and hardly waiting to aim smashed a .44 soft-nosed bullet into its spine, ten feet below the wicked head. At once there was a flurry of foam, and several heavy thumps against the boat's keel, shaking us as though we had run on a snag.
>
> With great difficulty I persuaded the Indian crew to turn in shorewards. They were so frightened that the whites showed all round their popping eyes, and in the moment of firing I had heard their terrified voices begging me not to shoot lest the monster destroy the boat and kill everyone on board, for not only do these creatures attack boats when injured, but also there is great danger from their mates.
>
> We stepped ashore and approached the reptile with caution. It was out of action, but shivers ran up and down the body like puffs of wind on a mountain tarn. As far as it was possible to measure, a length of forty-five feet lay out of the water, and seventeen feet in it, making a total length of sixty-two feet. Its body was not thick for such a colossal length-not more than twelve inches in diameter-but it had probably been long without food. I tried to cut a piece out of the skin, but the beast was by no means dead and the sudden upheavals rather scared us. A penetrating foetid odour emanated from the snake, probably its breath, which is believed to have a stupefying effect, first attracting and later paralysing its prey. Everything about this snake was repulsive.
>
> Such large specimens as this may not be common, but the trails in the swamps reach a width of six feet and support the statements of Indians and rubber pickers that the anaconda sometimes reaches an incredible size, altogether dwarfing that shot by me. The Brazilian Boundary Commission told me of one killed in the Rio Paraguay exceeding eighty feet in length!

Fawcett's son, Brian, edited his father's memoirs and published them (Fawcett, 1953). Accompanying the story cited above, he (Brian Fawcett) provided a footnote (page 93) stating: "When this serpent was reported in London, my father was pronounced an utter liar!"

South African herpetologist Vivian FitzSimons (1953:346–347) commented on the size of big snakes to a reader of Fawcett's, in response to a letter sent to the editor of *African Wild Life* magazine.

> Sir, — Following on the letter by Miss Fay Lennox in the last issue of African Wild Life, (Vol. 7, No. 3), in which she quotes a statement from *Exploration Fawcett,* regarding the gigantic size of the anaconda, it may be as well to emphasize right away that stories relating to length and size of snakes, based on visual evidence only, are notorious for their gross exaggeration and unreliability. In actual fact, from all the authenticated records available, it can be stated that the anaconda (or water boa-constrictor) seldom exceeds 30 ft. in length, and stories of specimens reaching up to 100 ft. and more must be regarded as apocryphal.
>
> According to official scientific records the longest snake living today is the reticulated or regal python, of Asia, which is known to attain a length of 33 ft. At the

same time it is universally conceded that the Anaconda, with its more massive body, is certainly by far the largest of the world's living snakes, but by no stretch of imagination "may weigh 5 tons" (the average weight of a full grown elephant!) as recorded by Gunther in his book *Inside Latin America*. . . . Transvaal Museum, Pretoria. V. Fitzsimons

Supersnake stories that intermittently appear in the literature take place in Brazil, and often mention the "boundary commission" or persons associated with it. It seems likely that these are variations on Percy Fawcett's story that have been exaggerated and recycled. Perry (1970:97) recalls a " . . . legendary battle near Tabatinga on the Solemoes, or upper Amazon.." with a 130-ft. snake, and a 1954 incident when the Brazilian army killed a 120-ft. snake near the French Guiana-Brazil border.

In 1933, officials of the Brazilian Boundary Commission reportedly killed another supersnake; its length varies depending upon the reporter telling the story. It was photographed and the picture placed on Brazilian postcards and the photographer was apparently stationed in Manaus (Figure 3–1). The following account is taken from an undated (post-1937) book by an anonymous author, entitled *Vagabondage Through the United States of Brazil*, by Sinbad—the vagabond sailor—1936–1937. The account starts on page 439. We have not seen an original of this, a typescript of this section is in the K. P. Schmidt Library, Field Museum of Natural History. We include this lengthy quote here because it contains elements of many of the super-

Figure 3–1. A Brazilian postcard ca 1932 reportedly showing a supersnake. Note the humans in the background appear dwarfed, not because the snake is huge but because of the angle from which the photo was taken. Also note the reflection in the snake's eyes, which gives them a glowing appearance. This so-called supersnake is clearly an anaconda, *Eunectes murinus*. *Photo from Anon. (n.d.) in the K. P. Schmidt Library, Field Museum of Natural History, Chicago.*

snake stories reported by Heuvelmans (1958) and Perry (1970), and makes the point about the connection between supersnakes and a boundary commission, this time on the Venezuelan-Brazilian border.

> Above all, the Amazonian waters contain the largest amphibious snakes in the world called "Sukurijo" (Anaconda). The largest live one, so far found and killed, had a length of 32 metres (about 107 feet). It was slowly moving it seems towards the river, probably after having devoured a bull, and having slept and digested it as is their habit, when, a Commission of Limitation of the boundaries between Venezuela and Brazil, in 1932, happened to arrive, and its somewhat sleepy attitude facilitated its killing with some ease. Herewith is the photo which I obtained in Manaos from the photographer who developed the films of the Members of the Boundary Commission. Its size and proportions may be gauged by comparing the two men who are sitting or standing near it. Its full length in the picture is not seen because a large part of it (so I was told) was lying on the other side of the slope of the high river bank. The portion in the picture represents about half its full length. Its skin was abandoned as these people have no interest in such things. On the back of this photograph the following description is given in the Portuguese language:—

> "Killed on the Brazilian Frontier/Venezuela — weighing 3 tons. Length 32 metres by 1.25 metres thickness. Killed by the Brazilian Demarkation Commission on the frontier in the year 1932."

> It is a matter for conjecture as to whether this monster could be compared to the mythical monster of Loch Ness! Its horrid huge eyes are frightening. The Brazilians call such eyes "Pharols" (Lighthouses). They say that its eyes shine like miniature lighthouses when it crosses a river, hence this appellation. I never got a chance of seeing anything like this. It is not so very easy. The immensity of the surroundings, and the absence of facilities and guides, precludes the realization of such ambitions. The skin has large scales. I bought the skin of a newly killed one at Cuyaba. It measured 9 metres long and 1 metre wide. It had large scales. If monsters of this size are in the upper section of the Amazon, there must be still larger ones in the lower section which is extremely broad and immensely deep. They prefer deep bays and still waters, according to the information given me. It is a fact that they swallowed even the largest crocodile.

This author continues with a long discourse on supersnakes, and includes a translation of a newspaper article describing encounters with 30- and 50-meter supersnakes with glowing eyes and magnetic gazes in a way guaranteed to keep small children and timid adults in their houses at night.

Heuvelmans's (1958:296) book, *On The Track Of Unknown Animals,* notes that a second specimen of this supersnake species was killed at Fort Abuna in the Guaporé territory with 500 machine-gun bullets; it was measured at 115 feet. Again, a photograph of this snake was supposedly taken. Perry (1970:98) devoted an entire chapter in an attempt to build a case for a South American supersnake, but offers only the same outrageous stories reported by Huevelmans, and cites Loch Ness monster hunter Tim Dinsdale's opinion that the photographs of the Abuna specimen are genuine. Dinsdale also adds to the myth by stating that the large eyes, large mouth and thickness " . . . at the sixth convolution and not at the normal fourth . . ." (note that convolution is a term that does not apply to any part of snake anatomy that we are aware of other than a loose coil of a snake's body) suggest it differs from any known giant snake. This is, of course, nonsense! We suggest that if the eyes and mouth look bigger it is undoubtedly due to bacterial decomposition which caused the carcass to bloat. Decomposition and bloating also most certainly account for any perceived increase in thickness at some part of the body, unless a large meal was recently swallowed.

The tract of country known as the Mallee Scrub lies between the junction of the Murrary and Darling Rivers in northern Victoria, Australia; it is not known to contain any giant snake currently known to science, but reports of the 30–40 foot Mindi or Mallee snake extend back to the early 19th century. Like other supersnakes, this mythological beast is known for its size, swiftness, and totally disgusting odor. In the September 13, 1880 issue of the *Proceedings of the Royal Society of Tasmania,* Mr. C. M. Officer, a nonbeliever, comments on why it has alluded capture (in Gould, 1884:180):

> No one, however, has ever seen one, for the simple reason that to see it is to die, so fierce it is, and so great its power of destruction.

We have only touched on the supersnake stories here and we are aware that there are others. Real giant snakes are spectacular creatures in their own right and there is no need to use imagined supersnakes to add to their attraction. Perry (1970: 99–100) and, more recently, Dinardo (1993:275–276), have invoked the "science does not know all" ploy, citing the recent discovery of large, previously unknown animals as a way of insinuating that supersnakes are potentially real.

Does this then mean that all species of large snakes are known to science? Australian herpetologist Graham Gow described the Oenpelli python, *Morelia oenpelliensis,* from Australia's Northern Territory in 1977 and Smith described *Liasis olivaceus barroni* in 1981. Thus, large snakes living in remote places may have escaped the attention of zoology beyond 1996. But there is a large credibility gap between describing a new species of python that is 4–5 m long (and may reach 7–8 meters) based upon specimens, and accepting hearsay evidence for a giant snake that is 30–40 m long! A scientific attitude must include not only a healthy skepticism, but a respect for established paradigms, a willingness to change opinion, and a loyalty to reality. Therefore, should a skull, a skin, or a live supersnake become available, we will be more than willing to reconsider our position. Now we are interested in moving ahead with the investigation as to how big snakes actually do get based upon available evidence. We will put aside the outrageous and examine stories that have credibility based on what is known about snake biology—there are interesting stories of huge, real snakes ahead.

Ancient Giants?

The question of how large prehistoric giant snakes were is legitimate and likely to be asked by anyone familiar with other prehistoric giant species. If snakes over 20 feet exist today, how large might they have been in the past? Evidence for real prehistoric snakes that approached the supersnakes in size is absent from the fossil record. Snake skulls are relatively fragile and few ancient snakes are known from skulls; however, snake vertebrae are small, hard, and more abundant than skulls in sedimentary rocks. There are three fossil genera based upon vertebrae, ribs and some skull material that are remarkably similar to each other in the position of a blood vessel that passes through the socket of each vertebrae, upturned lateral processes on each vertebrae, overall vertebrae shape, and massive articulation facets of the ribs. The latter characteristic suggests a very bulky body. These characters make these ancient snakes quite distinct from modern boids and all are placed in the sub-family Madtsoiinae. *Wonambi naracoortensis* is a southern Australian Pleistocene form that may have reached a length of 6.13 meters (Smith, 1985:156–158; Barrie, 1990:148). *Madtsoia bai* is a 7–8 meter fossil form from the Paleocene of Patagonia (Hoffstetter, 1959:384). And, the North African *Gigantophis garstini* (Anderson, 1906:306–312) may have reached 9 meters. Thus, if huge prehistoric supersnakes did exist, science has yet to find the evidence. What is even more interesting is that these lengths fall well within the sizes of the largest modern boids.

Snakes, Sex, and Size

About two-thirds of the snake species which have been examined for sexual size dimorphism have females that are longer than males, and females tend to be larger than males in species that are viviparous (live-bearing as opposed to egg-laying). Hy-potheses to explain the differences in size between the sexes are not lacking. Some snake species exhibit a sexual size difference at birth, whereas other species have both sexes starting out at the same size but with one sex, often the female, growing faster and maturing later than the male. This may be controlled by different feeding or metabolic rates, or sex hormones may actually slow growth in male snakes (see Shine, 1993, for a review). How sexual size differences are controlled in the giant snakes is unknown at present, but female giant snakes are larger than males. The anaconda's dimorphism is relatively well known, with males considerably smaller and more slender than females (Lopez, 1984). Gustav Lederer (1944:363–398) described male reticulated pythons as smaller and more slender than females, and Richard Shine (in litt. to RWH) has observed that all *Python reticulata* over 5 meters that he has examined have been females. The largest reticulated python maintained in captivity was probably the Highland Park Zoo's female named Colossus. There is a discrepancy in the literature about the sex of Colossus; Barton and Allen (1961:84) reported it as a male, while Minton and Minton (1973:207) stated it was a female. We investigated this with the help of Ray Pawley (personal communication to JCM). He contacted William B. Allen who was present at the autopsy of Colossus, and he confirmed that Colossus was indeed a female. The male scrub pythons examined by Shine and Slip (1990) showed a mean body length of 191.7 cm, while the females had a mean body length of 232.5 cm. Barker and Barker (1994:38) suggest these lengths are small for the species and they may be biased being based on museum specimens (people tend to collect smaller specimens that can be more easily stored). They noted Barnett (1993) had a captive-born animal grow to 477 cm in 4 years. Broadley (1983:67) noted that female *Python sebae* are proportionally heavier than males of the same size. Thus, the largest specimens of any of our giants are probably going to be females.

Adaptive Radiation, Bell Curves, and Giantism

All things are relative, especially the body sizes of animals. What makes one ani-mal a dwarf and another a giant is the relationship of their size to each other. Consider human body size: a person may be 8.9 feet tall or 1.8 feet tall (McFarlan, 1991:5,9) as a full-grown adult; these are size extremes of a bell curve, and most of us fall somewhere in the middle. Thus, any variable characteristic for any population of organisms can be expected to fit a bell curve. Of course, sample size is important; if only 10 individuals are sampled the curve produced will probably not look like a curve based upon one thousand individuals.

Animal species and populations are the products of their ancestry, and within a group of related species body size can be expected to vary, with some small species and some large species. Variation in body size is one way animals can partition resources. Larger animals feed on larger prey, smaller animals feed on smaller prey; similarly, animals may divide the habitat with one species or population using forest while another uses grasslands; some live in the forest canopy, others live on, or in, the ground. Thus, within the South American boid snake fauna there are small and large ground-dwelling species and small and large canopy dwelling species. Five members of South America's boa fauna (1 species of *Boa*, 2 *Corallus*, 1 *Epicrates*, 1 *Eunectes*) have shared a long history, and the wide differences in their sizes is probably a response to competitive pressures; i.e., if all species attained the same size, and all lived in the same area (as they do), then all five species might be competing for the same food resources. If that were the case, it is unlikely that all five species could coexist in the same geographic area and given habitat. An average sized adult boa constrictor (*Boa constrictor*) is about twice as long as an average sized adult emerald (*Corallus caninus*) or common (*C. hortulanus*) tree boa or rainbow boa (*Epicrates cenchria*); similarly, an average sized adult anaconda is about twice as long as an adult boa constrictor. By using different habitats, or different adaptive zones (trees, ground level, rivers) of a given habitat, and by exploiting prey of different species and sizes, the boines are able to coexist with minimized potential competition from one another. Because the Neotropics harbor a continuous and overlapping range of prey sizes, boines were able to evolve into several species likewise spanning a wide range of overlapping sizes. The largest species thus gained access to food resources not available to smaller predators. It is even likely that the common anaconda's competition for food does not come from other snakes, but from large carnivorous mammals, such as the jaguar, that also prey on caiman, turtles, capybara, and deer along waterside habitats. The common anaconda and the jaguar have widely sympatric distributions in South America (Henderson, 1994).

Which environments and environmental conditions favor large body size? Some giant reptiles are restricted to small islands; e.g., the world's largest tortoises and the Komodo monitor (the largest member of the lizard family Varanidae). "Dwarf" tortoises and "dwarf" monitor lizards also occur, but these occur on continental land masses where other close relatives coexist, and size differences may allow species to avoid competing with each other. Large body size in tortoises may be a way for them to escape predation, and at least one species of South American tortoise (*Geochelone denticulata*) has individuals which are quite large (Pritchard and Trebbau, 1984:225). Auffenberg (1981:289; also see Diamond, 1987) has suggested that the Komodo monitor evolved its large body size to feed on stegodonts (pigmy elephants) with which it coexisted during the Pleistocene. The giant snakes have relatively large geographic distributions and occur on both insular and continental land masses, and questions that deal with why they are giants must consider the advantages of being able to eat large prey. Snakes with a larger body size can feed on larger prey than smaller snakes. Giants, therefore, can eat small prey, but they can also eat large prey.

A shift to large prey allows a population of large snakes to avoid competing with smaller species, and smaller individuals of the same species. It makes the snake more flexible (adaptable) in its choice of prey size, and at the same time allows the snake to take in a huge amount of energy and nutrients at one feeding episode.

Near Giants from Australia and New Guinea

The scrub python (*Morelia amethistina*) is one of the less well known of the seven species of snakes possibly attaining the minimum length of 20 feet required for inclusion in this work. Worrell (1963:97) wrote, "L. Robichaux, of Cairns, in 1948 measured a 28-foot specimen killed at Greenhill, near Cairns. Pythons over 15 feet are uncommon." Cogger (1975:358) states, "Average length 3.5 metres; Worrell records a giant specimen of 8.5 metres." Recently, however, Australian snake biologist Richard Shine (1991:46) has stated that this species exceeds 8 meters in length.

The Oenpelli rock python (*Morelia oenpelliensis*) attains a length of at least 4.5 m, and Gow (1989:65) predicted it may reach 7 or 8 m based upon the fact that its eggs are huge (110.5 x 60 mm), almost twice the size of the scrub python's eggs. A third Australian-New Guinea species that may break the 20-foot mark is the western olive python, *Liasis olivaceus barroni*. Shine (1991:46) stated that it can reach 6.5 meters, or slightly more than 21 feet.

McDowell (1975:41) makes a passing comment about the size of the Papuan python, *Apodora papuana* (= *Liasis papuanus*): " . . . I suspect that if *Liasis papuanus* were known from as many specimens as *Python amethistinus* [= *M. amethistina*] it would be found to exceed that species in size." The basis for this comment is not known, but he does note that an American Museum specimen known from a skin carried a collector's note stating it was 14 feet 5 inches before skinning. O'Shea (1996) considered *Apodora papuana* "an extremely powerful python species well capable of killing and devouring large prey . . . and although rivaled by the amethystine python for the title of longest New Guinea snake, it is without doubt the heavier species."

Size of the Anaconda, *Eunectes murinus*

Opinions on the size attained by anacondas have been offered by many herpetologists and zoologists, some of whom actually had field experience and personally measured them. One of the earliest was physician, scientist, and politician Edward Bancroft (1769:203–205) who described a 33-foot anaconda killed in Guyana. It is unclear if Bancroft actually saw the snake, or merely related information given him by others. His attribution of the power of fascination to the snake was a commonly held belief at this point in history.

> One of the largest of this class of animals ever seen in America, was lately killed on the Plantation Amsterdam, in this colony [Guyana], belonging to Mess the heirs of Peter Amyatt, Esq; in Amsterdam. It measured thirty three feet some inches; and in the largest place, near the middle, was three feet in circumference. It had a broad head, very wide mouth, and large prominent eyes: From the middle it gradually tapered to the tail, which was small, and armed with two claws, like those of a Dunghill Cock, and in the mouth was a double row of teeth. On

the middle of the back was a chain of small black spots, running from end to end; and on each side, near the belly, another row of spots, similar and parallel to those on the back; and below these several large black spots centered with white; the rest of the body was brown. In its belly was found a small wirrebocerra, or deer, so far dissolved by the digestive liquor of the stomach, that no part of it would hang together. The viscera were covered with a great quantity of fat, of which a considerable part was tried and preserved for external application, for pains, bruises, etc. part of which was dispensed almost over the whole colony. A smaller one was soon after killed on the plantation Dalgin, lying on the opposite side of the river. Their bite is not venomous. When their stomachs are full, they lye still till their food is digested; it was in that state that both of these were shot in the head. They are said to have the power of fascinating, or attracting animals within their reach.

Experienced tropical naturalist and entomologist Henry Walter Bates (1863:236) related his experiences with large anacondas. Note the moderate size reported.

> I measured skins of the Anaconda afterwards, twenty-one feet in length and two feet in girth. . . .
> There appeared to be no doubt that this formidable serpent grows to an enormous bulk, and lives to a great age, for I heard of specimens having been killed which measured forty-two feet in length, or double the size of the largest I had an opportunity of examining.

Alfred Russell Wallace (1853:464), biogeographer and Charles Darwin's coauthor on a landmark paper on natural selection, also reported reasonably sized anacondas, but suggests legends of larger specimens may be accurate. He wrote:

> The largest specimens I met with myself were not more than from fifteen to twenty feet long, but I have had several accounts of their having been killed, and measured, of a length of thirty-two feet. They have been seen very much larger, but, as may be supposed, are then very difficult to kill and secure, owing to their tenacity of life and their aquatic habits. It is an undisputed fact that they devour cattle and horses, and the general belief in the country is that they are sometimes from sixty to eighty feet long.

Harvard zoologist Thomas Barbour (1926:11) commented on large anacondas. He is clearly skeptical about very large anacondas, but acknowledges an open mind about the controversy.

> Questions about the largest snakes are difficult to answer. The tales of the Amazonian voyagers who say that they have seen snakes fifty or sixty feet long one cannot believe. Yet there is no doubt but that there are larger Anacondas in the Amazon and its tributaries than have yet been caught, especially about the great swampy Ilha de Marajó which lies at the Amazon's mouth. These snakes may reach the reported maximum of fourteen meters (forty-six feet). It is doubtful if this is really so. A specimen of this size was once reported to Dr. Afranio do Amaral, the principal authority in South America. No such specimen has ever actually been saved, though a ten-metre skin is preserved at Butantan in Brazil.

New York Zoological Society (= Bronx Zoo) reptile curator Raymond Ditmars (1931:42–43) commented on the size attained by anacondas, noting that a 19-foot

anaconda was 36 inches in circumference and weighed 236 pounds. A 17-foot anaconda Ditmars weighed had a mass equal to that of a 24-foot reticulated python—
illustrating that anacondas have great bulk. He suggested that the largest anaconda
reaches a maximum length of 25 feet, while suggesting that the reticulated python
attains a maximum length of 33 feet. Naturalist William Beebe (1946:20) had considerable field experience in South America and reports the largest anaconda he
found to be relatively small compared to many other descriptions.

> The anaconda is the giant among American serpents with an accredited length of
> 29 feet, but the largest taken by us was close to Kartabo (British Guiana
> [= Guyana]), where one of these boas measuring 17 feet, two inches was shot
> from a branch overhanging the water a mile down river.

Ralph Blomberg (1956:93) searched for large anacondas, but failed to find them.
At one point he believed that he had actually found some evidence for huge snakes
only to be disappointed.

> I had been told that the commander of a certain Ecuadorian military post on
> the Putumayo River owned an anaconda skin measuring more than 10 meters—
> about 33 feet. So I looked him up.
> "That's correct," he said. "Actually 12 meters."
> "But do you have it here?" I asked. . . .
> . . . "Sure, I have it here." He ordered a soldier to bring it.
> "Here was something of a sensation! A new record, I thought. Theodore Roo-
> sevelt had offered $5000 for a skin or skeleton only 30 feet long.
> "The solider brought the skin, and we unrolled it on the floor. It measured ex-
> actly 6 meters—only half the length the commander had claimed.
> "That's a bit disappointing," I said. "Only 6 meters!"
> "Its hard to believe," answered the commander, laughing. "I thought it was
> 12, and it looks like 12, doesn't it?"

Blomberg realized the lure of a good story, and the inclination of people to exag-
gerate snake size, comparing big snake stories to that of an amateur fisherman's ability to add inches or feet to the fish that got away. Chiszar et al. (1993) noted media
reports consistently exaggerating the weight of a captive 24 kg python that killed a
human male, listing weights between 27–54 kg, despite the fact that the correct
weight was available.

Paul Fountain's (1904:107–108) account is similar to that of many explorers' nar-
ratives of big anacondas, but his estimates of size are quite moderate and he comments on the seduction of over-estimating the size of a large snake.

> In some marshy ground I killed an anaconda which was just over twenty-four feet
> in length, and this is the largest serpent I have seen in any part of America. It was
> an immense reptile as thick as a man's body, being forty-two inches in girth in
> the thickest part. A single bullet in the head was sufficient to kill it. An attempt
> to preserve the skin of this immense creature failed. Before the serpent was killed
> it looked much bigger than it proved to be, and I realised how easy it is to exag-
> gerate the size of any creature we have not had the opportunity of accurately mea-
> suring. Big things, while still at large, look much bigger than they really are; and
> there seems to be an almost irrepressible tendency in the human mind to exag-
> gerate the size of any animal which is of abnormal bigness. . . . Anacondas of

thirty feet long certainly have been found; and it is possible, I am told, that they occasionally exceed this length by five or six feet; but beyond that length it is extremely improbable that snakes have been found in South America, or any other country. . . . I have made a most careful examination of some of the least-known forests of the Amazon Valley, where a white man had never before penetrated, and if there were monsters there of forty of fifty feet in length I cannot think I should have failed to find them. Possibly in some obscure spots an anaconda may prolong its existence until it attains a length of nearly forty feet; but if so, these are very exceptional cases; and I cannot learn that any museum possesses a skin of anything like this length; and most of the skins in museums have been stretched while still moist. Indeed, it is almost impossible to skin an anaconda without, more or less, stretching the skin.

Colombian biologist Federico Medem described seeing a large anaconda between 30 and 40 feet and estimated its length by comparing it to the canoe he was using. He also provided a secondhand report of a 10.25 m specimen killed on the lower Río Guaviare in southeastern Colombia (Oliver, 1958:24).

Trinidad newspaper editor R. R. Mole (1924:237) reported what he knew about the size of Trinidad anacondas. Some of the specimens he discussed may be the same ones described by Ditmars, since Mole was a regular supplier of snakes to the Bronx Zoo and a friend of Ditmars.

It is recorded that one killed near Irois (Trinidad) in 1810, or 1812, was 32 feet in length. This is quite possible, for there are museum specimens extant which are 33 feet. Much larger ones have been reported from time to time. The *longest* example I have seen was by no means the biggest. In the flesh it taped 17 feet 3 inches, but weighed only 105 pounds. The *largest* I have seen was 16 feet 6 inches It was brought from Guaico in a box and was immediately weighed. Snake and case scaled 300 lbs. When the captive had been removed to more commodious quarters the container was put on the scales and was found to be 68 lbs. The animal was therefore 232 lbs. which far exceeds the weight of several 24 foot pythons of which there are records.

The Guyana Museum in Georgetown had two directors at different points in time that had field experience with large anacondas. J. J. Quelch (1898:297) reported seeing a large anaconda's head in the waters of the Essequibo River, from a distance of 5 feet. He estimated the head as being twice the size of a 20-foot specimen. On 30 May 1921 Vincent Roth (in Oliver, 1958:23–24) described an experience with a large anaconda on the Barima River.

Just below the Five Mile Itabo there was a shout of "Look big camoodi." At a sharp point of the bank a large tree had fallen into the river, carrying a large piece of the bank with it. This earth stuck up out of the water and formed an islet right off the point. In the shallow water between lay exposed in the sunshine a portion of an immense water-boa, as thick around as a pork barrel. The rest of the great snake was in the water. At first I reckoned that, having swallowed some large animal, the immense reptile was in the state of coma usually associated with the digestive periods of these creatures. As it subsequently turned out my surmise was correct. Going within thirty feet of it I observed large flies hovering over and settling on the huge body and, naturally, concluded it was dead. I gave orders to go on when the Indian girl remarked — 'Sometimes they does have flies on them when they living Sir!' At this intelligence I decided to put a bullet into the beast and ascertain whether it was alive. The first shot decided the matter quite definitely. The great body swayed and plunged out into deep water, but the part where the gorged stomach was refused to sink, so I pumped in bullet after bullet as the helpless mass rolled over and over on its own axis. Although the head did not appear to be more than a foot long, the whole serpent was longer than our boat, and that was 28 feet . . . I put that snake down as at least 34 feet as in its writhing on top of the water some 20 to 25 feet away from the boat, to which it was more or less parallel it projected at least 3 feet beyond the bow and stern.

Brazilian army officer, explorer, and anthropologist Candido Mariano de Silva Rondon was awarded medals by the American Geographical Society, The National Geographic Society, and the Explorers' Club (Oliver, 1958:25). On one field trip he encountered a group of Indians who had recently killed a large anaconda and Rondon measured it "in the flesh," (we take this to mean it was not a skin) and he found it to be slightly in excess of 38 feet.

The Brazilian herpetologist Afrânio do Amaral believed (1948; 1976), based on historical accounts (including some that we have cited here) and other anecdotal information, that *Eunectes murinus* attained a length of 14 meters " . . . (talvez 14) metros . . . "; (Amaral, 1948:237).

Up de Graff (1923:71) provided details of encounters with two very large anacondas. The first snake discussed was measured at 30 feet. He wrote:

> While bathing one morning, I stepped on what I took to be the bottom of the pool, when suddenly I felt it heave under me. Some of the Indians were in with me at the time. Thinking that I had stepped on a stinging ray, with which such rivers are infested, I struck out for the bank as hard as I could, shouting the news. The Indians on the bank ran for the canoe, armed with pointed sticks to spear the fish. One glance into the water showed them what really lurked there. Undaunted they attacked it with their spears. The huge reptile, which turned out to be thirty feet long, to our great surprise did not put up a fight for its life. Judging from my later experiences, I think it must have just taken to the water after one of its comatose periods, a theory borne out by the fact that we found an almost totally digested deer in its stomach, although it is unusual for these monsters to return to the water so soon. Having killed it finally with a shot which cut it in two, about three feet from the head, we dragged it ashore. The seven of us had a hard task to drag out the still squirming body and deposit it on the sand-bar. We skinned it. We had to work all day to complete the operation, slitting the skin from end to end along the snake's under side and tearing it inch by inch from the flesh. The work was not even over when at last we had hacked away the last of the clinging carcass.

Up de Graff's second (1923:79–80) encounter with a monster anaconda occurred on Ecuador's Río Yasuní. His estimate suggested to him that this snake was between 50 and 60 feet, and he described how he compared the snake's length to that of the canoe. Thus, this snake falls into the supersnake-size category, but it lacks the other characteristics of supersnakes. While his recounting is dramatic, it is not outlandish, it does not appear to be exaggerated, and it is tempting to take this account at face value—but there is no evidence the snake was the size he suggests it was, and an error in estimation cannot be ruled out.

> There lay in the mud and water, covered with flies, butterflies and insects of all sorts, the most colossal anaconda which ever my wildest dreams had conjured up. Ten or twelve feet of it lay stretched out on the bank in the mud. The rest of

it lay in the clear shallow water, one huge loop of it under our canoe, its body as thick as a man's waist. I have told the story of its length many times since, but scarcely ever have been believed. It measured fifty feet for certainty, and probably nearer sixty. This I know from the position in which it lay. Our canoe was a twenty-four footer; the snake's head was ten or twelve feet beyond the bow; its tail was a good four feet beyond the stern; the center of its body was looped up into a huge S, whose length was the length of our dugout and whose breadth was a good five feet. It is worth noting in passing that Waterton speaks of these reptiles being killed up to forty feet in length while, he says, the Spaniards of the Oroonoqui positively affirm that they grow to be seventy or even eighty feet long, and that such monsters will kill the strongest bull.

This account did not go without criticism. Kermit Roosevelt, son of Theodore Roosevelt, wrote the foreword to Up de Graff's book (pages xiv-xv) and he takes exception to the size of the anaconda in the above story. He wrote:

One point on which my own experiences are at variance from those of Mr. Up de Graff was in the maximum length reached in an anaconda. I have often heard tell of snakes forty or fifty feet long but I have never encountered one, nor seen the skin of one. Many of our companions in Brazil told of meeting with snakes of great size, and when my Father offered five thousand dollars reward for the skin and vertebra (or either alone) of a snake of more than thirty feet, our comrades considered the money as good as in their pockets, for Father set no time limit on the offer and only required that the specimen be turned over to the nearest American Consul, who would then forward it to him. That snake is still at large! There may be snakes of more than thirty feet, no one can definitely deny their existence, but they must be exceedingly rare.

Turtle biologist Peter Pritchard (1994:37–39) commented on the statistical probability of huge anacondas.

The anaconda is not a rare snake, and thousands of specimens have been measured (Petzold, 1983). A series such as this would be sufficient to document the size-distribution of adults of the species, which would be expected to follow a bell-shaped curve. The curve may be asymmetrical in that it may attenuate more gradually on the right rather than the left (an adult anaconda may be ten feet longer than the mean mature length, but would not be ten feet shorter), but in general, we would expect a progressive and rapid falling-off in the number of individuals in size categories increasingly displaced from the modal category. Yet, even without having the actual data at my fingertips, we can be sure that such a histogram would indicate that 20-foot anacondas are rare, 25-footers extremely rare, and 30-footers unavailable in any museum or zoo in the world, and it is not inappropriate to conclude that 35- to 40-footers probably do not exist.

At least a few authors (Heuvelmans, 1958; Perry, 1970) have suggested that huge anacondas have not been brought to natural history museums or zoos because of the transport problems involved. However, Pritchard (1994:38) wrote:

Huge crocodilians are even heavier and harder to handle than giant snakes, yet Spix and Martius were able to collect two large black caimans from the Lower Amazon as long ago as 1819, and their skeletons were prepared and kept. Indeed,

most of the older natural history museums have skulls (at least) of huge crocodilians, shot for "sport" in remote parts of the tropics and subtropics a century
or more ago—and it is by measurement of these skulls that we unfortunately learn
that the animals themselves may not have been nearly as big as they were alleged
to be.

    In the majority of 'monster snake' anecdotes, the snake in question is killed.
Travellers of the past, and of today, in Amazonia, the llanos, or the Guianas generally carry at least one cutlass or machete, usually several, and there is no great
difficulty in decapitating a dead snake, placing the head in warm water or on an
ant nest, and having a clean skull within a very few days. Somehow, this is never
done! (Why spoil a good story?)

The available evidence indicates that *Eunectes murinus* attains greater lengths in
those portions of its range occurring in rain forest habitat than in the llanos. We offer
the following hypothesis, based on the potential for differential encounter rates of prey
of predictable size, to explain this distributional pattern. The llanos supports huge
numbers, often in large social groups, of small- to medium-sized prey species (e.g., turtles [*Podocnemis vogli*], lizards [*Iguana iguana*], caiman [*Caiman crocodilus*], many
species of water birds, capybara [*Hydrochaeris hydrochaeris*]), and smaller numbers
and much lower densities of large prey items. It seems unlikely that small- to medium-
sized prey is a limiting resource, and that is what *E. murinus* will most often encounter,
kill, and consume in the llanos. Attaining a maximum size greater than about 5–6 meters confers no advantage. Conversely, along rain forest rivers vertebrate prey distribution is more patchily distributed, and, therefore, less predictable. An ambush foraging top predator must be able to capture and kill whatever comes along, be it agouti
(*Dasyprocta*), peccary (*Tayassu*), or small tapir (*Tapirus*); it can only do so by having
the size and strength necessary to kill large prey, and to also be able to ingest it. By attaining lengths that approach or exceed 7–8 meters, rain forest anacondas have the potential to overpower and consume very large prey.

Doubt About a Long-standing Record-sized Snake

    In 1944, Emmett R. Dunn, a professor of biology and a noted herpetologist at
Haverford College who had extensively investigated the herpetofauna of Colombia,
published a paper written in Spanish on Colombian snakes that contained the following statement (translated in Gilmore and Murphy, 1993:185–186):

> My friend Mr. Robert Lamon, geologist of the Richmond Oil Company, has
> told me that he killed and measured an example [of anaconda] of eleven and one-
> half meters on the llanos [of eastern Colombia]. I have also heard of examples of
> 14 meters [45 feet] but the statement of Mr. Lamon is not 'second hand' but di-
> rect [first-hand, original] and dignified with credit [credible, reliable].

James Oliver, in his 1958 book *Snakes in Fact and Fiction,* considered this to be
the best evidence that anacondas achieve this incredible size. He wrote:

> This is no estimate. Lamon's story is the nearest I [Oliver] have been able to get
> to a firsthand account of the actual measuring of a large Anaconda. When I talked
> to Dunn about the report, he stated emphatically that he knew Lamon and that
> his veracity was beyond question. Dunn queried him about various details of the

story and the method of making this measurement of a snake in the flesh—not the skin— and in a relaxed position. What more do we need for an authentic maximum record?

Oliver added some details about Dunn's discussion with Lamon and the events that surrounded Lamon's encounter. Oliver (1958:24–25) wrote:

> Lamon encountered the snake while he was leading a party exploring for oil in the llanos of the upper Orinoco River in eastern Colombia. The party stopped one day to lunch along the bank of a river, when someone noticed the body of a tremendous snake in the water. The party carried only .45-caliber automatics, but fired a number of rounds toward the snake. When its writhings ceased, they dragged it out on the bank and measured it with a steel surveyors tape. They then went back to their interrupted lunch, and following the meal they again became involved in their work. When they finally returned to skin out their prize, it was gone! Apparently their shots had merely stunned the snake.

Raymond M. Gilmore, former Curator of Mammals at San Diego's Natural History Museum was interested in the record of this large anaconda and tracked down Lamon in 1954. He corresponded with Lamon and received the following letter from him dated 19 May 1954. This information was not published until 1993 (Gilmore and Murphy, 1993:186).

> I do recall the Meta [River] anaconda which I killed and measured. But that was a long time ago and details have escaped me. I remember measuring the beast with a four-meter stadia rod, and, if my memory serves me right, it required three lengths of the rod to obtain the dimensions, but I could not swear to this in that it may have been almost *two* lengths of the rod [emphasis his].
>
> However, this occurred sometime in about 1939 or 1940 just before I met Dix Dunn in Colombia. Therefore the measurement must have been fresh in my mind, and, if so I reported it to Dunn, I feel confident that the 11.5 meters is correct. I also recall [that] I measured girth of the beast but unfortunately notes that were made as to measurements of the girth and length have long since been lost.

Clifford Pope, author of *The Giant Snakes* (1961:154) wrote,

> The most convincing recent measurement of an anaconda was made in eastern Colombia by Roberto Lamon, a petroleum geologist of the Richmond Oil Company, and reported in 1944 by Emmett R. Dunn. However, as a field measurement, it is open to question. Oliver's 37.5 feet is partly based on this report and can be accepted as probable. However, many herpetologists remain skeptical and would prefer a tentative maximum of about 30 feet.

Thus a snake accepted by some herpetologists as the largest recorded anaconda at 12 meters, is most likely slightly less than 8 meters, still an impressively large snake, but not the monster 12-meter-long serpent reported by Dunn.

The *Guinness Book of World Records 1991* (McFarlan, 1991:85) accepted a report of an anaconda 27 feet 9 inches killed in Brazil about 1960. We have no knowledge of this specimen, or the source of this information, and cannot comment on it (Table 3–1).

Table 3–1. Summary of Reported Sizes for the Anaconda, *Eunectes murinus*

Source	Size	Determination
Amaral (1948:237)	14 m	?
Bancroft (1769:203)	30 ft	h
Beebe (1946:)	29 ft	h
Blomberg (1956:97)	23 ft	m
Ditmars (1931:43)	25 ft	?
Fountain (1904:107)	24 ft	m
Lamon (in Dunn, 1944:183)	37.5 ft*	m
Medem (in Oliver, 1958:24)	10.25 m	h
Mole (1924:237)	32 ft	h
Quelch (1898:297)	37 ft	h
Roth (in Oliver, 1958:23)	34 ft	e
Rondon (in Oliver, 1958:25)	38 ft	?
Up de Graff (1923:71)	30 ft	?
Up de Graff (1923:80)	50 ft	e

*Probably in error, see text.

Note that we have omitted supersnake records. The determination column records if the snake's size was measured (m), estimated (e), or based on hearsay (h); a question mark (?) denotes lack of information.

Size of the Indian Python, *Python molurus*

The accounts of the size reached by this species are not nearly as numerous or exaggerated as those for the anaconda. The Indian python (also frequently called the Burmese python, or rock python), *Python molurus,* is a very well known species based upon captive specimens, and because of this its near-maximum size is also likely to be well known since some of these captives are pampered with all the food they can eat.

Consider the following comments on the size of this snake taken from the literature.

> The python was 18 feet in length and the span of the skin, after removal of the leopard was 22 inches. (Begbie, 1907:1021)

> . . . 7000 mm as a maximum. The maximum girth at the thickest is about 900 mm. . . . This is about the biggest and thickest snake of India. It weighs up to a maximum of 250 lb. (Deoras, 1965:97)

> . . . usually attains to 15 feet but an occasional specimen might be 20 feet long and weigh 250 lb. (Deraniyagala, 1955:7)

> . . . nearly seventeen feet. (Fife-Cookson, 1887:32)

> . . . the Manager, showed me with great pride, an enormous python in a box, length between 21 and 22 feet. (Forsyth, 1911:277)

> Most adult pythons from West Pakistan measure 8 to 10 feet. The largest python brought to the Karachi Zoo from West Pakistan during my stay in the country measured 15 feet and weighed 115 pounds, according to data supplied by Dr. A. A. Quraishy; it was certainly an impressively large snake. (Minton, 1966:117)

The most detailed information we have on the size of this snake comes from Frank Wall (1912:452–453) who summarized size records for *Python molurus*. This account is almost identical to the one published in 1921.

It is difficult to say with certainty to what length the python may attain. It seems probable that many of the great lengths given by travelers and sportsmen were guessed at, and the snake not actually measured. The creature is very thick relative to its length, perhaps three or four times the girth of a Russell's viper of similar length, and five or six times that of a dhaman (*Zamenis mucosus*). If a python's length were judged from its girth, the estimate would grossly exceed the real measurement.

Specimens of 10 feet are not very uncommon, as will be seen from the following records, and there is little doubt that it exceeds 20 feet. In this Journal [Vol. x, page 69] Ferguson records an 18 foot one from the Ashambu Hills, and Major Begbie [Vol. XVII, page 1021] one of similar length killed near Baksa Duars. Other specimens of like proportions have been recorded by the late D. Ferguson in Ceylon [Reptile fauna, Ceylon, p. 22], and in the Pioneer from Rajshai (Rajapur) [3rd July 1907]. I saw the skin of a specimen of the same length in the possession of Mr. A. M. Harry in Assam. Mr. Prince of the King's Own Shropshire Light Infantry shot a female in the United Provinces in 1906 which measured 18 feet 3 inches. In *Land and Water* (August 10th, 1866, or 67?) one is mentioned from Mussoorie of 18 feet 9 inches. Tennent [*Nat. Hist of Ceylon* II, p. 153] refers to a specimen brought him in Ceylon that taped 19 feet. Another reported of a similar length was encountered by Captain George and Mr. Delsuage when shooting in Ceylon. This was captured and brought to Colombo, and exhibited in 1885 when I saw it. Jerdon [Journ. As. Soc., Bengal, XXII, p. 526] saw a 19 foot specimen killed in Travancore, and Dr. Elmes told me of one he shot in Assam (N. Lakhimpur District) of the same size. A specimen measuring 19 feet 2 inches in our Society's collection, shot by the late Maharajah of Cooch Behar in Assam was originally reported in this Journal [XIII, p. 718] as a Malayan python (*P. reticulatus*). Captain Percival [*The Island of Ceylon*, 1805, p. 311] says he saw one in Ceylon 22 feet long, and the specimen mentioned by John Ray, and stated by him to be in the Leyden Museum was, he states 25 feet (I have not been able to get confirmation of this from Leyden, but notice that Dumeril and Bibron refer to one in that Institution 20 feet). Elliot [Rept. Brit. Ass. 1870, Trans., p. 115] claims that it grows to a length of 30 feet . . .

The weight of a python is remarkable, the specimen of *molurus* killed by the Maharajah of Cooch Behar, which measured over 19 feet, scaled 200 pounds (over 14 stone). . . .

A length of just over 10 m is also cited by DeRooij (1917:22), but she does not state where the specimen came from, who measured it, or provide any other details regarding the animal. A 10-meter, or 33-foot *Python molurus* does not seem very probable. We suspect that specimens stated to be this size originated with the article by Wallace Elliot, and noted in Wall's account above. Elliot reported the story about a 30-foot python killed on the Malabar Coast from Sir Mark Cabbon, Commissioner for the Kingdom of Mysore. Cabbon, in turn, had heard the story from a respected friend, a Parsi merchant. The snake had reportedly eaten an Indian bison or gaur. Cabbon took a serious interest in the story, interviewed eye-witnesses, and, since their stories agreed in detail that the snake was more than 30 feet long and that it had swallowed a bison calf, he accepted the story. Oliver (1958:28), however, felt that, despite the respectability of the witnesses, they lacked the needed critical attitude to properly evaluate the size of a large snake (Table 3–2).

Table 3–2. Summary of Reported Sizes for the Indian Python, *Python molurus*

Source	Size	Determination
Begbie (1907:1021)	18 ft.	?
Cooch Behar *	19 ft.	m
Deoras (1965)	7 m	?
Deraniyagala (1955:7)	15–20 ft.	?
Elliot *	30 ft.	h
Ferguson *	18 ft.	?
Fife-Cookson (1887:32)	17 ft. (may be skin)	?
Forsyth (1911:277)	21–22 ft.	h
Jerdon/Elemes *	19 ft.	h
Minton (1966:117)	15 ft.	m
Percival *	22 ft.	?
Prince *	18 ft. 3 inches	m
Tennent *	19 ft.	m

Note that we have omitted supersnake records. The determination column records if the snake's size was measured (m) or based on hearsay (h); a question mark (?) denotes lack of information. *Denotes information from Wall (1912:452–453)

Size of the Reticulated Python, *Python reticulata*

The reticulated python rivals the anaconda for length, but stories about huge individuals are not nearly as common as they are for the anaconda. This may be due to the more slender build of *Python reticulata*. That is, if a 20-foot anaconda and a 20–foot reticulated python were coiled side-by-side, the impression the observer would have is that the anaconda is longer, and larger, due to its bulk. Unfortunately, we found that very few experienced herpetologists have had firsthand field experience with this species, and that most of them comment on its size based upon stories in the literature and on hearsay.

East Indian naturalist Otto Beccari (1904:34) commented on the size of the reticulated python on the islands of Borneo and Singapore.

> The Malays assert that the biggest of these snakes are capable of swallowing a deer . . . On one occasion whilst at Singapore I saw the remains of a gigantic python: a Chinaman passed by the verandah where I was, carrying in two big baskets the transverse sections of the animal's body, some of them quite equal to a man's thigh. The Tuan Muda spoke of a python which he caught, measuring just 19 feet in length, which had a monkey in its stomach . . .

Nelly DeRooij (1917:20) stated that this species attains a length of 9 m. Stanley Flower (1899:655) wrote about it in Indochina.

> A friend told me that when the wooden floor of his stables in Bangkok was being repaired during 1897, in a cavity underneath a large python was found and killed, which measured over 6.09 metres (or 20 feet) in total length. One killed at Matang, Perak, the skin of which measures about 6 metres, is in the possession of Lt.-Col. Froude Walker, C.M.G., who told me the python had been known to kill and eat pigs. Another killed at Simpang (Larut district), Perak, measuring 6.7 metres (or 22 feet), is now in the Taiping Museum. Dr. Wilson, Senior Medical Officer in Johore, told me of a python killed at Muar about 1889, which was 6.85

metres (or 22.5 feet) long and 228 mm. (or 9 inches) in diameter. And Mr. L. Wray, jun., has measured one killed near Taiping, Perak, about 1896, which was in the flesh 8.2 metres (or 27 feet) long, and when skinned and stretched 10 metres (or 33 feet). Cantor writes: 'In 1844 one was killed at the foot of Pinang, which a gentleman informed me measured more than 30 feet.'

Ridley (1899:196) also wrote on Malayan reticulated pythons.

> One of the commonest is the python (*P. reticulatus*), the Ular Sawah of the Malays. It is perhaps the largest snake in the world, a specimen measuring 40 feet having been reported as obtained by a scientific expedition in Manila. Pythons of 20 feet in length are by no means uncommon here, and specimens of 26 feet are occasionally met with, but accurate measurements of large ones are still required.

Hoogerwerf (1970) discussed the size of *P. reticulata* in Java, suggesting that modern specimens are smaller, probably due to overhunting: "Opinions differ greatly about the length that the python can attain, but in Java specimens exceeding a length of 5 meters probably are exceptional nowadays." The Chancellor-Stuart-Field Museum Expedition of 1929 visited Sumatra in July and August of that year and obtained two large specimens of reticulated python, a 24-foot male and a 21-foot female (with a clutch of 81 eggs) (Anon. 1930:89). Specimens of similar size were taken by the Menage scientific expedition in 1892 in the Philippines, one snake was 22 feet 8 inches and another 22 feet 6 inches (Anon. 1903:149).

Malcolm Smith (1943:110) commented on the size of reticulated pythons, and he also believed it to be the largest snake in the world.

> The Reticulated Python is the largest snake living today, the South American Anaconda running it closely for second place. Authentic measurements of specimens that have been killed show that it reaches a length of 27 or 28 feet. Greater lengths have been recorded, but they cannot be relied upon.

University of Kansas herpetologist Edward H. Taylor (1965:669) commented on the size of reticulated pythons in his book on Thailand snakes and compared it to the anaconda.

> In literature this creature is widely known as the python and is probably the largest (longest) serpent known. Specimens measuring 25 feet are not especially rare and specimens reaching a length of 30 feet have been reported, perhaps authentically.
>
> The South American anaconda also belonging to this family closely approaches the size of the python, and where specimens of equal length are compared the anaconda may be the heavier and more bulky species.

One account that many of the above authors referred to was that of Spenser St. John (1863:256–261) who wrote about his travels in northern Borneo. He mentions a 19-foot specimen killed and its body brought to Kuching where it was measured by a Mr. Ruppell. He also mentions a 24-foot skin which was taken from a snake that carried off a dog and was subsequently tracked down by the dog's owner; this has been erroneously cited as a 24-foot snake by some authors. In another incident in 1853, a 26-foot snake was killed (and subsequently alluded to in many of the accounts mentioned above). But here is what St. John (1863:258) actually wrote.

> Mr. Coulson immediately skinned it, and shortly afterwards, brought it up to the consulate. When I measured it, it had lost exactly two inches and was exactly twenty-six feet in length.

Thus, St. John was discussing a skin, not a whole snake. However, St. John does relate a story about a monster reticulated python that attacked a man. The snake was killed and measured at seven Malay fathoms, which would be 35 to 37 feet. St. John confessed that the largest reticulated python he had killed was a mere 14 feet.

Raven (1946:38–39) believed that the reticulated python was the largest snake and related the following story from an unidentified locality in Sulawesi (formerly the Celebes). This story appears to be the basis for all, or most, references to 33-foot reticulated pythons. Raven and Raymond Ditmars were friends and Oliver (1958: 28–29) makes a case for Ditmars' support of the maximum length of *P. reticulata* as 33 feet, because of the following story. Hard evidence and critical details, however, appear to be lacking. Yet it appears that the *Guinness Book of World Records 1991* has accepted this record (McFarlan, 1991:84) as the world's largest snake. The *Book of World Records*'s date of 1912, and the reference to a mining camp in the Celebes, all match this story, but the length of the snake is given as 32 feet 9.5 inches instead of the 33 feet quoted below (Raven, 1946:39), and is most likely the result of converting 10 m to feet.

> ... men at the mine told me of a huge python one of their natives had killed a few days before my arrival, and showed me a very poor photograph of it taken after it had been killed and dragged to camp. The civil engineer told me it was just ten meters (33 feet) long. I asked him if he had paced off its length, but he said no, he had measured it with a surveying tape.

Probably the largest, most reliably documented length for a reticulated python was for Colossus, a snake in excess of 28 feet that lived at the Pittsburgh Zoo. Colossus was received by the zoo on 10 August 1949; its origin was unknown but it was shipped to the United States from Singapore according to Barton and Allen (1961: 840), and they hypothesized a Malayan origin for the specimen; Pope (1961:162), however, stated it was from Thailand (Siam). On arrival at the zoo it was 22 feet long. Barton and Allen (1961:84–86) discussed the captive history of this snake and noted that the most accurate size data were obtained on 24 February 1954 when it was found to weigh 295 pounds (this was shortly after its 4.5-month winter fast). The snake was measured by working a tape measure along its back, and a measurement of 27 feet was obtained. On 15 November 1956 it was measured at 28 feet 6 inches; thus it had grown 16 inches in 33 months. Merle J. Cox (1991:108) wrote that the reticulated python has been reported as exceeding 10 meters and that he had seen one a few centimeters less than ten meters. When one of us (JCM, personal communication) asked Cox about this specimen, he replied that it was at the Pittsburgh Zoo, and the snake was named Colossus.

However, another large reticulated python was apparently kept at the Mesker Zoo in Evansville, Indiana from 1931 to 1948. Davis (1974) reported a python measured by Alvin Short, an Evansville taxidermist, at 33 feet 7 inches and weighing 670 pounds. This is the greatest weight reported for any snake that we are aware of and we suspect it is in error. Colossus, a well-fed, 28.5-foot zoo specimen weighed only 320 pounds at death. It is improbable that an extra 5.1 feet could more than double the weight of one of these snakes. The mounted snake was damaged in 1950 when

Table 3–3. Summary of Reported Sizes for the Reticulated Python, *Python reticulata*

Source	Size	Determination
Anon. (1903:149)	22 ft. 8 inches	m
Anon. (1930:89)	24 ft.	m
Beccari (1904:34)	19 ft.	h
Flower (1899:655)	6.09 m. (20 ft)	h
Mayer (1920:854)	32 ft.	h
Minton and Minton (1973:194)	28 ft. 6 inches	m
Raven (1946:38–39)	33 ft.	m
Ridley (1899:196)	20–26 ft.	h
Smith (1943:110)	27–28 ft.	h

Note that we have omitted supersnake records. The determination column records if the snake's size was measured (m) or based on hearsay (h).

vandals broke into the Evansville Museum and cut up the skin and stole the head. Unfortunately, it is not clear if the snake was measured before or after it was skinned—we suspect the latter.

Mayer (1920:854) makes a passing comment about a reticulated python he caught and sold to " . . . Cross of Liverpool . . ." Cross apparently measured the snake and found it to be 32 feet.

According to Tweedie (1957:32) the greatest authenticated length recorded for a *Python reticulata* is 28 feet and he believes stories of individuals exceeding 30 feet are well within the bounds of possibility. A recent report (Anon., 1988) of a *P. reticulata* from Great Nicobar Island that was 33 feet long was not accompanied by documentable evidence.

Frank Buck (1932:103) alluded to the longest *Python reticulata* skin on exhibit anywhere as one from Cotobato Province, in the Philippines that was on display at the Bureau of Science in Manila. Buck stated that the 33-foot long skin was stretched during mounting, and its real length was probably about 30 feet (Table 3–3).

Size of the African Python, *Python sebae*

A large specimen of African python reported in the literature by numerous herpetologists (Auerbach, 1987:152; Branch, 1984:236; Cansdale, 1961:16; Doucet, 1963:227; Minton and Minton, 1973:197) was an animal shot in 1932 near the Ivory Coast town of Bingerville. Branch (1984:236) discussed the size attained by some of the larger *Python sebae* reported, including the Ivory Coast specimen.

The largest African rock python on record appears to be a 9.8-metre snake killed in a garden hedge at Bingerville in the Ivory Coast in 1932. However, full details for this specimen are lacking, and cannot now be verified. If it existed it would have been a truly formidable snake. Next is a specimen measured by the famous English herpetologist, Arthur Loveridge, whilst on a collecting trip to Lake Victoria in 1927. The fresh skin measured 9.1 metres and even allowing for extensive stretching, must have come from a snake well over seven metres long. George Cansdale (another Englishman, for those who think veracity can be judged by its source!) also measured a fresh skin of 9.1 metres from a West African snake. In the southern part of its range (subspecies *natalensis*) the rock python is smaller and a snake of 5.8 metres from the northern Transvaal bushveld is the largest recorded in southern Africa.

Broadley (1983:67) discussed age, length, and weight of *Python sebae*. Note that he apparently doubts the credibility of the length of the specimen discussed above, because he does not include it in the discussion.

> The maximum age attained by pythons is uncertain, but there are cases on record of individuals reaching 20 to 25 years in captivity. Although lengths of 8 metres have been claimed in the past, these must be accepted with extreme reserve as most of them are based on skins, which it is known can be stretched to a quarter as long again as their original length. In any event, it is most unusual nowadays to find a snake exceeding 5 metres, while the average length of adults can be put at 3–4 metres, of which the tail comprises from one eighth to one tenth. The girth of a 6 metre specimen may be as much as a normal man's waist, while a 4 metre snake averages about 40 cm. There is considerable variation in weight according to conditions and sex (females being proportionately heavier than the males). A 4.3 m female weighed 41 kg when just received by the Durban Snake Park. On the other hand, well fed 5 m specimens in captivity have been known to reach as much as 55 kg. In nature, with its normal hazards and periods of winter hibernation, it probably takes a snake 10 to 15 years to reach full maturity, but in captivity—with suitable conditions of feeding, regulation of temperature and consequent obviation of hibernating periods—a length of 2.5 m has been attained in as short a time as 3 to 5 years from the date of hatching.

Richard Burton (1864:96) wrote about the size of *Python sebae* in west Africa. All things considered, his size estimate is quite conservative, but he does cite John McLeod's more liberal estimates.

> . . . the python has exceeded, I am told, nineteen feet in length. Dr. M'Leod says that in Dahome many have been found from thirty to thirty-six feet long, and of proportional girth, but he does not say that he saw them.

Cansdale (1961:16), in discussing the size of *Python sebae,* reported sizes similar to those of other authors, cited the Bingerville specimen, and provided a view on the frequency of different size categories within the population.

> There will always be arguments about the size of big snakes. African Pythons 10 ft long are quite common; specimens up to 15 ft. are not very rare, but a python of over 20 ft. is distinctly unusual. On two occasions farmers in my area killed pythons that were probably close to 20 ft. long, though certainly not more than that. A mining engineer working in north-west Ashanti told me of one that he had shot measuring about 24 ft. in length; this was the largest of which I had personal knowledge, but I have no doubt that larger pythons exist in all West African territories. I can find few reports of giant pythons from other parts of West Africa, but there is an authentic record of a 32 ft. 8 in specimen from Bingerville in the Ivory Coast in 1932. This seems to be by far the longest yet found anywhere in Africa.

Others writing about the size of large African pythons appear to have overlooked John Duncan's (1847, 2:154–157) description of an encounter with a 31-foot *Python sebae* which he measured in West Africa.

At fourteen miles [presumably from the town of Gooba], while crossing a swamp of no great magnitude, we were met by a number of women. . . . they informed us of the extreme danger of passing any farther, till an enormous snake which they had just met should retire. They stated that this reptile had taken up his position in a large tamarind-tree, whence they said he had been in all probability compelled to retreat after a combat with a panther, which they said invariably practiced one particular mode of attack. Whenever they come unexpectedly upon one of these reptiles, they pounce upon its tail, and thus prevent it from coiling itself round its prey. Then with its claw it secures the head, which is immediately brought round to release its tail. However, I never witnessed an attack of this sort, and must leave my readers to judge of the truth of this assertion. One of the party offered to go back and show us the enormous snake, and several others of the party volunteered their services also.

Accordingly we proceeded about six hundred yards . . .

It appeared this reptile had descended the tamarind, and had ascended a much larger tree of a different description. I immediately dismounted, and unstrapped my double-barrelled carbine . . . I took steady aim at the neck, just behind its head, and fired the charge of slugs effectually . . . I then took my sword, which I had sharpened equal to a razor, and cut the head off at one stroke; but even then the people would not venture to touch it with their hands to pull it down, till I gave them a piece of small cord, which I invariably carried in my pocket. This was fastened round the body, and they then succeeded in pulling it down.

The monster was of the boa tribe, and measured thirty-one feet long, but the natives told me they had seen them much larger. . . .

Another account of huge pythons in West Africa comes from anthropologist Mary Kingsley (1897:546). She wrote:

I am assured by the missionaries in Calabar that there was a python brought into Creek Town in the Rev. Mr. Goldie's time, that extended the whole length of the Creek Town mission-house verandah and to spare. This python must have been over 40 feet. I have not a shadow of doubt it was. Stay-at-home people will always discredit great measurements, but experienced bushmen do not, and after all, if it amuses the stay-at-homes to do so, by all means let them; they have dull lives of it and it don't hurt you, for you know how exceedingly difficult it is to preserve really big things to bring home, and how, half the time, they fall into the hands of people who would not bother their heads to preserve them in a rotting climate like West Africa.

The largest python I ever measured was a damaged one, which was 26 feet. There is an immense one hung in front of a house in San Paul de Loanda which you can go and measure yourself with comparative safety any day, and which is, I think over 20 feet. I never measured this one. . . .

Harvard herpetologist Arthur Loveridge (1929:17) had firsthand field experience with African pythons, discussed measuring large skins, and provided an opinion on how large they get.

I am quite prepared to believe that this python may attain a length of thirty feet. I have measured a freshly-removed skin that was exactly thirty, though in the flesh such a monster would probably not be very much over twenty-five feet. This reptile had been speared by natives on the bank of the Ngeri Ngeri River near Morogoro. Two other skins which I purchased in the same locality each measured eighteen feet. The two largest living pythons, which I have kept in captivity, measured fourteen and twelve feet respectively; the weight of the latter when brought to me was exactly thirty pounds but when, some six months later, it left me for a bush life, it must have been nearer forty.

Pitman (1974:68) commented on this python in Uganda, and reported a 20-foot specimen, as well as smaller individuals.

Newly hatched African pythons slender, average about two feet (610 mm); some little thicker than ordinary pencil, others about finger thickness. Growth in captivity fairly rapid, may reach length eight feet (2428 mm) and weight ten pounds in five years, full maturity in ten to fifteen years. . . . Biggest authenticated Uganda measurement 18 feet (5486 mm), size adults usually varies 11 (3653 mm) to 15 (4560 mm) feet. Largest measured personally, 13 feet (3962 mm), contained partially digested, half grown female situtunga (marsh antelope). Large Uganda examples include—estimated 20 feet (6096 mm), Busingiro, Budongo Forest; 17 feet 4 inches (5284 mm) biggest (smallest 9 ft. 2 ins., 2794 mm) of 10 from near Mityana; and 16.5 ft (5029 mm), Entebbe. Skin measurements unreliable, even when not unduly stretched quarter as long again as living reptile. On island Victoria Nyanza near Entebbe, one (female presumed) seen estimated fully 15 feet (4560 mm), many hatchlings in vicinity. . . .

Sweeney (1961:43) commented on this snake's size in his book on the Nyasaland herpetofauna, and suggests large specimens are rarer at the time of the writing than in the past.

The python attains a maximum length of about 24 feet, but such a length would be phenomenal today. Any specimen exceeding 15 feet in length would be exceptional. The longest specimen caught in the Lower River was some 13 feet (3,925 mm). Altogether in eleven years in Africa I have recorded personally 26 mature specimens, the largest of which was a specimen in the southern Sudan which measured 4,650 mm (15.5 feet). The mean size of specimens over 5 feet in length was approximately 2,400 mm. All these specimens were measured alive or freshly killed, and for most, three measurements were taken and the mean found. However, specimens of 18–19 feet have been recorded recently, one specimen of some 19 feet in length being on exhibit at the London Zoo.

Van Rompaey (1985:250) wrote a letter to the editor of *African Wildlife* and submitted a photograph (Figure 3–2) of a specimen said to be 11 m long.

I remember having in my possession a photograph which could possibly be of interest to your readers. I enclose a duplicate of this photography, the original of which has the following words written on the back: 'Boa—11 m. Veau—43 kg. Luluabourg 1953.'
    I do not know who took the photo; it was presumably taken in 1953 near Luluabourg (now called Kananga) in Zaïre. By 'boa' is, of course, meant python; 'veau' is French for 'calf'. If the data are correct the half swallowed 43-kilogram calf would not be exceptional but the alleged length of this rock python (*Python sebae*) would be, with its 11 metres a new record. Unfortunately there is no way to check these data.

Actually there is a way to estimate the size of the snake in the photograph, because a human is standing alongside of the snake and the person's shoes are visible. As-

Figure 3–2. An African python, *Python sebae*. Written on the back of the photo was: "Boa—11 m. Veau—43 kg. Luluabourg 1953." Presumably the photo was taken in 1953 near Luluabourg (now called Kananga) in Zaïre. "Boa" undoubtedly means python, "veau" is French for calf. The photo is significant for two reasons. First, it shows the extreme degree to which a snake can extend its jaws when swallowing. Second, the stated size, if accurate, makes it one of the longest snakes on record, but see discussion. Photographer unknown. *Courtesy of H. van Rompaey.*

suming that the shoes are 10 inches long, and taking that distance into the portion of the snake visible in the photo it goes 22 times. Thus, there are about 220 inches of snake visible, or about 18.3 feet. It is highly unlikely that the snake is much more than 23 or 24 feet (or 7 m). Even if the estimate is off by 25% the snake is still not close to 11 m, but it is still a huge animal. (Table 3–4)

Pritchard's Rule

Zoologist Peter Pritchard (1994:37–39) surveyed the ratio of minimum adult length to record length of many North American snake species listed by Conant (1975) and found the record length is about 1.5 to 2.5 times the minimum adult length. Based on Holmstrom's (1980) data, Pritchard believed that a small adult anaconda is 10–12 feet in length and that, therefore, the record length would not be expected to exceed about 30 feet and may actually be considerably less.

Thus, none of these snakes is predicted to exceed 8 meters (or 26.3 ft.) (Table 3–5). Although there is certainly evidence that some individuals of some species do exceed this length, the best of which is the near-10-meter reticulated python named Colossus. There are several reasons for possible discrepancies. First, the minimum adult lengths are based upon captive animals reported in the literature, and the well fed and cared

Table 3–4. Summary of Some Size Records for the African Python, *Python sebae*

Reference	Maximum Size	Determination
Auerbach (1987:152)	10.0 m	h
Broadley (1983:65)	6.5 m	?
Burton (1864:96)	19 ft	h
*Cansdale (1961:17)	32 ft 8 inches	h
*Doucet (1963:227)	9.8 m	h
Duncan, (1847, 2:157)	31 ft	m
Kingsley (1897:546)	40 ft	h
Loveridge (1929:17)	30 ft	h
M'Leod (in Burton, 1864:96)	30–36 ft	h
*Minton and Minton (1973:197)	9.8 m	h
Sweeney (1961)	24 ft	h
Van Rompaey (1985:250)	11 m	h

*All refer to the same specimen, an animal about 32 ft long killed near Bingerville, Ivory Coast in 1932.

Note that we have not included supersnake records. The determination column records if the snake's size was measured (m) or based on hearsay (h); a question mark denotes lack of information.

for captive snake may achieve sexual maturity earlier than it would in the wild. Second, Pritchard's numbers were based upon North American snakes which are mostly in the family Colubridae, and members of the family Boidae may exhibit different growth and maturity curves. Third, there may be factors at work here that are unknown, or at least poorly understood, and Pritchard's Rule simply may not be valid.

Unclaimed Rewards for Big Snakes

Rewards for huge snakes were offered at the turn of the last century in England and Germany (Hagenbeck, 1910:179). Today, the New York Zoological Society (The Wildlife Conservation Society) continues to offer a steadily increasing reward for *any* healthy, live snake 30 feet or more in length, recognizing that the only potential candidate species are likely to be the reticulated python and the common anaconda (Conway, *in* Petzold, 1983). The Society does not even appear to have a rule against hobbyists overfeeding captive snakes to produce such a monster. The reward started many years ago at $1,000; subsequently it was raised to $5,000; then in January 1978 it rose to $15,000; and at the 1980 Members Meeting of the NYZS, William G. Conway announced that the reward had been raised to $50,000. To date, no 30-footer has been forthcoming. *Science Digest* ran an article on the unclaimed NYZS

Table 3–5. Estimated Maximum Lengths using Pritchard's (1994) suggestion that maximum size is about 1.5 to 2.5 times the smallest adult female length.

	Minimum Adult Size	× 2.5
Eunectes murinus	3.2m (10.5 ft)	8.0m (26.3 ft)
Morelia amethistinus	1.8m (5.9 ft)	4.5m (14.8 ft)
Python molurus	2.35m (7.7 ft)	5.9m (19.4 ft)
Python reticulata	3.04m (9.9 ft)	7.6m (24.9 ft)
Python sebae	2.50m (8.2 ft)	6.25m (20.5 ft)

reward in 1980, a series of letters collectively titled the "Longest Snake" was received between March 1981 and May 1982. We reviewed these letters and found them almost always to reference stories previously cited here, always unreferenced and undocumented.

We will close this chapter with two amazingly rational quotes from the "adventure" literature. The first comes from George M. Dyott (1929:144) who was sent to South America in search of the missing Col. P. H. Fawcett (who reported an anaconda in excess of 60 feet) and his party. One night in Brazil, Dyott observed an anaconda making its way down a river and

> . . . was fascinated by the sight of his great black bulk piling over the rocks in humping heaps. By moonlight he appeared to be every inch of forty feet long, which meant that in reality he must have been near twenty.

Another moonlight adventure was recounted by H. S. Dickey (1932:220), a medical doctor. He saw an anaconda that he felt was easily 30 feet long. It was eventually killed and it turned out to be 19 feet in length and 14 inches in diameter. He commented:

> . . . and was the largest boa I have ever seen. It looked, as I have said, to be thirty feet in length, when we first saw it as it emerged from the river. That was by the light of the waning moon. Perhaps the intrepid explorers who see these creatures as frequently thirty feet long and more, are affected by the moonlight also.

Summary

Stories regarding exceptionally large giant snakes are abundant, but often mixed with elements that suggest the story tellers are mixing facts with cultural myths. The scrub python, western olive python and Papuan python may have individuals which occasionally exceed 20 feet or 6.096 m. The Indian python appears to exceed 20 feet on occasion, but specimens approaching 30 feet seem improbable.

Which species of large snake attains the greatest length is not at all clear. Individual specimens of anacondas, reticulated pythons, and African pythons appear to approach, and possibly slightly exceed 30 feet on occasion. There is no doubt that *E. murinus* is the most massive snake species in the world, attaining weights greater than any other, and it seems that there are more authentic records of very long *Python reticulata* than for any of the other species.

The common anaconda and the largest pythons are as large as they are in order to exploit prey species that are otherwise unexploitable by a snake, and because other, smaller, snakes can't eat them, thereby alleviating possible competition for food resources. Perhaps the bottom line in the "controversy" surrounding which snake is the longest is that it doesn't really matter. It is more fun to argue and speculate about which is the longest, and if we knew for certain which species was the champ, we'd no longer have reason to discuss such an entertaining and enjoyable topic.

CHAPTER 4

FOOD AND FEEDING

> It [the anaconda] is also called "Cobra de Veado" because [it is] supposed to be fond of venison and Spix and Martius heard from M. Duarte Nogueira that it has attacked a man on horseback, and even swallowed an ox. A Brazilian gentleman assured me that in Maranhao he had seen the terrible reptile swimming across the stream with a pair of horns protruding from its mouth.

The above hearsay was reported by explorer Richard Burton (1869:180). The attack on a horse and rider can be easily explained as a defensive strike at a horse and rider that came too close to a large anaconda and threatened it. On the other hand, the attack on an ox seems highly improbable unless it was a calf. Regardless, these events are not unique in the popular literature, and we use them to set the stage for a review, discussion, and analysis of the diets and feeding behavior of the giants. Aside from, possibly, the literature discussing sizes of the giants, the kinds of animals eaten by the giants and how they kill those animals has generated more discussion than any other topic concerning anacondas and pythons.

John M'Leod, ship's surgeon and world traveler, recounted his adventures in the 1818 book *Voyage of His Majesty's Ship Alceste Along The Coast of Corea, to the Island of Lewchew With An Account of Her Subsequent Shipwreck.* Included is a story (pages 288–298) about a Bornean reticulated python that was going to be shipped to England aboard the *Caesar.* The snake, probably about 16 feet in length, was in a wooden cage on the deck of the ship, and six goats were on board as food for the snake. A goat placed in the snake's cage was described by M'Leod as trembling with agony and terror, and M'Leod continued with a discourse on how the goat met its horrible death. Watching the snake eat, M'Leod was unable to understand how the snake was capable of breathing and he suggested that it suspended its ability to breathe while it was doing so. He reported that the snake started to "droop" as the *Caesar* approached the Cape of Good Hope and correctly deduced that it was due to the cold weather; as the ship made its way toward St. Helena, the snake died. William Broderip (1826:215–221) subsequently refuted M'Leod's claims about the behavior of prey in the presence of a snake and discussed the breathing mechanism of snakes that does operate during feeding. However, M'Leod's book was widely read, and Broderip's critique was published in *The Zoological Journal.* This literary exchange points out the problem of the public obtaining accurate information and the strong emotions humans apply to the death of cute, fuzzy mammals in the coils of a cold blooded, reptilian killer. While many of us may laugh and criticize the attitudes portrayed in M'Leod's 180-year-old narrative, the anthropomorphic attitudes toward animals are not only alive and well, but flourishing in western culture today. This attitude needs to be replaced with the acknowledgment that humans, a large predatory and opportunistic species, exploit other life forms for their own survival. This exploitation should not be at the cost of extinction to other species, and attribution of human emotions to other species' behavior is an error.

Food is central to the biology and life history of all animals, and recognizing, locating, capturing, ingesting, and digesting prey are critical activities for their survival and reproductive success. In this chapter we examine what is known about food and feeding behavior of giant snakes, placing the information in perspective based upon current knowledge of snake biology. Giant snakes have been the subject of few field studies, so much of the information is based upon observation of captives, anecdotal field observations, and extrapolation of studies of other snake species.

How Do Snakes Recognize Food?

Giant snakes rely on several sources of sensory input to locate food, including vision, vibration, heat, and odor.

Prey detection occurs while a snake forages. North American queen snakes (*Regina septemvittata*), for example, are active foragers. On warm summer mornings they can be seen swimming along shorelines poking their heads under submerged stones and pulling newly molted crayfish out of their retreats (JCM, personal observation). In contrast, some snakes stay in one location for a period of time waiting for the prey to come to them. The largest pit viper in the world, the bushmaster (*Lachesis muta*), uses this sit-and-wait strategy. Greene and Santana (1983) followed a female bushmaster and found she used three hunting sites for 3–15 days. During a 35-day period she traveled 50 m and on the 24th day of observation she captured a rodent equal to 50% of her body weight. At this time the snake rested for 9 days before moving to a new hunting site. It has been estimated that a bushmaster needs only six meals per year for body maintenance and foraging. Most likely, large boas and pythons also use a sit-and-wait strategy (but on occasion may also employ an active strategy). A boa constrictor (*Boa constrictor*) was followed using radio telemetry on Barro Colorado Island in the Panama Canal Zone. The snake used the burrows of medium-sized mammals (switching burrows every 3–4 days) throughout a 12-day study, probably waiting for a burrow's resident to return, or for appropriate prey to pass nearby (Montgomery and Rand, 1978). Waiting for prey to approach within striking distance can be a long process, and snakes using this technique can be expected to go for extended periods of time without food.

The most detailed account of python foraging comes from Australia and is not based on one of the giants. Slip and Shine (1988) described foraging behavior in the diamond python (*Morelia s. spilota*), a species which attains a maximum length approaching 3.0 meters. Using radio telemetry, they found that, during the summer, adult snakes spent more than 80% of their time coiled (or loosely coiled, with the head positioned at the top of the coil and inclined at an angle of about 15° above horizontal), usually in a distinctive ambush posture near mammal trails (with the head toward open ground; i.e., toward the trail). Telemetered snakes found feeding had occupied the site for at least a day beforehand. In contrast to the amount of time spent foraging, the pythons spent about 15% of their time moving and 5% basking.

Some snake species have relatively good vision. Others, such as the blindsnakes and threadsnakes, have greatly reduced eyes which are often covered by skin and scales and probably act only as light detectors. Diurnal, active foraging snakes tend to have large eyes containing red and green color receptors; conversely, nocturnal snakes that ambush their prey tend to have smaller eyes, no color receptors and undoubtedly rely more on odor for detecting prey.

Many authoritative texts and articles suggest snakes cannot hear because they lack external ear openings and the anatomical structures associated with hearing in other vertebrates. However, snakes clearly do detect vibrations transmitted through the ground and water via their lower jaw bones and the portion of their bodies in contact with the ground. Additionally, snakes probably use their body to collect airborne vibrations and transmit the vibrations to their lungs. The role hearing plays in snakes detecting prey is poorly understood, but possibly is important.

Pits on the loreal scales of pit vipers and the labial scales of some boid snakes are used as infrared detectors. These allow the snake to detect amazingly subtle changes in environmental temperatures ($0.026°$ C; Bullock and Barrett, 1968) and, since most objects in nature radiate some infrared energy, the information collected by these pits may very well produce an infrared image in the snake's brain, allowing it to "see" in the infrared. Thus, even a blind pit viper or boid is capable of locating prey by its emission of infrared radiation.

Chemical-sensing, or chemosensing, is a complex sensory pathway in snakes because snakes analyze environmental molecules through their nostrils, as well as with its Jacobson's organ. Jacobson's organs are at two locations, one right and one left in the roof of the mouth. Molecules adhere to the tongue's surface when the snake flicks it, and are delivered to the Jacobson's organs when the snake retracts the tongue into the mouth. With these organs snakes obtain information about potential prey, predators, mates, and rivals, as well as directional information, right or left. All senses have roles in stimulating snakes to feed, but the single most important is odor, the chemosensory input. Chemosensing also plays a key role in understanding why these snakes, in rare instances, attack humans.

A 65 kg, 4.3 m, female anaconda at the Steinhart Aquarium in San Francisco died from the ingestion of plastic plants (Blasiola et al., 1982:10–14). Two weeks before its death the snake was seen gaping its mouth, and a few days after this the snake showed signs of weakness and anorexia. Plastic plants had been seen in the animal's feces, and upon death a necropsy revealed an obstruction in the colon caused by plastic plants. The authors do not give a reason for the snake swallowing plastic plants, but the snake was housed with a variety of South American fishes and it seems probable that fish odor on the plants resulted in the snake swallowing some of the cage decorations in error.

A classic example of a snake mistakenly ingesting an inappropriate item occurred at the London Zoological Garden (Anon., 1866:54) when a boa swallowed a large railway blanket instead of two rabbits which had been placed in its cage. Boulenger (n.d.:108) discussed the same incident and reported a story of an Indian python that swallowed two feet of a bamboo pole that was used to manipulate rats in the snake's cage. A Karchi zoo employee related a story to the Mintons (1973:215) about a *Python molurus* that swallowed a cloth bag containing two monitor lizards. The supervisor accused the employee of selling the lizards for their skins, but the bag and the lizards were found when the snake tried to pass the remains several days later. Odor is an all-important stimulus in snake feeding behavior.

Diversity of Food Eaten by Giant Snakes

Some snake species, including the giants, are very catholic in the kind of food they eat, preying on most or all major vertebrate groups: fishes, amphibians, reptiles (turtles, crocodilians, lizards, and snakes including members of their own species) birds, and mammals. Other species are very specialized for feeding on one or two very specific kinds of prey. For example, the aquatic North American queen snake (*Regina septemvittata*) feeds on newly molted crayfish as adults, while newborn individuals feed on dragonfly and damselfly nymphs. Experimental evidence suggests that queen snakes, as well as other species of snakes, are born with an innate knowledge of what they will eat. These specialized snakes may starve to death in captivity before they would eat fish, frogs, or some other animal, because their nervous systems do not recognize these other animals as food. The worm snakes and blind snakes (Scolecophidia) are mostly specialized for feeding on ants and termites. Other snake species are specialized for feeding on insects, spiders, scorpions, snails and slugs, reptile or bird eggs, or some other group of vertebrate animals.

Giant snakes eat a wide variety of vertebrates, both taxonomically and by size. None of the giant species appear to show any marked trophic specialization based upon what we currently know. This led Pope (1961:77) to write,

> Hundreds of species of mammals, birds, and fishes, not to mention numerous kinds of reptiles, if not amphibians, fall victim to these giants.

Humans may also be attacked and eaten, but these are rare events and accounts of giant snakes attacking humans will be discussed in Chapter 7. The general nature of the diet allows giant snakes to be opportunistic, taking advantage of almost any potential prey species of an appropriate size.

Invertebrates

Rarely, if ever, are invertebrates eaten by giant snakes, although Wall (1921:57) wrote about an Indian python, *Python molurus,* that apparently did so.

> The most curious meal that I have had reported to me was a double handful of earthworms, and a handful of the berry called by the natives 'jaman' (*Eugenia jambolana*). My informant was Mr. J. H. Mitchell, a planter in Assam. . . .

It is unclear under what conditions the snake ate this highly improbable meal, but the snake may have mistaken an odor given off by the worms and berries for a more normal prey item or, more likely, the story may be untrue. There are, however, several accounts of giant snakes ingesting fruit, and these will be dealt with below.

Fishes

Considering the highly aquatic habits of the anaconda and large pythons, fish would be considered likely prey; however, few reports exist which document fish in their natural diets. William Beebe (1946:20) is one of only a few authors to report fish in the diet of the anaconda. This is surprising considering the varied food taken by anacondas (Henderson et al., 1995) and the aquatic habits of the species. Beebe took 27 fish, including sharp-spined catfish and four species of armored catfish from three specimens.

Captive anacondas will eat fish. Michaels (1970:32) reported a 28 inch neonate that ate 51 minnows in a 3-month period. As it grew, it ate 25 to 40 inches of smelt per week and during one six week period this snake ate 135 inches (more than 11 feet) of fish.

Fish have also been reported in the diet of the African python, *Python sebae*. Bruton and Haacke (1980:263) discussed an incident at Lake Sibaya, Maputaland. Two pythons were caught in fish traps at a depth of 2 m off Crocodile Point at Lake Sibaya, both had gorged themselves on cichlid fishes in the trap before they drowned. It is likely that the other giants also occasionally eat fish.

Amphibians

Frogs and toads have rarely been reported as anaconda or python food in the literature; again, this is somewhat surprising given the preference for aquatic habitats by the giants. It is possible that smaller individuals may eat these amphibians, but it has not been documented. Wall (1921:57), however, related a second-hand account of a wild caught *Python molurus* that had eaten two or three toads, as well as a statement that a captive swallowed frogs. Cansdale (1961:18) suggested *Python sebae* will eat frogs when they are hungry, and Wall (1926:3–4) and Hoogerwerf (1970: 483) also record frogs in the diet of *Python reticulata*.

Reptiles

Turtles. The dermal bone composing the shells of turtles would be expected to make them unlikely prey for snakes, but Mole (1924:238) reported an anaconda regurgitating an aquatic turtle. Neill and Allen (1956:173) considered the upper and lower alveolar ridges of a tortoise voided by a reticulated python to have been secondarily ingested with a carnivorous mammal. This, however, seems unlikely since a carnivorous mammal is likely to eat only soft tissue; it is more probable that the whole tortoise was ingested by the python.

Crocodilians. Dermal bone is also present in large quantities beneath the skin of crocodilians which, combined with a large mouth full of teeth and powerful musculature, would make them unlikely candidates for giant snake prey. But reports of crocodilians being eaten by large snakes are frequent enough to suggest they may form a regular part of the diet of some populations.

A photograph published in the *Journal of the Bombay Natural History Society* (Anon., 1924:704) and *Overseas* illustrated a crocodilian killed by an anaconda on the Río Masparito, Venezuela. Based upon the photograph, the prey was probably the black caiman, *Melanosuchus niger,* and was said to be 10 feet long, while the snake was about 20 feet.

A 25-foot anaconda shot in Nariva Swamp, Trinidad contained a 6-foot spectacled caiman (Wehekind, 1955:10), and J. J. Quelch (1898:298–299), former director of the British Guiana (= Guyana) Museum, related an account of anacondas struggling to eat crocodilians, and he suggested they are eaten regularly. Photographs in several recent books also indicate giant snakes eat crocodilians; Halliday and Adler (1986:120–121) illustrate *Python sebae* constricting a Nile crocodile.

Lizards. Theodore Roosevelt (1914:228) related a secondhand account of an anaconda eating a common iguana (*Iguana iguana*), and Quelch (1898: 298–299) reported an anaconda feeding on a lizard of the genus *Tupinambis*, large omnivorous lizards that occur through much of South America.

Large monitor lizards (*Varanus* spp.) would also seem unlikely food for any snake as they have a mouthful of teeth, powerful claws, and behavioral traits which make them formidable prey. Yet literature accounts suggest large pythons feed on them with some regularity. Minton (1966:118) reported them eaten by Pakistani *Python molurus,* and Deraniyagala (1956:6) reported them in the diet of Sri Lankan *molurus.* Wall (1921:57) and Mash (1945:249) also cite captive *molurus* eating monitor lizards, and Brehm [*in* Hoogerwerf, 1970:483–484] mentions a 3-meter *Python reticulata* that had eaten a 1.65-meter monitor lizard. The African python, *Python sebae,* also eats monitor lizards on occasion (Branch, 1984:237), and FitzSimons (1930:31–32) described an incident at the Cape Town Snake Park which reads more like self-defense than predation.

> But one day a big, strong water monitor grabbed a python by the neck. The teeth of these lizards are strong but blunt, so although it had apparently been trying for some time to tear the skin of the python, it had not succeeded in so doing. The python, however, wearied at length of the lizard's attentions and, throwing three coils round its body, crushing it to death and forthwith swallowed it.

Snakes. Anacondas will eat other snakes, including other anacondas (O'Shea, 1994). Michaels (1970:32) reported a captive neonate *Eunectes murinus* eating a water snake (presumably *Nerodia*) with which it was housed. Also, captive reticulated pythons, *P. reticulata,* have been known to cannibalize cagemates; Ridley (1899:196–7) wrote,

> On one occasion five pythons were put together into a large cage. The biggest was a little over nineteen feet long, another was between 17 and 18 feet, and the other three were from 12 to 15 feet in length. The biggest snake ate all the three smaller ones in two nights, and attacked the remaining one, which however succeeded in beating it off, not without being wounded.

Thus, it is possible that all of these snakes are cannibals on occasion, and these incidents may be particularly common in the confines of the captive environment.

Parker and Grandison (1977:43) include a photograph of a *Python reticulata* constricting a king cobra (*Ophiophagus hannah*). The photo was taken in West Malaysia and appears as though it was taken in the field (rather than staged in captivity). It is unknown if the python ultimately ingested the cobra. The incident is especially interesting because *O. hannah* is a voracious snake predator. Wall (1912:460) commented on a similar encounter between a 10.3 foot hamadryad and a 7.9 foot python in Burma. The king cobra's snake-eating habits are well known and it is entirely possible that the cobra attacked the python and ended-up the prey in the first instance, while in the second human intervention ended the lives of both snakes.

Birds

Avian prey has been recorded in the diets of giant snakes many times, indicating that birds are routinely eaten by all of the giants. Often the species listed are domesticated and have gained notice because someone found a snake in their duck pond or hen house (Figure 4–1). Giant snakes that raid farmyards do little to improve their image for farmers who frequently hold the snake's life in their hands.

Figure 4–1. Boid snakes frequently feed on domesticated birds. *From Goodrich, 1870:402.*

The anaconda preys on a variety of wading birds; these birds occur in high concentrations, especially during the dry season, and probably often fall prey to foraging anacondas.

Wall (1921:57) commented on stories of *P. molurus* feeding on birds.

> Birds are frequently preyed upon by this snake. Mr. Thwaites mentions a peacock in the coils of a python in Ceylon, and Colonel Evans knew one in Burma to eat a pheasant (*Gennaeus lineatus*). One, when I was in Dibrugarh, was killed in the act of swallowing a chicken. Mr. Staunton killed one in Assam that had swallowed three of his ducks, and another made an unwelcome visit to Dr. Elmes's fowlhouse, accounting for five ducks, four fowls, and one pigeon of his stock, all of which had been swallowed, giving the snake a beaded appearance.

The feeding habits of *Python molurus* in Keoladeo National Park, Bharatpur, Rajastan were summarized by Bhupathy and Vijayan (1989:384), who reported 10 prey species, 6 of which were birds. A scrub python, *Morelia amethistina,* was found with a whistling kite in its stomach (Worrell, 1963:97).

Mammals

Like birds, mammals are reported as food in every general account of the feeding habits of giant snakes, and it becomes apparent that mammals most likely compose the bulk of the diet of giant snakes (except, possibly, *Eunectes murinus*). It seems probable that any appropriately sized mammal sharing the activity range of a giant snake is subject to predation. The size range and abundance of rodents and lago-morphs (rabbits) make them prime candidates as giant snake food, but many other mammals, including some quite unexpected, are eaten by giant snakes.

Accounts discussing anacondas frequently include rodents, dogs, deer, peccary, and domesticated pigs. Schomburgh (1922:330) described a 14-foot anaconda that had eaten a full grown "water hass." The water haas, or capybara (*Hydrochaeris hydrochaeris*), is the largest species of rodent in the world and it may attain a length of more than a meter and a weight of 65 kg (Emmons and Feer, 1990:204). Mole (1924:238) reported that anacondas have been known to kill dogs and deer, and one which was in his possession voided the horny claws of a tamandua. Tamanduas are anteaters that may weight up to 8.4 kg and frequently forage along streams (Emmons and Feer, 1990:32) where they may be encountered by *Eunectes murinus*.

The pythons of Africa and Southeast Asia have a wider choice of large mammals to choose from than the anaconda since the Neotropics have fewer large species. Thus, the variety of hoofed mammals, large wild cats, canids, ground-dwelling primates, and other medium to large mammals in the diets of *P. molurus, P. reticulata,* and *P. sebae* can be expected to be greater than those found in the diet of the anaconda.

Choices, however, may be particularly limited on small islands, and even more so on islands that have been recently covered with lava and ash from erupting volcanos. Dammerman (1948:348–349) described *Python reticulata* eating rats and chickens on Krakatau, and they were probably the most abundant prey available considering the condition of the island.

> Mr. Handl who stayed on Krakatau from 1917 until 1921 told us that his chickens were always devoured by the pythons. In January 1922 we found on Krakatau an adult specimen in a tree on the beach and two juvenile ones. In the stomach of one of these were remnants of a rat. In 1924 two rather large examples were caught, both males, one 3.63 metres and the other reaching a length of 2.94 metres. Their stomachs were empty.

Summaries of python diets also frequently include domesticated cats and dogs, rodents, ungulates, and monkeys (Figures 4–2, 4–3). This is due, in part, to the large sizes, as well as the economic and emotional bonds humans have to these animals. While working in Thailand, Flower (1899:655) wrote,

> In May 1897, a python [*P. reticulata*], 2820 mm (or 9 ft. 3 in.) in length was found in Wang Luang (the King's Palace); I was told it had swallowed a pet cat and then had become too fat to get away through the hole by which it had entered. On opening the snake I found a full-grown Siamese cat with a bell hung round its neck.

Young reticulated pythons living within the city limits of Bangkok commonly eat rats, and as they get larger domesticated cats are eaten more frequently than other domesticated animals; whether this is due to the greater abundance of these two species, or due to some learned or innate preference is unclear (Smith, 1914:9).

Bat roosts in trees and buildings may attract snakes. Deraniyagala (1955:6) reported a Sri Lankan *Python molurus* secured from a hollow tree trunk contained 35 horseshoe bats of the genus *Rhinolophus*.

Wild canids, as well as domesticated ones, may be eaten by large boids. Observa-

Figure 4–2. Domesticated animals are also frequent prey for large boids. This African python has recently swallowed a goat. *Courtesy, The Field Museum, Neg# 50712, Chicago.*

A LANGÚR IN THE COILS OF A PYTHON.

Figure 4–3. An Indian python, 12 feet 10 inches long was found and killed while it was constricting a langur monkey (*Presbytis* sp.) in the Canara Forest. *From Channer (1895:491).*

tions made by Singh (1983:32) suggest that *Python molurus* may have an important impact on the jackal population in some areas of India. He comments,

> In Sarapuduli [part of Corbett National Park], there were three families of jackals comprising 18 individuals. Two families with a total of 13 members were completely wiped out by pythons and the third family of 5 had only 3 members left. Dead and decaying jackals were seen on three occasions. The pythons had abandoned their kills, probably due to disturbances caused by the labourers engaged in uprooting lantana thickets in the area. It has been observed that, unlike other predators which generally return to their kills after the source of disturbance is removed, the python never returns to its kill once disturbed.
>
> At Dhikala (the main tourist complex of Corbett National Park) in January 1987, a python caught two jackals in its coils, one of which managed to escape, but the other was killed and eaten by the python. One week later, the second jackal was also caught by the python. There have been other incidents of the kind.

Walsh (1967:107–108) was involved in rescuing animals from an artificial lake that was increasing in size because of a new dam in Suriname. Dogs were often used in capturing animals which were to be removed to dry ground which would not be inundated. One day, one of the dogs plunged from a small island into the water in pursuit of a paca (*Cuniculus paca*), a rodent native to the Neotropics.

> Suddenly there was a swirl near the dog, then we heard a single, high-pitched yelp. A giant snake, an anaconda, a snake worshipped by the Bushnegroes as a god, was wrapping itself around him, and before we were even aware of what we were seeing, the dog sank in a clump of dying brush. The water smoothed, eddying gently.
>
> . . . Maybe we really didn't see what we thought we saw, or maybe the dog actually got loose and swam to shore. We searched the water where he was last seen, covered the island, scoured the shoreline and the submerging trees extended out from it. We searched until nightfall, but we saw not a sign . . .
>
> Weeks later one of the Bushnegroes told me that on the island the next day he saw a twelve-foot anaconda resting lethargically, hidden in a thicket—a huge bulge in its middle.

Of all mammals, the heavily armored ant- and termite-eating pangolins would be low on the list of species suspected as python prey. However, Neill and Allen (1956:173) presented evidence that pangolins are eaten by two of the giant snakes.

> On several occasions, both reticulated pythons and Indian rock pythons, *Python molurus* (Linnaeus), kept in captivity in Siam for an unknown length of time, were shipped to the Reptile Institute where, after three or four weeks, they voided masses of pangolin scales. These scales probably represent the indigestible portion of customary prey, judging from the frequency with which they appear in python scats.

Likewise, the spines of porcupines would seem to make these large rodents improbable prey, yet four papers (Wall, 1921:57; Deraniyagala, 1955:6; Mash, 1945:249; Bhupathy and Vijayan, 1989:384) list porcupines as *Python molurus* prey. And three authors (Bosman, 1705:311; FitzSimons, 1932:60; Broadley, 1983:66) list porcupines in the diet of *Python sebae*. These do not represent a single incident, but do represent observations made in the wild as well as captivity. The use of porcupine burrows by *Python molurus* suggests that pythons, at least *Python molurus* and *Python sebae,* and porcupines may have a more complex relationship than might be expected.

The scrub python is the least studied of the snakes under discussion. As might be expected, it feeds on the marsupial fauna of the long-isolated land masses of Australia and New Guinea. Gow (1989:63) mentions the agile wallaby as food for this snake; Worrell (1963:97) listed a bush rat and a long-nosed bandicoot from one specimen; and Martin (1995:76) added fruit bats, the common striped possum, and Bennett's tree kangaroo. It is the last species that drew Martin's attention to this snake, for while he was conducting a study of this poorly known, closed canopy-dwelling kangaroo in northern Queensland, a 3.3 m, 10.5 kg scrub python swallowed a 2.1 kg juvenile, female tree kangaroo with a radiocollar. Martin's observations, circumstantial as they are, suggest the scrub python may have a significant impact on Bennett's tree kangaroo populations. During a 44-day period he radio-tracked the snake by the kangaroo's radiocollar which was lodged in its gut. The snake had three periods of inactivity of 8–9 days each. The first inactive period Martin attributed to digesting a meal, the second period of inactivity was spent near a tree frequently used by another of Martin's radiocollared tree-kangaroos (a female with a juvenile). The juvenile disappeared, and Martin suspected the snake ate it, too, although he could not confirm this due to weather conditions.

Thus, Pope's assertion that almost all vertebrate species can be eaten appears to be an accurate assessment of the diet of these large snakes. No species demonstrates a preference for a particular prey type, and the generalized nature of giant snakes' diets appears to be a major contribution to their wide geographic ranges and continued survival despite widespread persecution, habitat destruction, and exploitation (Table 4–1).

Table 4–1. Summary of Prey Taken by Giant Snakes

Prey	Eunectes murinus	Python molurus	Python reticulata	Python sebae
Fishes	x			x
Amphibia				
Anura		x	?	
Reptilia				
Testudines	x			
Sauria	x	x	x	x
Serpentes	x		?	
Crocodylia	x			x
Birds	x	x	x	x
Mammals				
Chiroptera		x		
Primates	x	x	x	x
Carnivora	?	x	x	x
Perissodactyla	x	?	?	
Artiodactyla	x	x	x	x
Pholidota		x	x	
Rodentia	x	x	x	x
Lagomorpha		x		

The table illustrates the taxonomic range of prey taken by five species of snakes that attain lengths in excess of 20 feet. An "x" denotes a reliable record; a "?" denotes a questionable literature record.

Individual Preferences for Food

While each giant snake species may show no specific preference for food, individual snakes may exhibit such tendencies. The following accounts suggest that individual snakes may develop specific preferences or aversions for certain kinds of food. While individual preferences have not been documented in wild, free-ranging snakes, they have in captives. One of us (JCM) had a captive female reticulated python that consistently refused domesticated and wild rabbits, but would eat rats, squirrels, and chickens. It is difficult to be certain why one individual has specific preferences or aversions, but conditioning seems a probable reason. In captivity a snake may get used to a certain food and ignore all other foods offered, or the snake may have had an unfortunate experience handling a specific kind of prey and thus learn to avoid it in the future.

The finicky eating habits of a captive anaconda are described by Barton and Allen (1961:86):

> Our larger anaconda measured 16 feet 4 inches and weighed 108 pounds when it was received from a shipper in Belem, Brazil, on June 13, 1950. After shedding on June 24, it refused living pigs, rabbits, ducks and carp through an eight-week period until, on August 10, it accepted a small mallard duck. Since that date only waterfowl—mallard ducks, white Peking ducks and a snow goose—have been accepted . . .

The same authors (Barton and Allen, 1961:84–85) commented on a 22-foot reticulated python's food preference:

> After having rejected the fowl and rabbits offered it during its first two months, it accepted the first pig offered. This was on October 14 when it took a 15 pound suckling. Thus began a pattern of regular feeding that has continued until the present time. . . .
>
> This reticulated python has accepted nothing but pigs; rabbits, chickens and ducks have been refused on several occasions. When hungry, the snake strikes and seizes the prey with its mouth immediately upon the animal's introduction into the cage.

The story describing a *Python molurus* entering a chicken coop and selectively feeding on white birds is difficult to explain, unless it is untrue; remember, snakes use infrared and chemosensory information to locate prey. Wells (1923:216–217) wrote:

> At last we picked out about twenty good white Leghorns and the same number of black Minorcas, all of them fine healthy birds, and kept them away from the other fowls in their own special fowl house. One morning, when Luard went to let them out, all the white ones had disappeared and in the corner of the house was a huge python. The snake had entered at night through a small hole about six inches in diameter, and eaten all the white chickens, presumably because he couldn't see the black ones . . .

An African python was captured eating an impala. Subsequently, in captivity it refused rats, guinea pigs, cats, rabbits, and a dog over a 14-month period, but when offered a dead subadult impala, it was swallowed immediately. Apparently the snake did not associate being captured with the antelope in its mouth with the stressful experience of capture and captivity (Haagner, 1992–93:31).

Do Giant Snakes Eat Fruit?

No snake species is known to eat vegetation of any kind, but there are reports in the literature to suggest that they may occasionally do so inadvertently. Mookerjee (1946:733) described the very unusual situation of *Python molurus* feeding on mango fruit at a tea plantation near Siliguri, Darjeeling, India. Just before dark, some of the local laborers discovered the snake and killed it. He wrote:

> During the skinning of the snake, the oesphagus was also cut open, and four mangoes were recovered from it. The pericarp of these mangoes bore the marks of the teeth of the reptile, the fruits were otherwise intact. The length of the snake was 13 feet.
> After a detailed examination of the mangoes - found within the oesphagous of the snake, and also those obtained fresh from the tree, it was noted that they were infested with insect larvae. Each mango contained two or three larvae.

An African python with an apparent taste for tomatoes was reported to Rose (1962:270), and he followed with a quote from American herpetologist Charles Bogert who hypothesized that snakes might eat fruit if an animal odor was attached, and mentions that the German biologist Baumann had induced snakes to swallow such improbable items as cigars by coating them with secretions from a frog skin. A similar explanation was offered by Pope (1961:78). Fruit-eating snakes are difficult to explain, and Bogert and Pope's explanation is the most logical. Recall the snakes that swallowed the plastic plants and blanket and it is clear that an animal odor, or an odor that mimics that of an animal, may stimulate a snake to swallow unusual items.

Giant Snakes as Scavengers

Snakes, at least occasionally, function as scavengers. Again, if an object smells like food to a snake it is likely to eat it, and it is not surprising that dead animals are consumed if a snake fortuitously encounters them. Herpetoculturists have long known that almost any snake can be induced to take dead food in captivity, as long as it has the odor of an animal the snake recognizes as food. Wall (1912:462) commented upon *Python molurus* eating dead food.

> Usually in captivity live animals have until recently been given to the snakes in various zoological gardens, but now that it is known that pythons among other snakes will accept dead food, the order has changed. The fact that they would eat dead animals was noted 15 years ago . . . by Ferguson who says they will eat a dead rat, or rabbit, just as readily as a live one. He further states that under these circumstances it makes no attempt to constrict, but proceeds to swallow at once.

Evidence, albeit circumstantial, that free-ranging pythons will take dead food comes from an incident reported from The Gambia, West Africa. A dead, gutted, green monkey was left by primatologist E. Starin, but when she returned to collect the corpse it was gone. About 4 meters from where she left it was a 7-meter African python (Starin and Burghardt, 1992:57).

Hunting Techniques

Hunting from ambush has the advantage of letting the food come to the predator, so that the predator conserves energy. The disadvantage is that the predator may have to wait a long time depending upon prey density and activity. Therefore, snakes that utilize an ambush foraging strategy are usually stout-bodied with large heads and small eyes, are capable of swallowing large prey items, have cryptic coloration to avoid detection, and are capable of surviving long periods of time without eating. Snakes that actively forage for food tend to be slender-bodied, have smaller heads with large eyes, may be cryptic in coloration but may also have aposematic (warning) coloration, and require more frequent meals due to their active nature. Snakes that are trophic generalists, or switch prey types as they grow, may have combinations of these characteristics and may shift their hunting strategy with changes in size, season, or prey density. Clearly, the giant snakes have most of the characteristics predicted for ambush predators, but they have a generalized diet, and there is some anecdotal evidence that they actively forage on occasion.

Raymond Ditmars, the late curator of reptiles at the Bronx Zoo and the person who single-handedly popularized herpetological writing in the early decades of this century, had considerable experience with anacondas in zoos. He suggested that they use both sit-and-wait (= ambush) and active foraging techniques to capture prey; he wrote (1931:47):

> It lies in wait in murky waters, the neck reared and supported by the head really floating on the surface, nothing but the top and eyes protruding. Or it may glide through shallow water among reeds watching for prey ranging in size from agoutis, to capybaras or a young tapir, as the size of the hunting serpent may designate. It is also fond of waterfowl and may craftily stalk beneath them and seize them from below.

Similarly, Sweeney (1961:46) suggested *Python sebae* sometimes actively forages for food, while using ambush techniques at other times.

> In the evening or daytime it may catch its prey when lying in wait below a bush, in a tree or in reeds on a river bank, and it will rest in such places or in the water itself on hot days. At night it normally hunts its prey by scent and is very adept at catching sleeping animals without waking them.
> . . . The African python when undisturbed meanders over the ground very sluggishly and never hurries itself; when unmolested, or when chasing its prey (which it seldom does since it prefers to lie in wait for it), the python can move very quickly.

Ambush

Direct observations of anaconda foraging strategies in nature are sorely lacking. And as might be expected from the most aquatic of the giants, the anaconda hunts from watery hiding places. Explorer Paul Fountain (1904:108–109) does not actually describe seeing an anaconda capturing prey from ambush, but he suggests he has observed feeding.

As a rule (I think invariably) they capture their prey by surprise, lying in wait partly submerged in marshy places. They seize their victims instantly; and this is the only time when I have seen them display much activity.

He (Fountain, 1904:110–111) then described an anaconda hanging by its tail from branches to capture food and the sequence of events that occurred after the snake had captured its prey.

> The tail of the anaconda is prehensile; that is, he can use it to wrap round the boughs of trees when climbing; but I doubt if he can suspend the whole weight of the body on it. I have noticed that when they hang head downwards they always have more than one coil of the tail wrapped round the bough from which they are suspended. When they seize prey in this position, which they often do as it passes under the tree, if it is large of size they always come to the ground to eat it.

We are dubious of accounts of large anacondas hunting from trees. *Eunectes murinus* has a relatively short tail which precludes it from supporting a suspended body with a mass of 100–300 pounds.

A letter describing anaconda feeding habits from Robert Ker Porter accompanies a 19-foot specimen of anaconda to the "United Service Museum." The letter contains a considerable amount of erroneous information (Gosse, 1850:166–167), but this passage seems to agree with what we know about anaconda hunting behavior (although the language is clearly charged with emotion).

> Fish, and those animals which repair there to drink, are the objects of its prey. The creature lurks watchfully under cover of the water, and whilst the unsuspecting animal is drinking, suddenly makes a dash at its nose, and with a grip of its back-reclining double range of teeth, never fails to secure the terrified beast beyond the power of escape. In an instant the sluggish waters are in turbulence and foam, the whole form of the Colubra is in motion, its huge and rapid coilings soon encircle the struggling victim . . .

The African python, *Python sebae*, apparently also uses both aquatic and arboreal ambush sites. Pienaar (1966:146) wrote,

> . . . they will lie submerged—with only the nostrils and eyes exposed above the surface—for long periods. . . . From this vantage point they will frequently obtain their prey, which they seize by the snout as they stoop down to drink. They are also excellent climbers, often lying along overhanging branches from which they drop silently on some unwary prey animal passing below. The tail is strongly prehensile and is often anchored for extra leverage when they constrict their prey prior to swallowing.

Hunting postures, the time of day African pythons hunt, and the cryptic nature of pythons, were also commented upon by Stevenson-Hamilton (1947:319), a game warden in Kruger National Park.

> They are most active during the cool morning and evening hours; but they will catch their prey at all times of the day and night. Their favourite method is to lie concealed close to a game path, or stretched along the overhanging bough of a tree, whence they drop on to their prey as it passes below. They are very fond of water, and spend hours completely immersed, the head or nostrils only just show-

ing above the surface. Small animals coming to drink are frequently thus seized, dragged ashore, and swallowed. Should the water be a little discoloured, it is almost impossible to distinguish the snake when concealed in this manner.

In Natal, Isemonger (1956:47) observed an African python, estimated to be 15 feet, capturing prey from an aquatic hide.

> Once, as I lay watching, I noticed a family of bush-buck walking slowly towards a pool near which the snake was lying. On hearing the cracking of twigs, it became alert, lifted its head slightly, flickered its tongue and slid quietly in amongst the bushes next to the pool. At first I thought it had vanished, but as the buck drew closer to the pool and then started drinking, I could just see the snake re-arranging its coils to adopt a "striking" attitude.
>
> It remained in this attitude, watching the buck, and not moving an inch. When they had finished drinking and started to leave, one of the younger animals walked too close to the hidden snake. Instantly, it struck out, burying its teeth in the animals neck and held on. At first, I thought the buck would tear itself loose from the grip, as it pulled the snake quite ten yards through the bush with its initial rush, but the python held on.

Further verification comes from FitzSimons's (1930:32–33) description of a similar case of the African python hunting from ambush while submerged in water.

> Pythons, when hunting, often submerge in a pool of water wherein animals and large birds are accustomed to slake their thirst. At first sign of the intended prey the python withdraws its nostrils from above water, and, lying still, very still, at the bottom of the pool, awaits its chance. Five-ten-fifteen minutes and more may go by, yet it requires no fresh air to keep alive the sluggish fires of its body.
>
> Then like an arrow from the bow, the reptile makes its lunge, to secure a strong grip with its teeth. It matters not what part of the body is seized. The coils come into operation with such lightening speed that the victim has no time to struggle.
>
> I once saw a python grip and overpower a duiker buck in this way. The buck stepped into the shallows of the little pool of crystal-clear water. On the instant the submerged python gripped it by a foreleg. A piteous bleat; the lashing of the previously still water, lay the great python with the buck in its coils.

Tropical trees come into fruit throughout the year and frugivorous animals move from one fruiting tree to another in search of food. Thus, a fruiting tree is likely to have numerous birds, bats, rodents, and other mammals in the immediate vicinity. And, it is not surprising that snakes and other predators learn to use these animal magnets to their advantage. Wall (1921:50) reports a second-hand story of *Python molurus* using a fruiting tree for an ambush perch.

> Mr. Sharpe, D.S.P., in the Fyzabad District, told me in 1906 that he once climbed up into a banyan tree in dense jungle with his shikari, who told him that at that season, when the fruit was ripening, many animals, especially deer, visited these trees to eat the fallen fruit. After having been quiet for sometime, he noticed close to him a movement in what he had up till then taken to be an aerial root, but which on closer inspection proved to be a python suspended by its tail, and evidently established there for the same purpose that had actuated the sportsman. I have heard of pythons quartering themselves in hollow trees, and frequenting those on which egrets and night herons roost, to which at night the snake stealthily crept and successfully took toll.

Similarly, Shine (1991:164) stated that the residents of Kakadau Park in Queensland, Australia told him that large Oenpelli pythons, *Morelia oenpelliensis,* ambush native pigeons and fruit bats in fruiting trees.

Large snakes dropping out of trees on to unsuspecting prey has been depicted in Hollywood versions of tropical forests many times, but do snakes really do this? Snakes certainly hunt in and from trees, and a feeding attempt from a tree could accidently result in the snake falling or being pulled out of a tree by the prey. But, do snakes intentionally drop out of trees onto prey? FitzSimons (1930:65–66) presented an eyewitness account of an African python suggesting they do indeed.

> Lying concealed one day in the midst of a tangled leafy lair, I had focused my binoculars on some blue duikers daintily picking leaves from the foliage in a Natal forest glade. Suddenly a dark brown streak seemed to drop from amid a leafy branch. Next moment one of the beautiful little bucks was in the remorseless grip of a python.

Observations of captive *Python sebae* in Malawi support the assertion that pythons may ambush from arboreal perches (Burdett, 1971:11):

> However, should a python attack prey from a branch of a tree, it seems usual to suspend itself by the tail proper, or by the tail plus a portion of the body, and lift the victim off the ground while constricting it: under these circumstances the python normally swallows the prey while still hanging.

An observation reported from the Cape York Wilderness Lodge located at the tip of the Cape York Peninsula in Queensland, Australia, supports the idea that pythons hunt from trees and will relocate after making a kill. Low (1989:62) discovered a scrub python feeding on the carnivorous marsupial known as the northern quoll (*Dasyurus hallucatus*). The snake had an ambush site behind the Lodge's kitchen. During the day the 1.3 meter-long snake lay coiled on the ground at the base of a shrub, and at night it would ascend to a low branch of the shrub and wait for food. One evening, much to the dismay of some tourists, the snake captured a quoll. The interesting part of the observation was the prey handling reported by Low; he wrote:

> I sprinted to get my camera, and returned to find the python had transferred the quoll to its tail, and was now climbing higher into the shrub to escape the commotion.

Later that night, Low returned to the shrub to find the python again in position to ambush ground-dwelling prey from its arboreal perch.

This brings us to the incredible story and drawing presented by La Gironiere (1853:222) which involves similar prey handling from an arboreal perch by a *Python reticulata* in the Philippines; he wrote:

> Several times, when passing through the woods with my Indians, I heard the piercing cries of a wild boar. On approaching the spot whence they proceeded, we almost invariably found a wild boar, about whose body a boa had twisted its folds, and was gradually hoisting him up into the tree round which it had coiled itself.
>
> When the wild boar had reached a certain height, the snake pressed him against a tree with a force that crushed his bones and stified him. Then the boa let its prey fall, descended the tree, and prepared to swallow it.

Figure 4–4. In the Philippines, a reticulated python, *Python reticulata,* hunting from a tree captured the pig and was hoisting it up when discovered. *From La Gironiere (1853:222).*

This account was accompanied by an illustration (Figure 4–4) which at first appears quite contrived; however, in light of other descriptions of prey handling by pythons, such as that described by Low for the scrub python, La Gironiere's observations may have some credibility.

As might be expected, birds are also taken from arboreal perches. Thomas (1985:229) observed a green spotted dove land on a fallen tree, expecting it to fly down to the water hole below to drink. As the bird landed, a *Python sebae* seized it in its mouth, constricted it while hanging downwards from the branch, and ingested it. The snake then resumed its original position, presumably in anticipation of another meal.

Thus, giant snakes do hunt from trees and take a variety of prey. The question of whether or not snakes drop out of trees onto prey remains unresolved, but there is some evidence that they may do so.

Active Foraging

The body form and other characteristics of giant snakes do not fit the model for active foragers. However, there is ample evidence that giant snakes do sometimes actively forage for food, and many of these accounts involve the snakes taking domesticated or captive animals from cages. Clearly, an anaconda or python cannot sit-and-wait for a caged animal to come to it. Allen (1963:1) wrote,

> Anacondas hunt mostly by night, swimming around the lake margins and grabbing anything they can locate.

Amazonian explorer and entomologist Henry Bates (1863:235–236) described an event suggesting that anacondas actively forage for food.

> We had an unwelcome visitor whilst at anchor in the port of Joao Malagueti. I was awoke a little after midnight, as I lay in my cabin by a heavy blow struck at the sides of the canoe close to my head, which was succeeded by the sound of a weighty body plunging in the water. I got up; but all was again quiet, except the cackle of fowls in our hen-coop, which hung over the side of the vessel, about three feet from the cabin door. I could find no explanation of the circumstance, and, my men being all ashore, I turned in again and slept till morning. I then found my poultry loose about the canoe, and a large rent at the bottom of the hen-coop, which was about two feet from the surface of the water: a couple of fowls were missing. Senhor Antonio said the depredator was a Sucuruju (the Indian name for the Anaconda, or great water serpent, *Eunectes murinus*), which had for months past been haunting this part of the river, and had carried off many ducks and fowls from the ports of various houses. I was inclined to doubt the fact of a serpent striking at its prey from the water, and thought an alligator more likely to be the culprit, although we had not yet met with alligators in the river. Some days afterwards the young men belonging to the different sitios agreed together to go in search of the serpent. They began in a systematic manner, forming two parties, each embarked in three or four canoes, and starting from points several miles apart, whence they gradually approximated searching all the little inlets on both sides of the river. The reptile was found at last, sunning itself on a log at the mouth of a muddy rivulet, and despatched with harpoons. I saw it the day after it was killed; it was not a very large specimen, measuring only eighteen feet nine inches in length and sixteen inches in circumference at the widest part of the body.

Stories of snakes taking caged or restrained animals suggest active foraging (Beccari, 1904:33–34; Mjöberg, 1930:82–83; Jensen, 1980:18). In an unusual case, Starin and Burghardt (1992:57) described free-living *Python sebae* preying on captive animals in a small zoo on five occasions that led to the death or removal of the snakes by Conservation Department personnel. The snakes preyed upon a neonate harnessed antelope, a male bushbuck, a gazelle, a patas monkey, and a green monkey. These incidents suggest the snakes found the caged animals while actively moving about, not waiting in ambush. Furthermore, Starin and Burghardt (1992) observed snakes engaged in "moving" much more often than any other activity (e.g., coiled up, stretched out), suggesting that active foraging may be a commonly employed hunting mode.

Additional, but equivocal, evidence of active foraging in *Python molurus* comes from a single radio marked individual in Shui Hau, Lantau Island, Hong Kong (Goodyear, 1994:71–72). The snake (2.7 meters total length) was displaced 170 meters after it was captured in a chicken coop. After several days of longer movements (some >100 meters/day), perhaps due to being displaced, the snake made shorter movements (usually <100 meters/day, and often under 20). On 2 days it was observed partly or completely submerged in abandoned rice paddies. On the nineteenth day of observation it ate something, and short movements followed ingestion. Thus, there is evidence here of both ambush (submerged in rice paddies) and active foraging, but because the snake was originally displaced, the data must be treated cautiously. Longer movements may have been made in order to change ambush sites.

More substantial, unequivocal, evidence comes from the same snake as described in the previous paragraph. Goodyear (1994:71) reported that an old Chinese woman found the *P. molurus* in her oven-size, free-standing chicken coop.

> Apparently the snake had entered through a hole, eaten the two mature chickens within, and was unable to exit through the same hole . . . The woman vigorously explained in Cantonese (though her pantomime was sufficient) that we could recover the chickens by holding the snake's head under water. Additional stimulus proved unnecessary; after it was removed from the coop the snake quickly regurgitated and the delighted old woman departed with the chickens.

Obviously, the snake could have located the cooped chickens only by active foraging.

Barker and Barker (1994:39) state that "Scrub pythons [*Morelia amethistina*] are notoriously fond of chickens, so much so that they are occasionally killed as pests by some farmers . . . " This information also indicates that scrub pythons may be finding the chickens by active foraging. Certainly if the chickens are kept in a coop, and if that is where the predation occurs, the snakes are locating them by actively searching.

In Sarawak, St. John (1863:256) reported an incident suggesting *Python reticulata* also actively forages for food on occasion. A 19-foot specimen entered a closely-latticed space under a Dayak house, killed and ate a pig, and found it could not escape through the wooden bars.

Perhaps some of the strongest evidence of active foraging comes from observations of *Python molurus* hunting for Bengal monitor lizards reported by University of Florida herpetologist Walter Auffenberg (1994:405). At Keoladeo Ghana National Park, India, Auffenberg saw tracks made by pythons hunting for sleeping lizards during the night. The snakes moved from one monitor burrow to the next, following fairly direct routes, suggesting that they knew where the burrows were located. The pythons apparently stop at each one only long enough to inspect it for sleeping lizards.

Although not strictly related to foraging mode, the following information nevertheless pertains to locating prey. Madsen and Shine (1996) discovered an intriguing predator/prey relationship between Australian water pythons (*Liasis fuscus*) and the dusky rat (*Rattus colletti*). Although the water python is not one of our giants (they reach a maximum length of about 3.0 m), the predator/prey relationship is interesting and we don't know enough about the ecology of our giants in order to say that similar relationships don't occur. Dusky rats are the major prey species of *L. fuscus* at Fogg Dam and its adjacent floodplain in the wet-dry tropics of northern Australia. The distribution and abundance of the dusky rat varies seasonally: During the dry season the rats live in soil crevices in the floodplain, but wet season flooding forces them to higher ground (primarily to natural levee banks). Madsen and Shine determined that python and rat abundances on the floodplain were significantly correlated through time. That is, both attained a maximum during the dry season and fell dramatically during the wet season. Although activity of the pythons was centered around the dam during the dry season, all of the 25 radio-marked snakes moved away from that area during the wet season (most migrated to the vicinity of levee banks on the floodplain up to 12 km away from their dry season range). The seasonal migration of the water pythons allowed them to efficiently utilize a migratory prey species (i.e., the dusky rat) that would otherwise be unavailable for much of the year.

In another reference to prey-related python migrations, Whitaker (1993:88) related that *Python molurus* living in the Parmodhan Forest Division in Nadia District, India, seasonally migrate as far as 30 km from the forest to villages where they find dogs, chickens, and wild prey, such as hares and mongooses. This information lacks the quantified data of Madsen and Shine, and fails to report the causative factor or factors for the migration.

Charming Prey

The idea that snakes charm or mesmerize prey is quite old. In these stories the snake has some telepathic hold over the prey which causes it to freeze, or be drawn within striking distance.

Paul du Chaillu (in Hartwig, 1878:623–624) attributed this power to a python (Figure 4–5), almost certainly *Python sebae*.

> I shall never forget that one day, as I lay ill under a big tree, I spied an enormous snake folded among the branches of another tree not far away from me. My attention had been drawn to that tree by the cries of a squirrel. The snake was charming the poor little squirrel. How nice the squirrel was; how beautiful its little tail; how black and shiny the ugly creature was, and what a contrast with the green leaves of the trees. Part of the body was coiled on the limb of the tree. How fixedly he looked on the squirrel. His head was triangular, and he belonged to that family of snakes that spend the greatest portion of their lives on trees. Nearer and nearer the squirrel came; louder and louder were his chipperings; he tried to run away but could not. At last he came within a foot of the snake. There was a pause; then suddenly, like a flash of lightening, the snake sprang. The poor little squirrel

Figure 4–5. An African python, *Python sebae*, charming a squirrel. *From Hartwig, 1878:624.*

was in the folds of the ugly reptile, and I soon saw his body gradually disappearing into its inflated mouth, and the broken silence of the forest resumed its sway.

A story about an anaconda using its breath to lure prey is described by Juan and de Ulloa (1807:399–400) and they hypothesize the actual nature of the serpent's exhalations. Toxic, or intoxicating, breath stories may have originated from snakes that had food fermenting in their gut; the odor produced is exceptionally strong but does not have the properties described here.

> Its breath is asserted to be of such a nature as to cause a kind of drunkenness of stupidity in man or beast, which has the misfortune of being within the bounds of its activity; and thus causes the animal involuntarily to move till it unhappily comes within reach of the serpent, which immediately swallows it. This is the vulgar report: and it is added, that the only method of averting the danger, is on first feeling the breath to cut it, that is, to stop it by the interposition of another body, which hastily intervening, cuts the current of the blast and dissipates it. Thus the person who was moving on to certain destruction, is enabled to take another path, and avoid the fatal catastrophe These particulars, if thoroughly considered seem mere fables: as indeed the learned M. de la Condamine intimates; and the very circumstances with which they are decorated, increase their improbability.

But, in my opinion, with a little alteration in the circumstances, what seems to shock credibility, will appear natural and founded on truth.

That its breath is of such a quality as to produce a kind of inebriation in those whom it reaches, is far from being impossible; the urine of the fox is well known to have the same effect; and the breath of the whale is frequently attended with such an insupportable factor as to bring on a disorder in the brain. I therefore see no manner of difficulty in admitting that the breath of this serpent may be of that intoxicating quality attributed to it; and may be considered as an expedient for catching its prey, as otherwise the creature, from the slow movement of its body, would be utterly incapable of providing itself with food; whereas, by this delete-rious smell, the animal may be thrown into such horror and perplexity, as to be unable to move, but remain fixed like a statue, or faint away, whilst the snake gradually approaches and seizes it. As to what is related of cutting the breath, and that the danger is limited to the direction in which the serpent breathes; these are tales, which to believe, would imply an utter ignorance of the origin and progress of odours. In short, the vulgar errors, propagated by these rude nations, have gained credit among the Spaniards, merely because none has had the curiosity or resolution to put them to the test of experience.

The Jirara Indians of the Orinoco believe the anaconda overcomes its prey in a similar manner, and provides a reason why individuals should not travel alone when in anaconda country. Roth (1915:370) wrote:

As soon as it hears a noise, it raises its head, and a yard or two of its body, and when it sees its prey, be it tiger, calf, deer, or man, it takes aim, and opening its terrible mouth, emits so poisonous and foul an exhalation as to fix the victim, stupefy him, and render him unable to move. For this reason, no one dares to travel alone by himself, either for fishing or hunting, no matter where the jour-ney may be: at least two have to go in company, so that in case the buio, hidden or discovered, should take aim at one of them, the other, either with his hat, or with a tree-branch, which will shake and cut the air intervening between his friends and the monster.

Additionally, Lange (1912:218–225) reports a story of an anaconda luring a hu-man for the purpose of devouring him, but this will be discussed in Chapter 7.

There is no evidence that any snake has the ability to charm prey, but what most observers are actually seeing is the innate defense behavior of many animals to "freeze" when confronted by a predator. These animals have evolved a behavior that relies on their cryptic coloration to conceal them from a visually oriented predator. However, this may not work well with snakes because they are also using chemosen-sory and heat sensing abilities to locate their prey, and the prey animals may use the behavior at inappropriate times (e.g., when they are not well concealed by their col-oration). Thus, "freezing" in the presence of a snake may very well work to the prey's disadvanatge when confronted by a snake.

The Strike

A snake's strike does not have to be particularly powerful, but it does have to be accurate in order for it to be successful, and the snake must be able to judge its distance from the prey. The purpose of the strike from a large constrictor is to anchor the 80–110 strongly recurved teeth in the body of the prey so that a coil can be drawn around its body for constriction. In other words, the strike serves to gain purchase on a victim's body. But, is a strike powerful enough to stun a large animal?

Savage (1842:245), writing about the strike of the African python, concluded that the attack is so sudden and violent that the victim is often prostrated and stunned. He went on to say that a bull was so injured in an attack as to be beyond recovery. He then makes the totally erroneous assertion that the tail does not have to be anchored (Figure 4–6) to an object for the snake to strike because,

> The hooks or claws near the anus are sometimes protruded, it is said (and the evidence is wholly satisfactory) and inserted in the ground or under roots, thus affording a fulcrum which gives inconceivable force to the blow.

The use of the anal spurs as a fulcrum to anchor the snake during a strike is pure fiction, and anyone familiar with snakes is aware of the tiny and fragile nature of these structures. The idea that they could secure the weight of a snake's lunging body to the ground is absurd, let alone the idea that they would add significantly to the force of the strike.

Forsyth (1911:277–278) related a story about the hunting behavior of *Python molurus* which is at least thirdhand and suggests that prey is stunned by the force of the strike; this is undoubtedly exaggerated.

Figure 4–6. An illustration from a 19th-century handbill advertising a museum display in London. Note the tail wrapped around the tree trunk as the snake constricts its prey, this behavior was once believed to be necessary for the snake's success in killing in its prey. *Courtesy, The Field Museum Library, Chicago.*

In *Forest Life and Sport in India*—(Eardly-Wilmot)—as to the attack of the Python on its prey, the Author writes:—"It may therefore well be the case that the blow of a heavy python would be sufficient to stun a passing deer until it could be enfolded in the grip of the snake, and that this method of hunting may supplement the sudden and more deadly attack from overhead."

In reference to these remarks, the following notes are interesting. A few years ago on one of my many visits to Jamrach's collecting Depot, in Entally, Calcutta, Scott, the Manager, showed me with great pride, an enormous python in a box, length between 21 and 22 feet. I asked Scott how such a huge brute was captured? He told me that two of his collectors were in the Khasyia Hills looking out for captives. One of the men when high up in a tree making his way to a nest happened to look down and saw this python hanging from a branch, slowly swinging with its head a few feet from the ground. The man said he was very frightened and made not a move. All at once the python became rigid; by and by the bird-nester heard the rustle of leaves not far off and recognized that it was the footpath of his fellow collector, by whistling he was able to signal to him to give the tree a wide berth. Soon the snake began swinging very slowly, then it again became rigid, and the light patter of a deer was herd and a barking deer came in view and within striking range of the python "when like a shot it was sent flying:" and there it lay almost motionless. In a little the python got down to the ground and glided over to, and lay on, the deer. In a short time the operation of swallowing began. During the process of swallowing, the two men made a basket, and the snake had resigned itself to rest, the basket was worked over it and the making of it completed; over this another basket was made, and in the double basket it reached Calcutta. The men said they had no trouble in getting it into the basket.

The strike from a large snake may, however, knock the prey off balance, particularly if the prey is relatively small compared to the snake. Sweeney (1961:46) commented on the strike of *Python sebae*.

When it strikes, as it does with a very wide gape to its jaws, it fastens its teeth firmly in the prey, while the force of the thrust often knocks the animal off balance. At the same time the python rolls over, twisting itself round and round so that its body encircles the animal it has caught.

The measured speed of a snake strike was reported by Oliver (1958:74–75) and Minton and Minton (1973:217) as about 20 ft/second, comparable to a boxer's jab.

There is some evidence that anacondas, and perhaps the other giants, do not necessarily have to strike before they constrict. Mole and Urich (1894:505) described a captive juvenile anaconda seizing a rat without biting it:

The first [rat] was sitting on the edge of the tank, and the snake, instead of seizing it with his teeth as these reptiles usually do, slid up over its back very gently and quietly, and then threw round it several coils without once biting it.

Constriction and Swallowing

Boid snakes, as well as others, constrict their prey in order to hold on to it so that it does not escape, and to kill it. This usually occurs by the snake grabbing the prey with its mouth and, if the prey is small enough, rolling the prey into a coil or two of the snake's body. Some authors have stated that these snakes must have their tails anchored to accomplish constriction; observers of captive snake feeding know better. Burdett (1971:11–12) observed captive *Python sebae* in Malawi, and repudiates this idea.

> Contrary to a fairly common belief, pythons do not need an anchorage for the tail in order to constrict prey. Indeed, they can coil the entire body around an object (prey or enemy) in reverse, e.g. should the head be held or trapped, in spite of the rearward pointing of the scales.

Note that this does not mean that constricting snakes do not sometimes anchor their tails to some nearby object, but this is not a requirement for constriction to occur.

The exact cause of death from constricting snakes is controversial. Authors often use the term "crushed," implying or overtly stating that many bones are broken during constriction. Ridley (1899:197), however, describes a reticulated python as crushing a swan without breaking any bones. Likewise, Hay and Martin (1966: 151–152) examined two female kob (a small antelope) killed by African pythons, specifically looked for broken bones, and found none. Furthermore, McCarty et al. (1989) examined a human child killed by a python and found no broken bones. Thus bones of prey are not broken during constriction, at least not with any frequency.

Exactly what is the cause of death from constriction? British herpetologist Frank Wall (1912:462–463) commented on what causes the death of the prey during constriction by *Python molurus*.

> The habit of constricting is characteristic of the whole family—boas and pythons alike. The snake, roused to activity by the sight of food, advances toward its prey often with quivering tail and makes a sudden dash at it with open jaws, which are no sooner closed upon its victim than it throws a coil or two—according to the size of the quarry—round it, holding it as in a vice until its struggles have been completely ceased when it relaxes its embrace and proceeds to swallow it almost always beginning at the head. Dr. Chalmers Mitchell says, "there appears to be no special attempt to crush the prey, to suffocate it or to break its bones." I certainly agree that there is no attempt to crush with the intention of breaking bones, and so making the mass more easy to deal with, but if the victim is not suffocated how is it killed? My belief is that the vigour of the embrace is such that the victim's chest is incapable of expansion, and asphyxia results, or what amounts to the same thing the heart cannot beat against the pressure to which it is subjected.

McLees (1928:105) also suggests that suffocation may not be the specific cause of death; he wrote,

> . . . the snakes which kill their victims by coiling around them and squeezing them to death by a contraction of the coils, do so by placing the most powerful coil around the victim's body over the victim's heart. The coils are then quickly tightened until the pressure interferes with and finally stops the heart's pulsations, which means, of course, that the victim is dead. The process may be assisted somewhat by the incidental deflation of the victim's lungs, but death is too speedy to be accounted for by this suffocation alone.

Others suggest that prey is killed by suffocation. Hardy (1994:46) surveyed herpetological texts and found that 22 of them stated that constricting snakes kill prey by suffocation, while five others stated that suffocation combines with a circulatory impairment mechanism that results in death. Hardy concurs with McLees (1928: 105) that suffocation is not the primary cause of death in constricted prey, and that impairment of the flow of venous blood into the heart followed by irreversible cellular hypoxia of brain and heart are most likely the major causes of death. He reported that death occurs in 45 to 180 seconds and he concluded:

> ... death by constriction is most likely the result of circulatory arrest followed by rapid tissue hypoxia of vital organ systems. Although suffocation occurs simultaneously with circulatory arrest, it is not the proximate cause of death. This hypothesis is based upon general physiological principles and awaits controlled testing. In the meantime, "circulatory arrest" is a better bet than "suffocation." It is not simply semantics because physiologically there is a significant difference.

Do Snakes Shape Their Prey Before Swallowing It?

Pycraft (1905:123) concluded that prey captured by pythons was reduced to a crushed and mangled corpse of the shape of a sausage. Stevenson-Hamilton (1947: 320) discussed *Python sebae* and suggested that the prey's body is manipulated into an elongated roll, with the limbs protruding straight fore and aft. Oliver (1958:41) supported this idea stating he had seen a small python repeatedly pulling and stretching a bulky chicken it was attempting to swallow. On this point Rose (1955:80) was skeptical and appeals to anonymous authority by stating that those with considerable experience deny that it does more than cause heart failure and suffocation by continued pressure.

Some Erroneous but Nevertheless Interesting Killing Methods Attributed to Giant Snakes

Probably the most bizarre method of killing prey reported in folklore about any giant snake is that described by Bancroft (1769:205) for the common anaconda among the Amerindians of Guiana.

> When they encounter larger prey, the Indians say they [the anacondas] kill it by inserting their pointed tails into the rectum; hence the white inhabitants call it the sodomite snake.

Roth (1915:370) asserted that the Pomeroon Arawaks still hold this belief.

Father Vernazza, a missionary in Brazil, described a method of feeding used by the anaconda to U.S. Navy Lieutenant William Lewis Herndon (in Oliver, 1958:16) which suggested this large boid acts like a vacuum cleaner.

> He never seeks or follows the victims upon which he feeds; but, so great is the force of his inspiration, that he draws in with breath whatever quadruped or bird may pass him, within from twenty to fifty yards of distance, according to its size.

Pliny the Elder (in Aymar, 1945:73) proposed a quite specific behavioral repertoire used by *Python sebae* for capturing African elephants, and offers an explanation why elephants are so often found to be blind! He wrote:

The serpent has little difficulty in climbing up to so great a height, and therefore, watching the road, which bear marks of their [the elephant's] footsteps when going to feed, it darts down upon them from a lofty tree. The elephant knows that it is quite unable to struggle against the folds of the serpent, and so seeks for trees or rocks against to rub itself. The serpent is on guard against this, and tries to prevent it, by first of all confining the legs of the elephant with the folds of its tail; while the elephant, on the other hand, endeavours to disengage itself with its trunk. The serpent, however, thrusts its head into its nostrils, and thus, at the same moment, stops the breadth and wounds the most tender parts. When it is met unexpectedly, the serpent raises itself up, faces its opponent, and flies more especially at the eyes; this is the reason why elephants are so often found blind, and worn to a skeleton with hunger and misery . . .

Frank Buck (1932:125) tells a story about a jungle explorer who, suddenly coming upon a python that had poised itself for an attack, saved his life by dashing for a convenient clearing where there were no trees stout enough to provide the would-be killer snake with sufficient tail leverage. Apparently the explorer couldn't dash far enough or fast enough to just get away from the python. Buck felt the "sheer absurdity" of the story would be obvious

. . . if the reader could see a big python coiled around a deer, wild pig or other animal and watch the huge reptile's muscular contractions as those deadly coils tighten up on the victim, pressing harder and harder until practically every bone in the creature's body is crushed. And while the terrific constricting power of the main part of its body deals destruction, the great snake's tail, instead of being wrapped around a tree, thrashes and switches about in all directions, pounding the ground until clods are pulverized to dust, leveling every standing blade of grass and bringing down all the shrubbery within reach.

So Buck rightfully labels the explorer's story as absurd, but then adds his own flights of fancy regarding the bone-pulverizing ability of pythons.

Flexibility of the Jaws When Swallowing Prey

The advanced snakes show an incredible ability to extend their jaws, skull, and ultimately their body, over large prey. Anyone who has witnessed a snake eating a large meal cannot help but be impressed by its ability to stretch skin, muscle and other organs around a large food item. An extraordinary story that clearly demonstrates this ability is presented by Jensen (1980:18–23); the snake involved is *Python sebae natalensis*. Mrs. Ansie Moolman found a python in her Thabazimbi, Transvaal, farm yard which had swallowed her tethered, pointer watchdog and two of her pups; a third dead pup, covered with saliva, was next to the snake. The 5-meter python was restrained by the dog's tether. The snake swallowed the dog head first, and worked its jaws and head between the collar and the animals neck, so that the collar slipped over the outside of the snake's body and held the snake in the yard by the chain and wire. W. D. Haacke, a Transvaal Museum herpetologist, hypothesized that the snake killed the female dog and at the same time threw a coil around each of the puppies. The amazing aspect of this story is that the 5-meter python was able to slip its head and its body through the narrow space between the dog's neck and collar. It is impossible to determine the exact amount of space available but, for purposes of comparison, Murphy has a 63-pound dog whose collar has 6.2 square inches of space between its collar and neck. Assuming that the dog in question had a similar amount of space, the 5-meter python must have done some serious stretching to squeeze its body between the collar and the dog's body!

Do Snakes Cover Prey With Mucus Before Swallowing?

A common, long-standing, misconception about the feeding behavior of snakes is that they lubricate their prey with saliva before swallowing it. It seems probable that this misconception developed because recently fed snakes may disgorge their mucus-covered prey when disturbed. The mucus covering is laid down as the prey is swallowed, not before as some authors state. Thus, in the story above, a dead, saliva-covered puppy was found next to the snake. Obviously, the snake killed the pup, swallowed it, and then regurgitated it. Anyone who has watched a captive snake eat knows that snakes do not cover the prey with mucus. Gosse (1850:166) quoted a letter describing anaconda feeding habits from Robert Ker Porter that accompanied a 19-foot anaconda to the "United Service Museum." It contains a considerable amount of misinformation.

> On its ceasing to exist, the fleshy tongue of the reptile is protruded (taking a long and thinish form), passing over the whole of the lifeless beast, leaving on it a sort of glutinous saliva that greatly facilitates the act of deglutination, which it preforms gradually, by gulping it down through its extended jaws . . .

An account of a buffalo being eaten by a python is also reported by Gosse (1850:181). No geographic area, or other clue, is given as to where this incident occurred. The story is said to come from the German Ephemerides who was supposedly a spectator. This is clearly a fabricated story. Note the story teller claims to hear bones breaking and see the snake spreading saliva on the prey, two observations that have no support from reliable authorities or personal experiences.

> The serpent had for some time been waiting near the brink of a pool, in expectation of its prey, when a buffalo was the first that offered. Having darted upon the affrighted animal, it instantly began to wrap it round with its voluminous twistings; and at every twist the bones of the buffalo were heard to crack. It was in vain that the poor animal struggled and bellowed; its enormous enemy entwined it too closely to get free; till at length, all its bones being mashed to pieces, like those of a malefactor on the wheel, and the whole body reduced to one uniform mass, the serpent untwined its folds to swallow its prey at leisure. To prepare for this, and in order to make the body slip down the throat more glibly, it was seen to lick the whole body over, and thus cover it with its mucus. It then began to swallow it at that end that offered least resistance, while its length of body was dilated to receive its prey, and thus took in at once a morsel three times its own thickness.

Frank Buck (1939:198), famous as a wild animal collector in the 1920s-1940s, described a *Python reticulata* capture, kill, and swallow a leopard, he wrote:

> . . . Before starting the operation [i.e., swallowing], however, a sort of mucous saliva is ejected over the food so that it becomes slick and can be drawn more easily through the enlarged mouth and into the body.

This assertion is totally without foundation. The saliva is laid down as the prey is swallowed, not before.

Before Swallowing

Giant snakes, as well as other snake species, usually swallow prey head first. How does the snake decide which end of the prey should be swallowed first? Mitchell and Pocock (1907:786–787) observed captive boid snakes feeding on dead prey, and they provide some clues as to how the snake determines which end should be swallowed first.

> After some time, during which an originally living prey would have been suffocated, or in the case of the anaconda drowned, the snake usually lets go its hold. It then passes its head all round the prey, playing over it with its forked tongue, and by some means other than that of sight, as the choice is made equally in the dark, perhaps by the sense of touch in the muzzle or lips, selects the head of the carcass to begin the process of swallowing. We have never seen a snake of the python group make a mistake in its selection of the head and snout to begin on, and it is plain that the lie of hairs, or feathers, the position of horns and the general shape of the body of vertebrates, justify the snake in its choice.

The skull itself may provide some orientation for the snake; possibly the shape, rigidity, or even the amount of heat produced by the head. Since the head-end of most birds and mammals is more streamlined (narrower), it may appear to be a less formidable starting point.

Diefenbach and Emslie (1971) performed experiments with the colubrid snake *Elaphe climacophora* in order to determine factors that influenced the direction of prey ingestion. They concluded that the most important factors were shape of the body and position of capture. Hair position (direction) and olfactory cues were believed to be of secondary importance. They also determined that the amount of time required for swallowing head first was significantly less than for tail first. Loop and Bailey (1972), using boids, colubrids, and viperids, determined that the probability of head-first ingestion of prey was strictly determined by a relation of the diameter of the prey to the diameter of the snake's head.

Swallowing While Submerged

R. R. Mole and F. W. Urich (1894:505–506) described a young, captive anaconda in Trinidad capturing prey and swallowing food while submerged.

> It kills full grown rats, sometimes launching its head out of the water a distance of 15 inches to seize them. The victims are always dragged back into the water, and there constricted and swallowed. After killing them the snake comes up to take air, but does not do so again until after the prey is swallowed, a process which it assists with a coil of the body round the corpse of the rat. Gorging occupies from 10 minutes to three quarters of an hour. This particular anaconda refuses food out of the water, but, upon a rat in a trap being held close to the edge of its tank, has darted into the open door and seized the rat and constricted it in-

side the trap, trying to drag itself back into the water at the same time. After he has gorged, the part of his body containing the rat is naturally much swollen and frequently floats on the surface, the other portions of the snake except the head being submerged. Mr. J. S. Wilson informs us he has frequently seen anacondas in the rivers of Demerara with a part of their bodies floating in this manner above the surface.

Wehekind (1955:10) also described a captive anaconda feeding on a mongoose with ingestion taking place underwater and taking a total of 17 minutes. Another captive anaconda was fed rats and always entered the water at feeding time. The author suggested that the water's buoyancy facilitated the snake's movements in maneuvering food into position for swallowing (Staedeli, 1961:6).

Size of Giant Snake Prey

Snakes swallow their prey whole as they have no mechanism by which they can bite off a piece of a whole animal or chew their food. And the size of prey is limited by the size of the snake's head, or more specifically, the gape of its jaws. Gigantic meals for giant snakes are expected, and many authors have stated outright, or hypothesized, that giant snakes will eat prodigious meals. Arnold (1993:87–115) examined numerous studies of snake feeding habits and found that as most snake species get larger they delete smaller food items from their diet. This survey included the study of one boid snake, the diamond python, *Morelia spilota*. According to Pope (1961:77,84),

> Only the largest vertebrates are immune to attacks by the hungry python or boa of gigantic dimensions. Almost any not too formidable creature weighing less than 125 pounds is a potential victim, horns, armor, and spines notwithstanding. . . .
>
> No authority to my knowledge has expressed a belief that a creature heavier than 150 pounds could be swallowed by even the largest python or anaconda, though two or three have stated that this figure is probably the ceiling.

This statement is conservative because there is at least one authentic case of a 37 kg *Python sebae* killing a 35 kg impala and beginning to swallow it. This strongly implies that an adult giant can handle prey that is at least 95% of its own body weight. Perhaps this is not surprising in light of pit vipers known to eat prey equal to 160% of their body weight (Greene, 1992:111). We know that some large anacondas may exceed 135 kg (300 lbs), so prey items in excess of 125 lbs (56.8 kg) are not out of the question.

While the stories of large pythons attacking oxen, horses, rhinoceros, or elephants may seem outrageous, snakes may sometimes misjudge the size of prey that they can consume, literally biting off more than they can chew (or, in this case, swallow). In these situations the snake may back off and abandon the meal, or swallow the meal and later die from internal injuries. Pitman (1974:69) observed that python ribs injured from swallowing large prey results in ossification of injury sites. Also, exceptionally large meals put the snake at risk from predation because the snake's ability to move away from approaching predators efficiently is greatly reduced. Indeed, many of the stories dealing with giant snakes are told by sportsmen or other people working outdoors who find a snake in the process of digesting a meal.

The Anaconda, *Eunectes murinus*

Much of the literature on truly large meals is based upon second- or thirdhand stories and much of it represents exaggeration and fabrication. One author may pick up a story from another and alter it, possibly even enhancing it for dramatic flair. Since anacondas are the largest snakes, at least in bulk, they may be expected to be capable of swallowing the largest prey.

Gardner (1849) [In Huevelmans, 1958:293] described finding a huge anaconda containing a horse. The size reported for the snake makes the story questionable, but would it be possible for a 37-foot snake to swallow a full-grown riding horse, which would weigh in the neighborhood of 1000 pounds?

> The largest [anaconda] I ever saw was at this place, but it was not alive. Some weeks before our arrival at Sapê, the favourite riding horse of Senhor Lagoeira, which had been put out to pasture not far from the house, could not be found, although a strict search was made for it all over the Fazenda. Shortly after this, one of his vaqueiros, in going through a wood by the side of a small river, saw an enormous *Boa* [anaconda], suspended in the fork of a tree which hung over the water; it was dead, but had evidently been floated down alive by a recent flood, and being in an inert state, it had not been able to extricate itself from the fork before the waters fell. It was dragged out to the open country by two horses, and was found to measure thirty-seven feet in length; on opening it, the bones of a horse, in a somewhat broken condition, and the flesh in a half digested state, were found within it, the bones of the head being uninjured; from these circumstances we concluded that the *Boa* had devoured the horse entire.

Andre (1904:178) commented on the anaconda's ability to consume an ox:

> There is a widespread belief among the inhabitants of Venezuela and Colombia that there are snakes forty feet long and as big as a barrel, and that these huge reptiles can crush and swallow an ox.

However, Fountain (1904:110–111) suggested anaconda prey size had been exaggerated.

> The stories of their having attacked bullocks and horses are not true. I am convinced that even a serpent of seventy feet long, supposing such to exist, could not swallow an animal the size of a bullock. It is only the largest anacondas that can swallow the small deer of these regions if full-grown. . . .
> . . . nor do anacondas attack jaguars and pumas for the purpose of preying on them, though I think that fights sometimes take place between these curiously matched creatures; for I afterwards found the carcass of a jaguar near Pastos Bons, Maranhao, which showed every appearance of having been killed by a constricting snake, which afterwards seemed to have made an attempt to swallow it, and failed on account of its great size. Anacondas do sometimes kill prey which is too large for them, and make desperate efforts to swallow it; but I know that the jaguar is very fond of snake's flesh, and frequently attacks anacondas, and the boas also, which are found in these forests, and no doubt he sometimes catches a tartar.

Although not an ox, Lopez (1984:109, 110) does provide photographs of an anaconda that had recently swallowed a calf. The length of the snake was not provided, but it appears to be in the 6-meter range.

American herpetologist and author Raymond Ditmars (1931:56) criticized the idea of huge meals for anacondas, and suggested a large anaconda would be satisfied with capturing a fifty-pound capybara. He believed the snake would probably be afraid of a full grown tapir and retreat from it, but would attack a young one.

Clark (1953:282) told a tall tale that is quite comical about force feeding an anaconda a 500 pound boar. This is from a nonfiction book on the personal adventures of the author, but this story is pure fiction.

> After feeding, the snake becomes comatose. It may not feed again for months. If an ant army finds it, all that remains is the skeleton of the reptile, for it is helpless if caught too far away from water. Anacondas not only could swallow a hundred-pound deer (a point often disputed by "experts" in Lima), but could actually swallow a domestic pig. When I voiced doubt, the patrone glanced at his men, then offered to wager $1000 (U.S.), payable in Lima, and he would furnish both pig and snake. . . .
>
> We strode up to the low bamboo fence and I saw a very large boar that must have weighed all of five hundred pounds. Now an Amazon boar can be a very dangerous animal, and this one had tusks. The patrone reached down and slashed its face with his machete, giving it a nasty wound. A double line of twenty Indians came running up, and I saw they held-straight out behind them so it could not constrict a snake at least twenty feet in length. It was coal black, with a yellowish belly.
>
> The snake was heaved over the fence and it landed on the boar. Instantly the boar attacked with its tusks, ripping into the monstrous coils, thicker than a man's thigh, slashing them so that the snake's flesh showed cotton-white, a bleeding and gory mess. All the time the pig was furiously grunting, but quite coolly going about the work of its butchery. The snake slowly raised its massive, flat head toward the boar, and apparently smelling the pig's blood, instantly struck. It had the boar by the long, upper snout where the tusks curled out, and it hung on, quickly thrashing the long, thick coil around the boar, until three coils were side by side, and then with a sudden and awful convulsion—squeezing.
>
> The boar stood upright on its feet for quite a long time, absorbing what must have been a terrible punishment as its ribs were cracking. Then suddenly it grunted, and crumpled. You could see the coils grasp now, creeping, feeling for a closer vice-like hold, and then—squeeze. Blood flowed from the pig's mouth, then its ears.
>
> After that the snake slowly uncoiled and started crawling away. The patrone had been fascinated, but now he was furious. He yelled at the Indians, and they leaped over the fence and laid hold of the snake, dragging it back to the pig, at the same time holding tight and stretching it out full length. This took all twenty of them, for the snake was bunching up and writhing, and the three men at the end of the tail were being knocked around. They finally succeeded in laying it out full length on the ground, and a big Indian placed his feet inside the lower jaw and with his hands stretched the upper jaw, exerting the great power of his brawny legs, shoulders and arms, opening the mouth and throat wide. The other two Indians were dragging the boar over, and now rammed its head inside, getting behind and pushing, actually stuffing that 500 pounds of pig into the snake by sheer force . . .
>
> Presently the snake took a mild interest, and the men loosened their hold. The snake began *pushing* its length *forward,* so that the pig gradually crept down into the neck. When the pig's hind feet had disappeared and the whole pig was well on its way to the snake's midriff, for it had now brought a coil up forward

to assist in the leverage, the patrone turned to me, "Well, señor, here is the address of my agent in Lima. You may send me your $1000 when you reach the coast."

I hadn't accepted the wager the night before, but there didn't seem much I could do about it. If I found El Dorado, I'd be glad to mail him a thousand dollars, but if I did not find El Dorado, he could go to hell. I put the card in my pocket.

The Indian Python, *Python molurus*

On 19 December 1906, at about 6 p.m., news was brought to Mr. Ralph and Mr. Debrulais, Assistant Engineer of the Bengal Duars Railway, that a huge *Python molurus* was lying in the Tondoo Forest between the Murti and Saldaacca Rivers, India. The 18-foot python had just eaten and was injured with seven lacerations, the first about 3 feet from the head, the last about 1 foot from the tail. The snake was killed, opened, and found to contain a leopard measuring 4 feet 2 inches from nose to rump. The big cat had been swallowed head first (Begbie, 1907:1021).

The native peoples of the Malayan Peninsula assert that pythons (*molurus* and/or *reticulata*) are known to have killed and eaten rhinoceros (Skeat, 1900:302). As improbable as this may seem, a newborn one-horned rhinoceros (*Rhinocerus unicornis*) weighs 34–75 kg (adults weigh 2–4 tons; Walker, 1975:1351), a prey size within the range of capabilities of a large python. Also, a smaller species (adults weigh about one ton), the Sumatran rhinoceros, *Didermoscerus sumatrensis,* inhabits the area and the neonatal weight for this species is remarkably light at 77 pounds or 35 kg (Schenkel, 1990:614), and certainly within the prey handling abilties of a large python.

On 3 November 1952, a Ceylonese newspaper carried an article describing a python (*Python molurus*) attacking a baby elephant, and noted that villagers had killed the snake (Deraniyagala, 1955:7). Considering baby Asian elephants weigh about 200 pounds (90 kg) at birth (Walker, 1975:1321) this snake attempted to swallow quite a mouthfull. This may be the same incident discussed by Oliver (1958:45–46) who does not state where the following episode occurred.

> A weird, terrifying jungle tug-of-war between a giant python and a calf elephant drew villagers from miles around to a clearing in the Manchils forest reserve near here, tribesmen reported today. The python seized the elephant by a hind leg and, mooring itself to a tree, started a fight to the death. The fight seesawed crazily around the clearing for hours, smashing the undergrowth flat as the elephant tried vainly to free its leg.
>
> Eventually the python swallowed the elephant's leg. Then came a deadlock. The elephant couldn't move and the reptile couldn't swallow any more. Villagers moved in, hacked the python to pieces with knives and axes, and freed the elephant. Seventeen years ago in the same forest villagers watched a three day tug-of-war between a giant python and a fully-grown elephant. The outcome was the same that time.

In Nepal, deer may be the preferred food of *Python molurus* (Dhungel, 1983:7–8). However, the probability of encountering these snakes while feeding on large animals such as deer are likely increased because of the longer time required for food handling, and the noise created by the snake and prey. Dhungel wrote,

One of their preferred foods seems to be the hog deer (*Axis porcinus*). At times they have even preyed on chital (*Axis axis*) which can weigh as much as 110 pounds, whereas the average weight of the hog deer is about 80 pounds.

The Reticulated Python, *Python reticulata*

In Borneo, Shelford (1917:88) observed a snake that had swallowed a pig, and his description suggests that the snake was probably in a life-threatening situation because of the size of the prey, and the degree to which the snake's body had to have been stretched.

> I have seen a specimen of 18 feet in length which had just swallowed a large pig; in this example the middle of the body was enormously distended, so that the skin was stretched almost to bursting-point, and the scales, instead of lying side by side and almost overlapping, were situated quite far-apart, and between them it was possible to see the hairs of the pig through the skin and stomach-wall of the snake. This power that snakes have of swallowing very large masses, is, as is well known, due to the loose attachment of the various bones by which the jaw apparatus is slung on to the skull, permitting a wide gape to be made . . .

Frank Buck gave two accounts (1935:219; 1939:196–197) of, obviously, the same encounter between a *Python reticulata* and a leopard. A "huge" python had been found coiled alongside a game trail on the edge of a clearing. Knowing that a leopard had been prowling nearby during the night, and hoping to capture an encounter between the python and cat on film, Buck sent native beaters into the forest in order to drive the leopard toward the waiting python. We present the 1939 account here.

> . . . I heard sounds of shifting leaves and the cracking of twigs as if some animal were coming towards us through the jungle on the run, and peering up the trail I saw it coming—the black leopard . . . I had hardly dared hope that the beaters would be able to rout him out of his daylight hiding place. Stealthy, graceful, self-confident, and wholly unsuspicious of the coiled threat that lay beside his path, the jungle killer came directly toward our cameras.
>
> He must have scented the waiting reptile, for as he came near he seemed to hesitate in his stride—only for an instant, but that was long enough. Like a coiled spring the great reptile lunged. With a snarl and a growl the leopard sprang into the air in an effort to avoid his antagonist. Like lightening shooting from the brush, the great hammerlike head of the of the python heaved and struck. He flexed huge jaws and caught the leopard by the neck, a coil of silver-steel muscle shot up and around the sleek black body. The leopard's scream was one of tortured savagery—blood-curdling. The fight was on. It was the most terrific battle I have ever seen, or ever hope to see—here was the law of the jungle in its most savage manifestation. The leopard unsheathed his claws and tore deep into the python wherever he could reach the sinuous, slithering body. The lithe black cat swung his body recklessly into the air in desperate efforts to free himself. Slowly, surely, silently, coil on coil of the python's long, unwinding strength, powerful and unbreakable, was looped like shiny armor plate over the sentient black, until only his head and tail were left in view. The leopard was completely smothered by constriction. He was dead in less than four minutes from the time the battle started.

In *Wild Cargo*, Buck (1932) presents a photograph of a *Python reticulata* coiled about a tiger (*Panthera tigris*). There is no accompanying text.

Buck (1932:130), while in Sumatra, encountered some Eurasians who had just killed a "huge" *Python reticulata* in order to get the hide. The snake had obviously just eaten a large meal, and Buck was curious to learn what it was.

> The python was quickly slit open and I soon beheld something even more un-usual than I had hoped for. The snake had swallowed a sambar stag [*Cervus uni-color*], antlers and all! The sambar stag is the largest of all Asiatic deer and this was a fair-sized representative of the species, weighing about 160 pounds. In making its kill the reptile had first crushed the life out of the animal in charac-teristic fashion and next had broken the antlers. Then, when the antlers lay back flat on the neck, the snake had swallowed the deer, nose first . . .

Large meals eaten by small individuals were described by Hoogerwerf (1970:483). Smaller snakes eating prodigious meals allow a snake to take in huge amounts of calories and nutrients, but pose risks to the snake's health. He wrote,

> Incidentally, pythons considerably smaller in size are capable of overcoming and devouring bulky prey. In May 1929 a large deer was found in a python 4.5 m long in the vicinity of Rangkasbitung (Bantam, West Java). Manupassa (1941) found a young muntjac 55 cm long and with a withers height of 35 cm in a python of about 4 m, and many times adult wild boar, sheep and goats were found as the prey of such small pythons. It is known that in nature antler-bearing muntjac have also been seized and devoured.

British herpetologist Malcolm Smith (1943:110) suggested reticulated pythons have a preference for small prey. This is most likely due to the higher frequency of en-counters with small prey, and the fact that even the largest snake attempting to take large prey places itself in a situation that is apt to increase the probability of injury.

A reticulated python, about 25 feet long, consumed an extraordinary amount of food in a week if Hagenbeck's (1910:180) story is to be believed. It was accepted as legitimate by Pope, but other parts of Hagenbeck's account make its validity and his story suspect. The python was given the following food items: a 31-pound goat, a 43-pound buck, and a 52-pound Siberian goat; thus, the snake consumed 126 pounds of food. Hagenbeck stated he heard deep groans coming from the snake af-ter this meal, and when a photographer was brought in to photograph the snake, it regurgitated the Siberian goat. Hagenbeck continued,

> I had it [the goat] dissected on the following day. It was found that the goat's neck had been twisted completely out of its articulations. The ribs had been so pressed that they had all broken off from the vertebrae.

The African Python, *Python sebae*

There are more food records available for this giant snake than any of the others. This may in large part be due to the number of hunters and travelers interested in Africa's animals that visit its habitats. Broadley (1983:66) hypothesized on the swal-lowing capabilities of *Python sebae*

> Although there is without doubt much exaggeration about the swallowing pow-ers of these snakes, nevertheless a 4 metre snake is quite capable of swallowing

prey up to 25 kg in weight, while a 6 metre snake in all probability could manage anything up to 50 kg.

Snakes may kill and eat multiple prey items when they are present. In nature this
may be in a nest or social group situation; often, however, this situation presents itself in farm yards with domesticated animals. Haacke (1981:16) related a story
about a large meal of goats for *Python sebae*.

> To further illustrate the enormous capacity of large pythons, attention is drawn
> to a short contribution and photograph in the latest issue of *African Wildlife* Vol.
> 35,4:33. A python about six meters in length was shot in about 1921 at Monze in
> Zambia after it had swallowed six goats. Admittedly two were lambs and the goats
> appeared to be of the rather stocky and small variety. However, a snake of such
> size, appetite and determination could probably also have handled a human being.

Haagner (1992:31) reported a *Python sebae natalensis* swallowing an antelope almost equal to its own weight. The female python was captured in the Manyeleti
Game Reserve during December 1986 while swallowing a subadult impala ram. She
measured 4.7 m and weighed 37 kg; the impala weighed 35 kg (94.6% of the
python's body weight).

Warden of the Transvaal Government's Game Reserves, Stevenson-Hamilton
(1947:320–321) suggests African pythons usually take smaller prey, as opposed to
large prey.

> Personally, I never knew a python to seize anything larger than a half-grown
> bushbuck, and that would, I should imagine, be about the limit of a twelve-foot
> serpent's capabilities. Natives say that a very large one can swallow an impala,
> but I must say I never heard of such a thing occurring in the Game Reserve, where
> they have seldom been found to have eaten anything exceeding in size a duiker
> or a steenbuck.

A photograph (see Figure 3–2) provided by Van Rompaey (1985:250) illustrated
a large African python in the act of consuming a 43 kg calf. The size of this snake is
discussed in Chapter 3, but it is extremely unlikely it was the reported 11 m length.
Spawls and Branch (1995:20) suggest African pythons can handle antelopes weighing up to 59 kg.

Digestion

The teeth of mammals and the crops of birds grind food and thereby increase its
surface area so that stomach acids can quickly liquify the food making it available
for enzyme actions. Snakes have no method to mechanically digest their food, but
folklore reported by Tennent (1861:304) suggests a fanciful behavioral mechanism
for *Python molurus* in Ceylon (Sri Lanka).

> The Singhalese assert that when it has swallowed a deer, or any animal of simi-
> lar inconvenient bulk, the python draws itself through the narrow aperture between
> two trees, in order to crush the bones and assist in the process of deglutition.

Observations on the time required by digestion of a captive *Python molurus,* and
its relationship to temperature were reported by Phipson (1887:165–166).

It will be seen that during the hot months the period of digestion averaged about eight days, whereas in the cold weather it became much slower, the two rats eaten on 21st December being retained until 28th February.

During the cold weather, from 21st December to 13th April, a period of 113 days, the snake refused food and remained in a very sluggish, sleepy condition. During this period of hibernation the temperature of the reptile fell from 82° (normal) to 73°, a fall of 9 degrees. Taking the temperature was a matter of considerable difficulty. The snake is very strong, and it often required as many as six persons to hold it still while the thermometer was inserted. The results are, however, of particular value, as such observations cannot be made in European menageries, where artificial heat has to be used.

The snake cast its slough four times during the course of the year: three times in the hot weather, at intervals of 2 months, and once after it had recovered from its hibernation.

Aspects of digestion by *Python molurus* were discussed by Wall (1912:465), including the anatomical parts of prey that cannot be digested by snakes.

In a vigorous snake every part of the animal swallowed is completely digested except epithelial structures such as hair, feathers, quills, teeth, the beak and claws, the scales of reptiles, the cornea, or in snakes, the disc before the eye which is the analogue of the eyelids in other animals. If the dung is inspected these structures will be found massed together, and often retaining in a wonderful degree the relationship occupied in the animal ingested. In sickly snakes, or in those whose vitality is impaired, when hibernation is approaching, bones will be found passed in a more or less imperfectly digested state. In the excrement also may be seen circular spaces which are believed to be casts from the snake's intestine.

Digesting snakes are often said to be sedentary after eating, and the suggestion that if the prey is too large for total ingestion the snake will wait around for some anatomic part to decompose is most likely in error. Somanader (1941:284) wrote,

. . . Investigation of a horrible odour has sometimes led sportsmen to the discovery of a python lying in a marsh digesting a spotted deer which it had swallowed up to the antlers, waiting patiently for the head to rot and drop off. While digesting large carcasses the python is comatose and sluggish in its movements, and half-hearted in defending itself . . .

However, a 13-foot African python that swallowed a female sitatunga did not remain in one location but frequently changed position, each time evacuating its colon (Pitman, 1974:70). An alternative reason snakes may not move after a huge meal was suggested by Wall (1921:61):

It is popularly supposed that after a large meal the python lies torpid, in a condition of satiety, until digestion has far advanced. I very much doubt if this is the true explanation of the disinclination of the snake to move in such circumstances. . . . I think it is much more likely that in many cases the snake is so distended that it is afraid to move on account of internal injuries it may receive in the attempt.

A digestion story that pushes the limits of credibility comes from, again, Hagenbeck (1910:189). A 14-foot Indian python swallowed four lambs within a 24-hour period, each weighed between 12 and 19 pounds, and, therefore, the minimum weight would have been 55 pounds. Hagenbeck wrote,

> After this performance the snake was so swollen by the gas evolved in its interior by the semi-digested lambs that it burst open for a length of about a foot, the two edges yawning apart to a width of a couple of inches.

He then continued to describe how digestion took 10 days, and suggested the snake actually survived this experience! What seems a more plausible explanation for the exploding snake is that a hoof on one of the sheep tore a hole in the gut and body wall.

Digestion in snakes is described as a "race with the foreign microbes that live in their prey's intestines" (Diamond, 1994:54). The race is for the food contained in the prey, and every experienced snake keeper knows what happens when the temperature drops while a snake is digesting a meal. The bacteria in the prey are able to decompose the prey's body faster than the snake can digest the meal. Thus the snake must regurgitate the food in order to keep the bacterial soup from entering its small intestine.

Digestion takes days to weeks in snakes, while the same process in humans requires only a few hours. The extended time is the result of the size of the food, a lower body temperature, and the inability to mechanically digest the food. Hydrochloric acid fills the snake's stomach and saturates the prey, slowly dissolving bone and connective tissue, so the prey is liquified. While the food is sitting in the snake's stomach the small intestine is prepared for receiving the prey by rapidly growing, doubling or tripling its weight within 24 hours. This growth increases the cells available to make the enzymes needed to digest the massive amount of liquid food it will soon receive (Diamond, 1994:57).

Do Giant Snakes Swallow Animals with Horns or Antlers?

Eating a particularly large meal makes a snake more vulnerable to predators, but what happens to snakes that ingest prey with horns or antlers? The following anecdotes suggest giant snakes have faced this problem more than once.

Charles Waterton (1909:216) reported an anaconda that swallowed a stag with horns. This description is highly unlikely because snakes almost always swallow their prey head first. In order for the story below to be correct, the snake would have had to swallow the deer back-end first—an improbable occurrence.

> A Dutch friend of mine by name Brouwer, killed a Boa, twenty-two feet long, with a pair of stag's horns in his mouth: he had swallowed the stag, but could not get the horns down: so he had to wait in patience with that uncomfortable mouthful till his stomach digested the body, and then the horns would drop out. In this plight the Dutchman found him as he was going in his canoe up the river, and sent a ball through his head.

Africa has a rich fauna of hoofed animals with horns or antlers. FitzSimons (1930:63–65) reported several incidents of African pythons swallowing prey with horns, and the aftermath of the ingestion.

But this python was enormously distended, and upon examination we found the horns of a Duiker ram sticking out fully two inches from its side. When the stomach of the snake was slit, the half digested body of the buck was disclosed.

Apparently the movements of the snake, after it had swallowed the buck, had caused the sharp horns to penetrate the stomach muscles and skin. But if the snake had not been violently disturbed, and if it had not met so untimely a death, the buck would have been digested, bones and all, and the horns would have worked out.

Later on I saw an instance of this. A python was captured unhurt, with a pair of Duiker buck horns protruding between its ribs. A slight pull detached them; the flesh of the snake had healed right up to the skin. Wounds in wild animals invariably heal rapidly, without any suppuration, unlike those of domestic animals and civilized human beings.

At Palapye, in Bechuanaland, a python nearly sixteen feet in length once constricted a full grown Duiker ram that had horns four inches long. The python swallowed the prey, hindquarters first, and the entire buck, horns and all, was worked down to the reptile's stomach. Subsequently the horns punctured the snake and protruded through the skin between the ribs.

When the snake's body was cut open, the appearance of the buck in its stomach showed that it must have been swallowed at least three days before the natives killed the snake.

. . . We found a python one day lying helpless, with the head and horns of an adult duiker buck protruding from the left side of its jaws.

The reptile had constricted and elongated the body of the buck to prepare it for the swallowing process. But instead of starting at the head it had begun with the hind quarters. And as the victim's body was forced down the throat of the snake, the hind legs doubled up under the abdomen.

South African herpetologist Bill Branch (1984:237) also commented on African pythons eating horned ungulates. He noted that the sharp horns of buck such as sitatunga and duiker may penetrate the sides of a python following ingestion, but that they usually fall off when the prey's head is digested, and the small wounds in the python's side soon heal.

Vulnerability to Predators During and After Feeding

It should be apparent by now that much of the early literature on giant snakes was produced by snake-human encounters which occurred because the snake had just eaten a large meal and could not easily escape to cover before it was discovered. Following are a few select anecdotes which illustrate this point.

During foraging, snakes may also expose themselves to predators, their movement making them more susceptible to detection. They may also encounter animals they are not prepared to deal with. Meercats are small, social, viverids of Africa, and looking at one, it would appear to pose little threat to the life of a large snake. However, these animals have evolved an elaborate, collaborative defense strategy when attacked by a predator. FitzSimons (1930:73–75) witnessed a fight to the death between a colony of fifteen bushy-tailed, or rooi (red), meercats (*Cynictis penicillata*) and an African python.

The snake had made an attack on a meercat colony on the veld, adjacent to a scrub-covered hillside. Issuing from cover, the python had entered one of the burrows, but, being immediately assailed-and most persistently-by the meercats it withdrew hastily and took up an attitude of defence.

Wildly excited, the meercats gathered round the python. Whenever a chance offered they made a sally, buried their teeth in the flesh of the foe, and jumped hurriedly out of danger again.

Presently the python made a lightening-like lunge and gripped a meercat in its powerful jaws. One coil went simultaneously round the victim, and its life was instantly crushed out of it.

But the stupid reptile held on to its prey while the other meercats were assaulting its body. Blood was oozing from its innumerable tears and bites in its flesh, yet it held grimly on to the little body within its coils.

Then, with a sudden sweep of its tail, it gathered up another meercat. Next instant I saw the little creature struggling and biting, with a lap of the python's tail round the body. The tail-grip tightened, the meercat gasped, impotently, for breath, and died-crushed by the steel-like grasp of that fearsome tail.

But meanwhile the surviving meercats had been tearing and biting at the body of the snake, and it was visibly weakening from loss of blood.

There is no need to describe the rest of that struggle in detail. After three hours of gallant effort the meercats had slain their foe and were lapping up its blood.

On seeing me approach, the victors scuttled away and down into their burrows. The python's body was torn and bitten in at least a hundred places.

A python that captured a young baboon fared better in dealing with the troop attack that followed than did the snake in the story above. Isemonger (1956:48) described the troop's attack on the snake.

The troop, though very scared, crowded round, barking, and every now and then one of the larger ones would dash in, give the snake a nip then shoot back to a safe distance. When they realised the python had no intention of releasing its prey they ambled off, but not before inflicting several nasty wounds.

Isemonger later saw the same snake and observed that the wounds were healing. However, meercats and baboons are not the only animals that will attack giant snakes in social groups: Dickey (1932:220–221) reported peccaries will also attack in unison.

From Guiana, Schomburgk (1922:330) reported a case of human predation on an anaconda during feeding. The time involved in handling large prey, and the disturbance created increases risk to the snake.

The gentleman was just then engaged in skinning a large boa constrictor [actually a large anaconda], *Boa murina* [= *Eunectes murinus*] that had attacked one of his pigs that morning, and for which it had now to pay the penalty with its life. It measured 18 feet. A few days later a second one was killed at the edge of the lake by one of the Indians fishing there. Attracted by a noise in the proximity he sneaked a bit closer and found the snake in ardent combat with a full grown water haas. In spite of the first ball piercing its belly it dragged the spoil, round which it was coiled, towards the water; it was only the second shot that freed the captive. The snake measured 14 feet; its skeleton is to be seen in the Anatomical Museum at Berlin.

When a large predator encounters a snake that has recently fed, the snake is at a decided disadvantage to defend itself. Singh (1983:31–32) described what must be a relatively infrequent incident: a *Python molurus* eats a pig and then encounters a tiger.

During June 1980 in Corbett National Park, a sub-adult tiger measuring 2.20 m in length and a 5 m python fought each other to death. An autopsy of the python discovered a wild boar in its stomach which had been swallowed whole. In all probability, the tiger had stumbled over the python and in the ensuing fight, the tiger died of asphyxiation and the python died of serious wounds inflicted by the tiger.

FitzSimons (1930:70–73) also related a similar hunter's story about an African python-leopard encounter that had results similar to the one above.

Humans have undoubtedly been major predators on large snakes, and Bosman's (1705:311) encounter with two porcupines and an African python makes this quite clear.

Some of my servants once going to the country beyond Mouree, found a snake seventeen foot long, and very bulky, lying about a pit of water, perhaps to divert himself; near which were two porcupines; betwixt which and the snake began a very sharp engagement, each shooting very violently in their way, the snake his venom and the porcupine their quills of two spans long, for with such they were armed. My men having seen this fight a considerable time, without being observed by the curious combatants (in the heat of battle) after having loaded their muskets, let fly upon the three champions to so good purpose that they killed them all, and brought them to Mouree, where they were devoured by them and their comrades as a very great delicacy.

Fasting

Sit-and-wait predators may have to go for extended periods of time between meals. Droughts, cold spells, declines in prey populations, and other changes in the local ecosystem may create a shortage of food for snakes and other animals. The ability of snakes to survive these unpredictable circumstances has been honed by natural selection over the millennia. Today, giant snakes, as well as smaller sized serpents, have the ability to survive long periods without eating. For a mammal who desires three meals a day, fasting for long periods is difficult to relate to. Snakes have a low metabolic rate and can therefore go without food for long periods of time. As previously noted, this is an adaptation to obtaining food from ambush. How long can giant snakes fast? The following passages suggest years. The literature contains many references to fasting snakes and in many cases the fasting period is less than a year. We have restricted the discussion here to fasts lasting more than 18 months (Table 4-2).

One of the longest fasts reported for any giant snake is that from Wucherer (1861:115) who discussed a fasting anaconda.

Eunectes murinus seems to possess an extraordinary capability of fasting; a friend of mine kept the largest specimen I ever saw in close confinement for three years, and it was never known to swallow anything during this whole period. It died much emaciated.

The 19-month fast of another anaconda is not as spectacular as the previous one, but supports the idea that these huge snakes can go for extended periods of time without food. Quelch (1898:300) wrote:

A specimen kept in a narrow-meshed wire cage in the Museum some years back refused to eat for nineteen months, though it would lie in the water for long intervals; and it seemed at the end of the time to be about as plump as it had been before.

McArthur (1922:1142–3) reported an Indian python fasting for 2.5 years (30 months) based upon a letter he received from a neighboring planter.

The python was a young one 9 1/2 feet long. It was caught, without being injured some time in 1911 or 1912. It was kept in a wire cage for 2½ years. During that time it ate absolutely nothing. It was tried with frogs, and a pigeon was in the cage for 5 or 6 days. The pigeon had to be removed as it started bullying the python. It had a dish of water in its cage always, but there is no absolute proof that it drank. During the 2½ years it changed its skin regularly and appeared in perfect health. At the end of the time it suddenly began to get thin and weak very rapidly, so we let it go in the jungle.

Wall (1926:86) reported a 23-month fast for a reticulated python.

That this python can exist and maintain its health for very long periods without taking food is exemplified by the remarkable instance of a captive specimen in Regent's Park, that refused food for one year, and eleven months after which it indulged in a meal and continued to feed normally.

A 3-year fast for an African python was mentioned by Pitman (1974:69), but no details were given. Another African python described by Sweeney (1961:46) fasted for 33 months.

FitzSimons (1930:28–29) described a captive African python that had been injured by rodents chewing on it. The snake had refused to eat during its 24 months in captivity. He wrote,

The wound healed perfectly, and the python doggedly kept to its fast. Fowls and guinea-pigs tempted it not at all, but I hoped that sooner or later it would give up its foolish hunger-strike. When once a python can be induced to eat in captivity there is no more trouble with it, at least in regard to taking food. Two years went by, and nothing stronger than water was swallowed. Yet the reptile was not in an emaciated condition.

Two more months fled, and I was about to make arrangements for taking the python out to the nearest kloof and releasing it, but it forestalled my good intentions by escaping.

Table 4–2. Summary of Fasts Reported for Giant Snakes

Species	Length of Fast	Source
Eunectes murinus	36 months	Wucherer (1861:113)
Eunectes murinus	19 months	Quelch, (1898:300)
Python molurus	30 months	McArthur (1922:1142–3)
Python reticulata	23 months	Wall (1926:4)
Python sebae	33 months	Sweeney (1961:46)
Python sebae	24 months	FitzSimons (1930:8–28)
Python sebae	36 months	Pitman (1974:69)

The hypothesis that fasting could be prolonged by lowering the temperature was proposed by Pope (1961:89). He suggests that chilling would induce hibernation and that in the cases cited above the snakes were maintained at "normal temperatures." This is arguable, and it may well be that the reason the snakes cited above refused food was that they were not maintained at temperatures high enough to stimulate feeding. Snakes kept in buildings, or in shaded cages, may not achieve body temperatures high enough to consume and digest food.

Summary

Although no thorough study exists on the diet of any of the giants, it is possible to make some generalizations about feeding behavior and diet based on what we do know.

The four giants are probably largely sit-and-wait (ambush) foragers, but will often employ an active foraging mode; that is, a combination (or continuum) of foraging modes may be employed by any individual giant snake.

The time of hunting may, apparently, occur at any hour of the day or night. Branch (1988a:51) has observed that African pythons hunt primarily at dusk or after dark, but Starin and Burghardt (1992) encountered pythons routinely during daylight hours, and usually during the afternoon. We suspect that there may be a continuum of activity in giants, depending on season, age group, etc.

All of the giants are trophic generalists, taking a wide taxonomic and size range of vertebrate prey including fishes, amphibians (probably rarely), turtles, lizards, snakes (including conspecifics), crocodilians (caiman and crocodiles), birds (ground-dwelling, ducks, wading species), and mammals (bats, anteaters and pangolins, carnivores, a wide variety of rodents including capybara and porcupines, deer and antelope, primates including an occasional *Homo sapiens*). Since snakes are gape-limited, for any given species of giant, larger individuals have the option of exploiting a wider range of prey species (taxonomically and by size); that is, a large giant can consume small and large prey, whereas a small giant is limited to small prey items.

Although the giants are capable of consuming prodigious meals (approaching 100% of their body weight), it is likely that most giants, regardless of size, prey predominantly on relatively small prey items (e.g., 25% or less of their own body weight), because smaller prey items tend to be more plentiful than large ones, and the giants are opportunistic foragers.

CHAPTER 5

SEX AMONG THE GIANTS

> But that which is most characteristic of the Boidae is the presence of two hooks
> or spurs, situated one on each side of the vent. These are undoubtedly of great
> use to the reptile, as helping the prehensile tail to maintain a firm hold on the
> branch of a tree, from which the long body depends, with the head bent up a lit-
> tle above the ground, watching for the approach of prey. But these spurs are un-
> doubtedly the rudiments of posterior limbs . . .

Gosse (1850:164) wrote the above statement, suggesting that the giant snakes and
their relatives are not limbless at all, almost 150 years ago. Thus we have giant
snakes *with* legs, albeit tiny ones (Figure 5–1). Tiny legs in giant snakes have stimulated the imaginations of earlier writers to suggest that snakes use these to anchor
their bodies when striking and are used in ascending trees (Savage, 1842:245). Some
African tribes believe the python thrusts these minute structures into the nostrils of
prey to cause suffocation (Rose, 1962:329), and in Sri Lanka the remnant legs are
believed venomous and that during constriction the snake stings the prey in the head
(de Silva, 1990:13).

Why do some snakes have vestigial legs? After all, boids (boas and pythons), worm
snakes (Leptotyphlopidae), blindsnakes (Typhlopidae) and the pipe snakes (Anili-
idae) all have traces of pelvic and lower limb bones. Vestigial limbs are evidence that
the ancestral snake was lizard-like or a lizard with reduced legs. We say this with considerable confidence because modern lizards with reduced limbs exist today in many
saurian families (Pygopodidae, Scincidae, Anguidae, Teiidae), and some of these look
so much like snakes they can pose temporary problems for herpetologists making
quick decisions about an animal's identity. "Descent with modification" is a well-worn
evolutionary slogan but one that has as much validity today as it did 140 years ago
when Charles Darwin wrote it. Evolution works by modifying old structures into new
ones, not by creating dramatically new structures from nothing, and a pattern seen in
some groups of organisms is one of degeneration; that is, loss or reduction of structures that are well-developed in close relatives. Current knowledge of molecular ge-
netics suggests that reduction or loss of certain features may be accomplished through
relatively simple mutations by turning specific genes on or off, and timing the activa-
tion switch during development. Thus, living snakes presumably closely related to the
ancestral snake(s) have traces of reduced limbs, while more modern snakes such as
the colubrids, viperids, and elapids have lost all traces of limbs. However, these limb
remnants are not without function in the boas and pythons.

Male boid snakes have longer spurs than females, suggesting that these structures
may have a function in reproduction, and indeed they do. Courtship, copulation, and
the role of the vestigial limbs in courting were described by Trinidad newspaperman
and herpetologist R. R. Mole (1924:237–238) for the anaconda. He wrote,

> These reptiles have been observed to couple in December and January, both in and
> out of the water. During this act the anal hooks, which are hardly ever used, come
> prominently into play. The male throws a coil or two round the female, which is

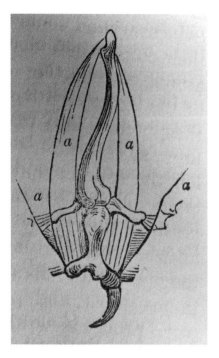

Figure 5–1. Remnant hind leg skeletal structure and associated musculature denoted by "a." No species information given. *From Martin (1843:226).*

usually the larger of the pair, and his claws are moved quickly, and scratch the scaley sides of his mate, inducing her to crawl forward slowly until union is established.

Reproductive behavior in the Indian python was described by Barker et al. (1979:469–470) in a captive colony at the Dallas Zoo. The courtship lasted 5 to 30 minutes, during which the male would attempt to align his body with the female as she slowly crawled forward. When the female would stop forward motion, cease tongue flicking, and raise her head to a height about 75 cm above the substrate, the male would initiate vigorous courtship. The female would hold her position for 10 seconds to several minutes, while the male would loop his body over the female's back and rapidly tongue flick the top of her head and back. The cloacas would then be aligned, and the male would begin vibrating his vestigial limbs 30–80 times per minute against the female's body in the region above her cloaca. At this point the female would sometimes become receptive, arch her tail, gape her cloaca, and the male would insert one of his hemipenes. During the 45–365 minute coitus, the male continued to stimulate the female with his spurs. Similar use of the remnant legs has been reported for the reticulated python by Lederer (1944:363), but it has not been reported for the African python or for the Australian scrub python.

Aggregations

Snakes may aggregate for hibernation, during mating season, and possibly at other times when food is particularly abundant in a given area. Den sites are often fissures in rock or deep burrows where the snakes can escape the cold of winter, extreme heat of summer, or very dry surface conditions. Tropical species such as the giants are generally believed to remain active year-round, although annual patterns of rainfall affect aspects of their ecology. There is evidence indicating that small congregations of giant snakes do occur. These may be in response to sexual or environmental factors.

Hunters discovered "eleven anacondas in a single tangle . . . the largest specimen was more than 6 m . . ." (Blomberg, 1956:97). Lange (1914:134–138) reported finding a pond-like hole in a forested swamp containing an aggregation of anacondas. In his highly emotional, macho, and undoubtedly exaggerated account, Lange and his companions shot most of the snakes, but made no attempt to count them or to assess why there were so many snakes at this location.

Lopez (1984:113, 116) reported "rollos de culebras" (rolls of snakes [anacondas]) made up of one female and several males in Venezuela. He also alluded to a liquid of strong odor secreted by the female and which acts as a sexual attractant for the males. He recounted a story in which a reproductive aggregation comprising one female and "muchos machos" (many males) of *E. murinus* was encountered. A member of the party wanted the skin of the female and killed her. The body of the female was then dragged a long distance across the savanna. The following morning, there were many traces of other anacondas where the female's body had been dragged the previous day. Apparently other anacondas, presumably males, were attracted to the pheromone (scent) trail left by the dead female as her body was dragged across the savanna (translation by RWH).

Recent field work in Venezuela has shown female anacondas attract numerous males that possibly compete with each other in an attempt to mate with her (Figure 5–2) (Thorbjarnarson, 1995).

Apparently the Indian python hibernates in all parts of India which have a cool season. Wall (1921:54) recounted a newspaper story of six *Python molurus* discovered in a stream bank cavity, all were between 10 and 12 feet long, and he cites other instances with less detail. A photograph in Bhupathy and Vijayan (1989:plate 1) shows at least six pythons near a hole in the ground, with three of the snakes entering the hole. At the dens (or python points) they observed 1–30 snakes during two winters, and found the frequency of mating and movement between dens high in February and March. Thus, denning appears to provide an opportunity for animals that are otherwise solitary to mate. References to aggregations of reticulated pythons (*Python reticulata*) appear to be absent from the literature. Starin and Burghardt (1992:58) observed clusters of 2–6 African pythons, but, again, only in the winter. They reported that the snakes were often intertwined, or one trailing another, and they concluded that this represented reproductive behavior. While aggregations at a limited number of "hibernacula" may be motivated by the need to escape environmental conditions, it does provide an excellent opportunity for mating, and reproduction may be the primary reason for these gatherings.

Incubation to Hatching

Temperature effects embryo growth rates and warmer temperatures cause reptile embryos to develop faster, while cooler temperatures result in slower embryonic growth. Anaconda incubation behavior was described by Holmstrom (1980:32). A

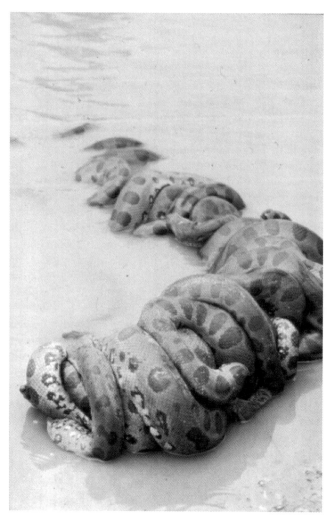

Figure 5–2. A female anaconda being courted by seven males. This kind of scene stimulated the phrase "rollos de culebras." *William Holmstrom.*

gravid female spent considerable time over a heating coil in her cage and a negative aspect of this behavior was the desiccation of her skin, which resulted in inhibiting shedding several times.

Live birth and egg-laying seem to be distinctly different modes of reproduction, but in snakes and lizards the line between live birth (viviparity) and egg-laying (oviparity) is far from being clear-cut. While it is true that snakes either give birth to young wrapped in extraembryonic membranes or produce shelled-eggs containing embryos in some stage of development, there is evidence to indicate that both of these methods may be used by different populations of a single species. Some species lay eggs, but the eggs hatch within a few days of being laid because the female retained the developing embryos in her body for some time before secreting an egg shell around the embryos and depositing them in a nest, others lay eggs shortly after they have been fertilized and the embryos undergo lengthy de-

Table 5–1. Egg Dimensions and Weights for Four Species of Pythons

Species	Egg Dimensions (mm)	Egg Mass (g)	Source
Morelia amethesitina	70–98×45–56	98–102 g	Barker and Barker (1994:40)
Python molurus	70.9–99×49–68	150–178 g	Acharjyo and Mishra (1975:562)
	85–120×47–52	165–207 g	Acharjyo and Mishra (1980:364)
	92×57	170 g	Coborn (1975:471)
Python reticulata	90–93×58–62		Hoogerwerf (1970:484)
	103–116×63–75		Hoogerwerf (1970:484)
	90–93×58–62		Kopstein
	115–103×75–64		(1938:131, 159)
Python sebae	77×56	132 g	Haagner (1993:38)
Python sebae	100 mm diameter	120–160 g	Branch (1988b:63)

velopment in the nest. Within many families and genera which are primarily egg layers, there are live bearers; thus viviparity has evolved many times in snakes and lizards. Boas are viviparous and pythons are oviparous; the common anaconda gives live birth, while the pythons lay eggs containing developing embryos. Table 5–1 summarizes egg dimensions and weights. The reticulated python produces the largest eggs.

A major advantage viviparous snakes have over oviparous species is the precise control of embryo temperature. A gravid female can orient her body during basking to warm the developing young, or she can place them in the shade or submerge them in cool water. The major disadvantage of viviparity is that the female must carry the weight and volume of the embryos wherever she goes. In the latter stages of pregnancy this may result in making her more vulnerable to predators, and the large mass of embryos reduces the room in the body cavity for processing food. Thus, gravid or pregnant boids frequently fast until egg-laying or birth is completed. Eggs placed in a nest are often abandoned, although this does not appear to be true with many, if any, pythons.

Gestation time is difficult to determine in snakes because females of many species have the ability to retain sperm. Holmstrom (1980:32) presented dates for anaconda courtship, matings, and birth which suggest anaconda gestation could be as long as 288 days or as short as 182 days. These development times are relatively long for snakes, but, in general, boids have long gestation periods.

Terrestrial birthing sites for the anaconda are suggested by Mole and Urich (1894:505) who report observations from a wild specimen.

> . . . one of five received from Pedernales, Venezuela, on the 12th of July, 1892. It was captured on the 1st of July of the same year. The mother, which was 22 feet long, was on that date observed on the bank of one of the mouths of the Orinoco, giving birth to young ones.

However, observations on captives suggest aquatic births may also occur. On the afternoon of 8 March 1976, Deschanel (1978:98–99) observed the birth of anacondas in their tank, the neonates began to swim immediately. Holmstrom and Behler (1981:354) also reported aquatic births in a captive anaconda. Table 5–2 summarizes reproductive data for the anaconda.

Pre-egg Laying Posture

Prior to egg-laying female pythons assume an unusual posture: lying on their sides or backs with their ventral sides pointed somewhat upward. Branch and Erasmus (1984:6) discovered an Indian python in this position and suggested the following:

> This initial frightening experience has subsequently proved to be a common occurrence in females during the latter half of egg development. Presumably it offers some form of relief to the mother from the weight of the increasing egg mass.

Table 5–2. Reproductive Data Summary for the Anaconda, *Eunectes murinus*

Size of female	Litter Size	Birth Date	Size of Young	Source
22 ft	30	1 Jul	"about 20 in"	Mole and Urich, 1894
	30–42	Jul–Aug		Mole, 1914
4.45 m	70			Belluomini et al., 1959
5.2 m	77			Belluomini et al., 1959
	82			Belluomini and Hoge, 1958
5.3 m	47			Belluomini and Veinert, 1967
4.2 m	24		0.73–0.76 m	Belluomini and Veinert, 1967
3.842 m	26			Belluomini et al., 1977
4.933 m	47			Belluomini et al., 1977
5.120 m	46			Belluomini et al., 1977
3.5	15	8 Mar	$\bar{x}$ = 75 cm/250g	Deschanel, 1978
19 ft./236 lbs.	72		38 inches	Ditmars, 1931
17 ft.	34		27 inches	Ditmars, 1931
3.2 m	27	5 Feb	800–855 mm $\bar{x}$ = 843.9	Holmstrom, 1980
3.8 m	30	30 Nov	855–900 mm $\bar{x}$ = 877.1	Holmstrom, 1980
3.3 m	23	8 Dec	730–765 mm $\bar{x}$ = 748 mm	Holmstrom, 1980
15 ft	4	8 Jan		Neill and Allen, 1962

Nesting

The Indian python has been reported (Wall, 1912:468) to nest in relatively open areas, as well as in tree holes and termite nests. Coborn (1975:471) suggested *Python molurus* may build a nesting mound; a 10-foot female Indian python laid 27 eggs on top of a mound of gravel which she scraped together from the cage floor.

Porter (1988:44) described the nest site of a *Python sebae natalensis* at Game Valley Estates, Hella Hella, Natal.

> On 4 February 1986 . . . a python was discovered coiled around a clutch of eggs. The nest was in an open 36 ha. field, far from the nearest thick cover, lightly concealed in 600 mm high *Panicum* spp. grassland. The nest was not disturbed after discovery, but when visited the next day it was found that all the eggs were broken and scattered and the python had left the area. A total of 30 eggshells were counted in the vicinity of the nest. The cause of the disturbance is unknown. It is strange that the site was chosen in such an accessible area as many more suitable sites were available within 50 m of the nest, including thick riverine bush, rocky outcrops and warthog holes.

Nesting sites utilized by *Python sebae* were described by Stucki-Strin (1979:154) as tangled bushwood, abandoned antbear holes, other animal holes, old termite hills, and deep rock crevices. Tables 5–3 through 5–6 summarize reproductive data for the largest pythons.

The Brooding Python Controversy

Old ideas die hard. The recent controversy over the ability of dinosaurs to control their body temperature is well known to the general public. But a lesser known controversy concerning the ability of female pythons to control their body temperature while brooding eggs is not so well known, although it began more than 150 years ago. We have pieced this story together based upon accounts in Valenciennes (1841), Hopley (1882), Benedict (1932), and Dowling (1960).

In March of 1832, M. Lamarre-Picquot read a communication before the French Academy of Sciences, describing an Indian python brooding its eggs with body heat,

Table 5–3. Reproductive Data Summary for the Scrub Python, *Morelia amethistina*

Size of ♀/ mass	Number of eggs	Date of mating	Date of egg laying	Date of hatching	Days of incubation	Size of Hatchlings	Source
2.1 m	7 (infertile)	?	October	-	-	-	Boos (1979)
2.1m	12	-	15 August	-	77–79	$\bar{x}$ = 64.5 cm/52.8 g	Boos (1979)
2.7 m	7	24 Sept.	26 Dec.	10 April	105	$\bar{x}$ = 54.1 cm	Charles et al. (1985)
3.9 m/5.5 kg	17	5–15 Oct.	7 Dec.	2–5 Mar	85–88	$\bar{x}$ = 63.3 cm/52.9 g	Grow et al. (1988)

Table 5–4. Reproductive Data Summary for the Indian Python, *Python molurus*

Size of ♀/ mass	Number of eggs	Date of mating	Date of egg laying	Date of hatching	Days of incubation	Size of Hatchlings	Source
2.35 m/7.7kg	13 (infertile)						Acharjyo and Mishra, 1980
2.5 m/8.9 kg	17 (infertile)						Acharjyo and Mishra, 1980
4.35 m	53	4–5 Feb	28 April	23–25 June	56–58	77–103 g 58.5– 66.5 cm	Acharjyo and Mishra, 1976
	about 100						Benedict, 1932
			Feb.–Aug. (in wild)				Bhupathy and Vijayan, 1989
	58						Black et al, 1983
10′	33		18 April	25 June	63		Coborn, 1975
8′6″	16		12 May	no hatching			D'Abreu, 1917
10′	15		May	no hatching	56		Forbes, 1881
	12–20						Leigh, 1951
	15–54 for 16 clutches x̄=29						Pope, 1961
		Oct.– March	Jan.– June	April to August	58–63		Ross and Marzec, 1990
	11						Stemmler-Morath, 1956
3.47 m/29kg	34	19 Feb.	13 June	11 August			Van-Mierop and Barnard, 1976a
2.7 m	23		15 Feb				Vinegar et al. 1970
	44				61–68		Vinegar, 1973
					57–71		Wagner, 1973
	8–107	Dec.–Feb.	March– June	58	average 2′5″		Wall, 1912
12′	48						Wray, 1862
	42	24–25 March			53	43–48 cm	Yadav, 1967

Table 5–5. Reproductive Data Summary for the African Python, *Python sebae*

Female Size	Number of Eggs	Date of Mating	Date of Egg Laying	Date of hatching	Days of Incuba-tion	Size of Hatch-lings	Source
	55	Aug.–Nov.			79–83	50–59 cm	Haagner, 1992:33
	30–50	all year			about 90	61 cm	Pitman, 1974
	28				49, 52		Joshi, 1967:311
	25		Dec.				Patterson, 1974:81
	23	4 Nov.		14 Feb.	81–88		Patterson, 1974:81
3.2 m	74			10 Feb.			Porter, 1987:37
	30						Porter, 1988:44
13 ft	39			Dec. 24		60–63 cm	Broadley, 1959:11
3.8 m	48				86–88		Branch and Erasmus, 1984:5
4.0 m	35	Oct.			76–79		Branch and Erasmus, 1984:5
3.2 m	32		Nov. 5				Branch and Patterson, 1974:27
3.5 m	37	13 Nov.	15 Jan.	1 April	75	63–65 cm	Dunn, 1979:91
16 ft	55	-					Stevenson-Hamilton, 1947:322

Table 5–6. Female Size and Clutch Size of Reticulated Python, *Python reticulata*

Female Size	Number of Eggs	Source
	more than 103	Hagenbeck, 1910:192
	24	Hoogerwerf, 1970:484
	16	"
	29	"
	38	"
	96	"
3.5 m	14	Kopstein, 1938:131
3 m	16	Kopstein, 1938:131
Nine females 10–26 feet	14–103, $\bar{x}=46.4$	Pope, 1961:139
	59	Wall, 1926:87
	96	Wall, 1926:87

Data on mating, egg laying, incubation, and other information are lacking for this species.

based upon observations made while traveling in India. This idea was contrary to the paradigm of the time, which said reptiles are cold-blooded and therefore unable to produce metabolic heat. Physician and anatomist André-Marie-Constance Duméril dominated European herpetology at the time, and provided Achille Valenciennes with the opportunity to disprove Lamarre-Picquot's idea that pythons could generate heat by assigning him to head a committee to investigate the controversy.

Figure 5–3. An Indian python, *Python molurus,* with eggs at the Jardin des Plantes in Paris. *From Goodrich (1870, 2:404)*

The committee ultimately rejected Lamarre-Picquot's findings and part of the problem was one of credibility: Lamarre-Picquot endorsed the ability of a snake to drink milk from a cow's udder.

Valenciennes' opportunity to make direct observations came when fifteen eggs were deposited on 6 May 1841 by a python in the Jardin des Plantes in Paris (Figure 5–3). The female python had been kept in a cage with several other *Python molurus* and she had been observed mating in January and February; on 4 April she shed. The normally gentle female became agitated on 5 May, striking at anyone who came near her; the first egg was laid at 6:00 AM, and fourteen more eggs were deposited by 9:30 AM. Using movements of her body, she collected the eggs into a cone-shaped pile, rested with her head on the apex of the cone, and concealed the eggs with her body so that none was visible. During incubation the female refused food, leaving her eggs only five times in order to drink. She remained with the eggs for 56 days. Valenciennes found the female aggressive and difficult to approach, but he set up mercury thermometers to monitor temperatures in the room, under the cloth, and between the coils of the snake. On 8 May, the room temperature was 23°C, the air under the cloth was 28.5°C and that between the snake's coils was 41.4°C -the greatest difference ever reported between a snake and its environment. As incubation progressed the temperature of the snake decreased, until 2 July when it was 28ºC, but it was always measurably higher than room temperature. Realizing the cage floor was heated by hot water pipes, Valenciennes recognized the possibility for errors in determining temperature and attempted to avoid them. The snake was warm and it showed a great desire to drink, so Valenciennes compared the brooding heat to a "state of fever."

In 1842 Lamarre-Picquot read a second paper suggesting that observations on a captive python in Transylvania supported his finding of heat production in brooding pythons. And later at the same meeting, Duméril summarized the situation and suggested that excretion from the snake and the liquid from broken eggs fermented and generated the heat. Duméril duplicated some of Valenciennes' experiments, but without a snake. He placed warm water in vessels below the apparatus used by Valenciennes, and draped a woolen cloth over the area, placing a thermometer within the cavity that was formed. After several hours the thermometer under the cloth was 10°C warmer than a thermometer outside the cloth. Duméril concluded that the heated water was the source of the extra heat.

Sixteen years later, in 1858, Lamarre-Picquot read yet another communication to the Academy, indicating that his remarks were misinterpreted, and that he meant to express the fact that only pythons incubated their eggs—not all snakes. Duméril spoke immediately afterward, questioning Lamarre-Picquot's credibility and recalling his earlier comments about snakes suckling milk from cows, and the inaccuracy of using the hand as a thermometer to express temperature in degrees. Despite these many problems, Lamarre-Picquot's observations were to be vindicated.

At this point the story of hot pythons broadens to include the African python, *Python sebae*. In 1861, Sclater (1862:365) observed a brooding female *P. sebae* in the Gardens of the Zoological Society of London, and he measured air temperatures as well as the skin temperatures of a brooding female and a male housed in the same compartment with specially made thermometers (Figure 5–4). He wrote: "It appeared to me that any decided difference observable between these two animals subject to exactly the same external conditions, could be only attributable to the incubation." His results suggested that the female python did indeed generate heat, and they appear below in Table 5-7.

Sclater's results were criticized because the two snakes were not close enough to each other, and for this reason Benedict (1932:91) considered Sclater's results inconclusive.

W. A. Forbes (1881:962–964) reported on another brooding female *Python molurus* at the London Zoological Park. The female incubated the eggs for about six weeks, at which time it became obvious the eggs were decomposing. During the brooding, Forbes used the same setup employed by Sclater, but he removed the male and placed him in an adjacent cage. Forbes's data also suggested brooding female pythons generate body heat, and he was the first to compare the female's body temperature to the inverse air temperature. He wrote,

> It would seem therefore that, if his observations are to be relied on, throughout the case recorded by Valenciennes the female developed a far greater amount of heat than ours did, though she was kept in a cage that was apparently considerably colder. As in this case more than half the eggs hatched out, it may be that the failure of our animals to do the same was due to the lack of heat.

Another attempt to measure "fevered" pythons occurred in Washington, D.C. Benedict (1932:102–114) measured the temperatures of a brooding python and obtained results suggestive of heat production by the female, but he left the issue openended because the temperature of the eggs was not measured and his observations

Figure 5–4. A pair of African pythons, *Python sebae,* with eggs at the Zoological Society of London. *From Cassell's Popular Natural History (ca. 1856, 4:51).*

were limited. Considering the conflicting reports, it is not surprising that it took more than 130 years to settle the question of heat production by the Indian python.

It was thermocouple technology that finally allowed the question of heat production by brooding female pythons to be resolved. Hutchison et al. (1966) monitored the temperature and gas output of a 2.7 m brooding female *Python molurus* in a temperature controlled room using thermocouples taped to the snake's skin. Environmental temperatures below 33°C cause the snake to spasmodically contract its muscles resulting in a "twitching." As the environmental temperature was decreased from 33°C to 25.5°C, the snake increased its rate of oxygen consumption. At 25.5°C the oxygen consumption of the brooding snake was 9.3 times higher than when the snake was not brooding. More clues to the brooding mechanism in this snake were reported by Vinegar et al. (1970). They found the heart rate of brooding females increased from three to five per minute when the temperature was raised from 17°C to 26.5°C, but increased to 16 beats per minute at 33°C. This increase is proportional to oxygen consumption at those temperatures. They also reported "false brooding" in a female *Python molurus*. A female was observed twitching at an irregular rate, similar to other females before they deposit eggs, the snake was placed in a metabolic chamber at 31°C, where she was expected to lay eggs—but did not. The contractions continued for three months. The authors hypothesized that brooding behavior, specifically the muscular contractions, is under hormonal control, and that the "false brooding" was the result of a tumor in the area of the brain that controls this behavior.

Table 5–7. Data from Sclater (1862) on *Python sebae* Heat Production

Date	Temperature of air in den	Temperature of male		Temperature of Female		Difference
Feb. 12	58.6	On surface	70.2	On surface	73.0	2.8
		Between folds	74.8	Between Folds	81.6	6.8
Feb. 23	65.4	On Surface	71.8	On Surface	75.5	3.6
		Between Folds	74.0	Between Folds	83.2	9.2
March 2	60.0	On Surface	71.6	On Surface	84.0	12.4
		Between Folds	76.0	Between Folds	96.0	20.0
March 9	61.0	On Surface	72.8	On Surface	89.5	6.7
		Between Folds	*	Between Folds	86.5	
March 16	66.0	On Surface	72.4	On Surface	77.6	6.2
		Between Folds	77.6	Between Folds	86.0	8.4

* Not observed, the male being very restless.
Temperatures in degrees F.

The ability to brood eggs has enabled *Python molurus* to extend its range farther north and into higher altitudes, areas that would otherwise be too cool for embryonic development (Vinegar et al., 1970). Vinegar (1973) took two clutches of *P. molurus* eggs, divided them into three groups, and incubated them at three different temperatures, 23.0, 27.5, and 30.5°C. The eggs at 23°C failed, showing no growth; eggs at 30.5°C hatched within 61–68 days, and eggs at 27.5°C showed elongated developmental times, and after 70 and 65 days were moved to 30.5°C. One of these eggs hatched on day 93; the hatchling had a malformed pattern, showed poor motor control, could not feed, and soon died. Vinegar noted brooding females maintained eggs at 32–33°C; the 30.5°C temperature used in this experiment probably represents the lower limit for optimum embryonic development.

Verification of heat-producing Indian pythons came from Van Mierop and Barnard (1976a:398–401) who observed a brooding female *Python molurus*. They found the mean body temperature of the gravid snake was 3.1°C higher than the mean substrate temperature (24–30°C), while the mean body temperature of the same snake when it was not gravid was only 1.1°C higher than the mean substrate temperature (24.4–29.5°C).

On the afternoon of 13 June, contractions of the body were counted at a rate of 8 to 10 per minute whenever the snake lay in a coil. By 2300 h the female had laid three eggs. The next morning the female was in a brooding coil, her body contracted at the rate of 34–36 per minute, the eggs were completely hidden from view, and the female was ventilating her lungs at a rate of 7–8/min. During the next 7 weeks her body temperature was maintained at an almost constant temperature, between 33–33.5°C in the morning and 34–34.5°C in the evening. The mean difference between body temperature and substrate temperature during this period was 6.2°C (4.1–7.4°C). Van Mierop and Barnard's snake did not leave her eggs during incubation to drink, eat, excrete, or defecate. This lack of movement was determined by markers placed around the female snake.

They identified three phases of heat production. The first occurs before egg-laying and cannot be attributed to basking. The second phase starts after the eggs are laid and is maintained for about 7 weeks during incubation. The third phase is when the body temperature starts to decline, lasting for about 10 days.

Later, Van Mierop and Barnard (1978:615–621) reported that oxygen consumption of the gravid female python increased as the frequency and strength of the body contractions increased. At an ambient temperature of 23°C the temperature differential was 8.3°C and oxygen consumption had increased to a mean of 169 ml of oxygen per kg per hour, 20 times that of the nongravid animal at the same ambient temperature. When the temperature was increased, oxygen consumption decreased. And they found that during the last 9 days of incubation the eggs used oxygen at a rate comparable to neonate snakes maintained at about the same temperature.

There is little doubt that *Python molurus* actually uses shivering thermogenesis to generate body heat, but what about *Python sebae, Python reticulata, Morelia amethistina,* and five other species of smaller pythons that have been observed by various authors to perform similar behavior. Do they produce heat? Vinegar et al. (1970) suggested that this behavior is highly species specific. However, there is conflicting evidence that *sebae, reticulata, amethistina,* and at least five other species are actually capable of producing heat by muscular contractions. Shine (1988:289–291) summarized the reports and suggested that almost all pythons probably use shivering thermogenesis to brood eggs, and that small sample size, interpretation of environmental temperature versus egg temperatures, and the kind of evidence used (temperature measurement versus muscular twitching) have confused the issue. Furthermore, he suggested that brooding females are capable of producing heat because of their massive lateral musculature which is apparently capable of sustained rapid contractions. But Spawls and Branch (1995:20) are emphatic that *Python sebae* does not generate heat by shivering.

Reproduction of Indus Valley *Python molurus* is timed so that the eggs are laid at the hottest time of the year (June and July), and Minton and Minton (1973:211) point out that an egg-cooling system would be more advantageous than egg-heating mechanisms for this population. They hypothesize that this mechanism may have originated in a cooler region or a cooler time period than the one this snake inhabits today.

A somewhat typical hatching event is described by Acharjyo and Mishra (1976:562–3) for *Python molurus.*

> On 22 June 1974 the python exposed her eggs in the middle and coiled around the eggs. Eggs began to crack and some newly hatched python heads appeared through the openings. The mother moved her head in the direction of the keeper when approach. The first young hatched on 23 June 1974 and the last ones on 25 June 1974. The incubation period was 56–58 days. . . .
>
> Before final hatching at frequent intervals some young pythons poked their heads and anterior part of their bodies out of the egg for distances of up to 10–30 cm. They retreated into the shell at the slightest disturbance. Complete emergence of a hatchling took about 10 minutes. 38 young hatched from 53 eggs laid (71.1%). Examination on 26 June 1974 of the rest of the eggs revealed that 4 embryos had died at various stages of development; 5 eggs showed no signs of development and were assumed to be infertile and 6 full formed dead embryos, with unabsorbed yolk failed to emerge.

A female scrub python (Grow et al., 1988) at the Oklahoma City Zoo basked under a hot spot on a branch and in a tank of warm water before her eggs were laid. Like the previous female, this one also twitched her muscles and kept the eggs about 3–4°C warmer than the ambient temperature. But she would also bask, collecting environmental heat and bring it to her eggs, and the shivering muscles would start only after her body temperature had dropped. This snake fed during the latter stages of incubation, contrary to reports for other brooding pythons. Boos (1979:88) described a captive female scrub python coiling around her eggs so that none of them touched the moss substrate. She was observed twitching her muscles during incubation, but no temperature increase was noted. This female also occasionally left the eggs to feed. A scrub python reported on by Charles et al. (1985:46) laid eggs on 26 December, and the female coiled tightly around them. Twitching and shivering muscles were not observed, but they reported a constant temperature of 30°C within the coils while the cage temperature fluctuated between 28–30°C. They removed the eggs from the female and artificially incubated them at 29–31°C. Hatching occurred 105–108 days later on 10–13 April. Ross and Marzec (1990:149) reported hatching in March, April, October and November for *Morelia amethistina*. Hatchling snakes frequently do not emerge immediately from the egg, but may stay put for a few days (Mattison, 1995:156). Shine (1988:291) cited an uncorroborated observation that newly hatched *Python molurus* return to their abandoned egg shells at night, where the female will coil around them and warm them with her muscular contractions.

Haagner (1992–93:33) found a gestation period of 107–115 days for *Python sebae natalensis*, observing posterior swelling, refusal of food, and increased aggression. Eggs were laid in November and December, at night or early morning, and one female took 3 hours and 17 minutes to lay 55 eggs. The eggs adhered to each other, but were separated for artificial incubation. Haagner placed 3–4 eggs in separate containers on moistened vermiculite, and incubated them at 30–31°C. Hatching occurred at 79–83 days. Hatchlings did not completely emerge from the eggs until 24–36 hours after they had been pipped. Haagner suggested oxygen deprivation as a possible reason for the low hatching success rate reported by some authors, and hypothesized that eggs left in a clumped mass, or in a small container, may be impacted by lack of oxygen towards the end of embryonic development.

Broadley (1959:11) described finding a nesting female *Python sebae natalensis* at the time of hatching.

> On 24.xii.56 a 13-foot ♀ was discovered coiled round her eggs in a hole in a bank beside a small dam near Umtali. Three newly hatched young were basking outside the hole. A coil of the mother was visible from outside. As I pulled out the big python the leathery shelled eggs split open and I had to remove handfuls of young snakes at intervals in order to avoid crushing them. Only three unruptured eggs remained and these hatched the same evening, bringing the total number of hatchlings to 39. This clutch appeared to be 100 per cent fertile. The hatchlings measured between 600 mm and 663 mm. in total length.

Postpartum Behavior

No snakes are known to administer postnatal or posthatching care. However, the common anaconda and its relative, the rainbow boa (*Epicrates cenchria*), come closest to demonstrating parental care after birth. The following accounts suggest that female *Eunectes murinus* may behave in a way that enhances the chances for her offsprings' survival. The behavior is suggestive of complex behavior not normally attributed to snakes, but bear in mind that it occurred under captive conditions.

A 15-foot anaconda from Guyana gave birth on 8 and 9 January 1959 to four living young and 19 large aborted eggs. Neill and Allen (1962:73) described the birth process and after it had ceased the female snake began to eat the aborted eggs. They wrote,

The method whereby the snake ate the aborative eggs was quite unlike the normal feeding behavior. The snake would press its nose to the concrete substratum, slowly following a trail of foetal membranes and birth fluids. . . . When the nose touched an abortive egg, the snake's tongue would flicker out a few times in exploratory fashion. Then the reptile would slowly open its mouth, and gently try to engulf the entire egg. This being difficult on concrete . . . , the anaconda would slowly push the egg until it was secured against some backstop. Then with considerable delicacy the snake would take the egg into its mouth. . . . Next it would tilt the head upward, also elevating the head and neck. . . . In this position the snake would slowly masticate the egg, and swallow the fragments. . . . During swallowing, the snake's tail was coiled and uncoiled a number of times, but the body remained motionless. After ingestion of the egg, the reptile would lower the head to the substratum, lie motionless for 5 or 6 minutes, then search for another egg.

. . . following a trail toward an egg, the snake encountered a small puddle of birth fluids and foetal membranes. This it tried to consume, by small, biting movements.

Holmstrom and Behler (1981:353–354) described similar behavior in a 3.2 meter female anaconda at the New York Zoological Park (now the Wildlife Conservation Park). Their observations included the female picking up a neonate in her mouth without damaging it, and another female swallowing one neonate and slightly lacerating another while holding it in her mouth. Those fetal membranes consumed were in the water and on the gravel substrate of their cage, and it is possible that the offspring were swallowed accidently when attempting to remove fetal membranes, or the adult mistook the young for the fetal membranes.

The function of this behavior is as yet unclear, but there is no shortage of hypotheses available. Neill and Allen (1962) suggested that some useful molecules may be recycled in this way, or that odors that may attract predators can be eliminated by this behavior. Groves (1980) observed a female rainbow boa (*Epicrates cenchria*) swallow a stillborn embryo, and prod each membrane-covered young with her nose. He suggested this behavior stimulates the young to exit the fetal membranes to reduce risk of predation. Proposing another hypothesis, he suggested that removal of dead young and birth debris reduces the risk of bacterial infection, noting that 10 of 27 neonate *Epicrates cenchria* developed an umbilicus infection. Additionally, Holmstrom and Behler (1981:356) hypothesized that removal of birth debris may stimulate rapid dispersal, promoting the survival of the young.

Summary

Reproduction in giant snakes is relatively well known under captive conditions, especially relative to other facets of their natural history. Because of the interesting behaviors associated with reproduction in boid snakes, and due to the demand for them in the pet trade, considerable work has been done. But little is known about the reproductive biology among free-living giants. Information on *Python reticulata* reproduction is amazingly sketchy considering its size and popularity in the pet trade. Work currently being done with *Eunectes murinus* in Venezuela, including observations of reproductive "rollos," indicates that there is much to be learned about the dynamics of courtship, mating, and genetic contribution in *Eunectes* social systems. A great deal remains to be learned about all of the giants.

CHAPTER 6

ENCOUNTERS

> The Xingu was visited in 1842 by Prince Adalbert of Prussia, with Count Oriolla and Count Bismark, . . . but very few persons know that the great statesman ever made such a forest-journey. I am reminded here of a wonderful adventure, which the two counts had with a big sucuriju snake. Oriolla gallantly 'threw himself at full length upon the creature, as it was sliding away, and thrust his cutlass into its back a few feet from the tail. The count vainly tried to stop the monstrous reptile, which dragged him along, though the cutlass had pierced its body and entered the ground beneath.' However, Bismark blew the snake's head to pieces with his gun; a summary method, which he afterward developed most fully. I wish, for glory's sake, that the sucuriju had been forty feet long instead of sixteen; it is a pity to spoil so good a story.

Brown's (1876:593–594) description of the encounter between Prince Adalbert of Prussia and a common anaconda in the Mato Grosso of Brazil has an ending that appears all too frequently in the "adventure" or exploration literature. It is obvious from the tone of the account that a rendezvous with a large snake assures one of a good story; apparently killing the giant makes for an even better story as will be demonstrated repeatedly in this chapter.

Human-snake encounters are often told in prose which relates more than just a story about seeing or killing a giant snake. These stories often contain elements which embody the writer's attitude towards snakes and, in a more general sense, nature. In the accounts that follow, the snakes frequently lose their lives. And not because a human's life is in jeopardy, or because these animals are being hunted to feed human families. The hunter is the hero conquering a dangerous beast, but the beast may represent nature, and conquering the beast has become symbolic of human desire to control nature. Subjugation of nature and the environment is viewed as a means to make it safe for those who come after. The stories that follow are remarkably similar, even though they span three centuries, three continents, and involve four species of giant serpents. The stories need little in the way of interpretation and we have, therefore, added little in the way of narrative. Although the prose differs, the attitudes toward the snakes and nature remain constant. In Chapter 8, we will examine the origins of this attitude toward snakes and nature in Western cultures.

The Anaconda, *Eunectes murinus*

Captain J. G. Steadman (1796:171–173) was engaged in repressing a slave revolt when he encountered a 22-foot common anaconda, while traveling in the Guianas between 1772 and 1777 (Figure 6–1).

> . . . having loaded my gun with a ball-cartridge, we proceeded; David cutting a path with a bill-hook, and a marine following, with three more loaded firelocks to keep in readiness. We had not gone above twenty yards through mud and wa-

Figure 6–1. A 22-foot anaconda killed and skinned by Steadman (1796).

ter, the Negro looking every way with an uncommon degree of vivacity and attention; when starting behind me, he called out, 'Me see snake!' and in effect there lay the animal, rolled up under the fallen leaves and rubbish of the trees: and so well covered, that it was some time before I distinctly perceived the head of this monster, distant from me not above sixteen feet, moving its forked tongue, while its eyes, from their uncommon brightness, appeared to emit sparks of fire. I now, resting my piece upon a branch, for the purpose of taking a surer aim, fired; but missing the head, the ball went through the body, when the animal struck round, and with such astonishing force as to cut away all the underwood around him with the facility of a scythe mowing grass; and by flouncing his tail, caused the mud and dirt to fly over our heads to a considerable distance. Of this proceeding however we were not torpid spectators, but took to our heels, and crowded into the canoe. The Negro now intreated me to renew the charge, assuring me the snake would be quiet in a few minutes, and at any rate persisting in the assertion that he was neither able nor inclined to pursue us; which opinion he supported by walking before me, till I should be ready to fire. And thus I again undertook to make the trial, especially as he said that his first starting backwards had only proceeded from a desire to make room for me. I now found the snake a little removed from his former station, but very quiet, with his head as before, lying out among the fallen leaves, rotten bark, and old moss. I fired at it immediately, but with no better success than the other time: and now, being but slightly wounded, he sent up such a cloud of dust and dirt, as I never saw but in a whirlwind, and made us once more suddenly retreat to our canoe: where now, being heartily tired of the exploit, I gave orders to row towards the barge; but David still intreating me to permit *him* to kill the animal, I was, by his persuasion, induced to make a third and last attempt, in company with him. Thus, having once more discovered the snake, we discharged both our pieces at once, and with this good effect, that he was now by one of us shot through the head. David, who was made completely happy by his successful conclusion, ran leaping with joy, and lost no time in bringing the boat-rope, in order to drag him down to the canoe; but this again proved not a very easy under-taking, since the creature, notwithstanding its being mortally wounded, still continued to wreath [= writhe] and twist about, in such a manner as rendered it dangerous for any person to approach him. The Negro, however, having made a running noose on the rope, and after some fruitless attempts to make an approach, threw it over his head with much dexterity; and now, all taking hold of the rope, we dragged him to the beach, and tied him to the stern of the canoe, to take him in tow. Being still alive, he kept swimming like an eel; and I having no relish for such a shipmate on board, whose length (notwithstanding to my astonishment all the negros declared it to be but a young one come to about it half growth) I found upon measuring it to be twenty-two feet and some inches, and its thickness about that of my black boy Quaco, who might then be about twelve years old, and round whose waist I since measured the creature's skin.

An encounter with a "big" anaconda was described by Gilmore (1925:300, 322–325) while searching for lost companions in French Guiana. He wrote:

We had paddled perhaps a half mile and were nearing the spot where Turp's track ended. Before us, to the left, a recently fallen timber lay half under water, its leaves and vines still verdant and hanging like an arras across the creek. In the center of this green mat, fifteen feet distant, I noticed a yellowish mass. I asked Morse, who paddled bow, what he made of it.

"I think its a dead fish or gator belly up," he answered.

"Better have a shot with your revolver," I suggested.

For a few seconds there was no sign of life. Then slowly the formless thing began to writhe. We remained with paddles suspended, fascinated. It was a full half minute before we realized that we had run upon an enormous snake.

Now from the screening leaves a wicked head with darting tongue was thrust, and we lost no time in getting our frail craft to the bank. There, temporarily abandoning it, we hacked our way through the vines with cutlasses, taking post behind a great limb of the fallen tree. Whenever the head came into view, we fired. Quickly the pool formed by the submerged branches was churned into yellowish foam by monstrous gyrations. At this point we would have sworn the snake was a half-mile long! Its girth was astonishing, and in one spot there was a distension four feet long and as thick through as a man's chest. This swollen portion showed that the monster had lately made a meal, and the sickening thought came to us that at last we had found either Turp or the boy.

The movements of the anaconda (for such it proved to be), the great non-poisonous boa of South America, at first resembled the slow revolutions of a mill-wheel, the head rising many feet above the water with a circular thrust, followed in its movements by the entire yellow-and-brown-mottled body, which revolved and sank again into the murky waters. Now the churnings and lashings gradually became slower, and after a few minutes the snake disappeared into a hole just below waterline on the opposite bank, leaving some ten feet of the posterior end suspended over a limb of the tree.

We decided that it would be best to make the tail fast with a stout chain that we carried in the canoe. In this way we might secure our quarry against escape and open the belly. So we cut a long pole and, removing our wrap leggings, plaited them into a rope and fastened one end to the chain and the other to the pole. Morse crept along the trunk until he reached a spot directly over the tail. It was a hazardous exploit; for he had no assurance that the snake would not turn to attack. As he was in the act of lowering the noose chain, suddenly, without perceptible movement from the tail, the heart-shaped head reared out of the water in sinuous menace just beside him and between him and us. The entire body then swished over the log, still with a rotary motion. Morse hastily dropped the grappling paraphernalia and made his way back to the protecting limb.

For twenty minutes the anaconda continued its revolutions while we, our scant supply of ammunition exhausted, awaited the effect of the direct hits we had already given with steel-jacketed bullets. At last the snake, almost at the end of its strength, again plunged beneath the far bank, and this time Morse was successful in looping the chain about its tail, which had remained exposed. Swiftly the line was drawn taut and fastened securely to the limb with the end of the manufactured rope.

All three of us clambered out on the trunk of the tree, intent upon opening with cutlass the distended portion of the body, which just showed above the water. Exhibiting that tenacity of life common to the great reptiles, the creature, shot in several places, began its struggles a third time. After deliberating a few moments, we decided to abandon the job for the present but to return when we might proceed with less danger.

The serpent was till feebly wriggling as we paddled away down the Creek Anglais and the Maroni. When we reached camp, most of the search-parties had returned from their fruitless hunts, and we were confirmed in our fears. Faith had not stood the test of seeing that lump in the snake's body. . . . . [Shortly after this the two lost people showed up.]

When the first excitement had passed, we remembered our snake and went back to investigate. It was quite dead, and Caiman, the hunter, dived beneath the water and after great exertion succeeded in noosing a rope fast about the head. By this means we dragged the great carcass clear of the stream. Of eleven revolver shots, seven had been effective. One, very likely the first, may have pierced the insignificant brain. Otherwise, I am sure the anaconda would have taken to the bush and escaped. A second had fractured the spinal column two feet below the head. The distended portion proved to contain the body of a wild pig, weighing close to a hundred pounds.

The skin of our snake, which we removed with hunting-knives, was at least one-eighth of an inch thick and of a texture that nearly defied our specially sharpened blades. We left the carcass, with its great sheath of rippling muscles stretching from head to tail, in the creek, for the delectation of the myriad fish or the 'gators, upon which the anaconda frequently battles. Thus were the scaly ones avenged! . . .

Aggregations of giant snakes were discussed in Chapter 5, and Lange (1914:134–138) was referenced. But here is the full, depressing, account of what happened when these "adventurers" stumbled onto what appears to be a mating aggregation of anacondas:

As we come to a pond-like hole in this profound forest-swamp, we are halted by a fearful sight. The hole is full of snakes!

There we behold a writhing mass of long, blue-grey snakes of all sizes and lengths, some no more than six or seven feet, others over three times that length. At first they do not notice us. They are partly sleeping, some with their bodies under the surface of the lukewarm, shallow ooze, while others, mounting on the bodies of their brother snakes, or half creeping and resting on the margin of the pond, are happy, so to speak, in the family bosom. Some of them are as thick as a man's leg, while others are thin and slender as eels. The whole mass of this snake nest, however, is at rest. A few of the smaller ones are lazily creeping in and out through the labyrinth of snake bodies.

It would, indeed, have been a nice predicament to have walked into the middle of this congregation! Another hour's delay on the hill itself, and it would have been too dark to distinguish anything on the ground. Walking into this heap of snakes not only would have been hurtful to one's aesthetic feelings, but it might have ended fatally for some or all of us, for we quickly recognized these snakes as *sucurujús* or anacondas, the illreputed boa-constrictor of the Amazon region. All depends upon a man's presence of mind as to what may happen when a constrictor makes his one quick and dangerous loop around his body or neck. If he is frightened and loses his wits (which is quite excusable under such circumstances), he is gone, but if he stands the choking grip of the snake for some seconds, enough to take his knife and gash the body of his enemy, preferably trying to sever or injure the spinal chord, then he stands every chance of winning, for the snake will loosen his gradually tightening grip to defend himself or will attack with another part of his body. The bite of even a large boa is not poisonous, nor very painful. On several occasions, I have been bitten by such boas and found the bite hardly worse than that of a domestic cat. The bite is made by the snake merely to secure a hold for its body simultaneously with its great constricting and paralyzing twist. Some caboclos say that the bite of the boa is poisonous in May and June.

I really feel quite safe as we stand there not twenty feet from the numerous reptiles, but my four men at first feel nervous and one is ready to run, but his father, Rodriguez, tells him to remain. Fica com Doutor, "Remain with the Doctor," he says. Again we survey the situation and now notice that none of the sucurujus are paying any attention to us; merely playing their bifurcated tongues in our general direction. I feel safe because I know that under such conditions the snakes will not leave their lair to attack a man. I tell the bucks that we will have some fun shooting into the heap, as I am forever on the look-out for a large skin to take home to the States to show my disbelieving friends. The boys readily assent and they fill their .44 Winchester magazines. Rodriguez's youngest son has no rifle, but carries an ordinary "trade-gun" of the old muzzle-loader pattern, and he pours a goodly quantity of black powder into the barrel with a shaking hand, chews some leaves for a wad, and pours a measure of buck-shot on top, closing this with another layer of chewed leaves.

Skelly stands next to me with my old military Mauser loaded with a clip of five cartridges, while I cram my Luger-pistol magazine with nine bullets. Then we take a few steps back, resting our weapons against tree-trunks, almost as one man let go.

The reverberations scare us almost more than they do the snakes. A tremendous commotion follows the volley and the snakes seem to tangle themselves up worse than ever. We shoot again, now without aiming in particular; and some of the long, unhurt bodies stream out like black ropes over the margin of the pool and vanish among the trees and ferns into the gathering darkness.

Only Skelly and I kept on firing. Rodriguez's son has cried out with pain of some sort and brother and father are attending to him. I notice, with a peculiar calmness of mind, that in spite of our evident carnage in the bunch of snakes there is not, by any means, such an infernal hissing and writhing as I expected. The snakes do not seem to hear the shots and many of them lie waiting, or inert, looking at us with their small, protruding, beady eyes, which we can see as we walk around reloading our guns.

The barrel of the muzzle-loader of young Rodriguez has burst with an overcharge and has torn some skin and flesh of his left thumb and ring finger. I order Skelly to take out the medicine chest, which we always carry with us, and as he is well versed in these matters he soon has some iodoform sprinkled in the wound and a tight bandage around it.

In the meantime I have emptied another round into the snakes and diminished the number considerably. The swarm is still in constant movement, but as it is getting late, and the fun is gone, we resolve to make our way home before it grows to dark. Besides we are anxious to avoid stepping on some of the escaping boas which cannot have gone very far, and in the gloaming they might not be visible in time to avoid them.

With a last glance at the disgusting mass of half-mutilated, half unhurt *sucurujús* we depart in the direction of the noise from the *cachoeira* rapid. It takes some time to find the path and more than once we imagine that we have some fugitive snake right under our feet. At the canoe we find the fellow Xininga very wide-awake for he has heard our many shots. When we tell him what it was about he just nods his head and makes no other comment.

Another disgusting story was reported by Lopez (1984:114–115). In Venezuela, at a site in the state of Apure, the owner of a ranch was bitten while molesting an anaconda that was in a "cave" on the bank of a narrow river. Apparently the bite became infected, and a supposed expert determined that the anacondas were venomous. Forty-seven anacondas that were grouped together, apparently some estivating and others mating, were drenched with 200 liters of gasoline, set on fire, and burned alive.

A more refreshing encounter with an anaconda was reported by Dyott (1929: 144–145). Traveling in Brazil on the Rio Sepotuba, and despite warnings from locals, he plunged into a pool that was believed to be the retreat of an anaconda.

. . . the next moment I was on my way out with all possible haste. I had trodden on what seemed to be a slippery log, but before I knew it that log gave a violent upheaval, and with a ponderous movement that set the water swirling about me, it slid off into the center of the river. I am still wondering whether the anaconda or myself was the more frightened.

Theodore Roosevelt (1914:54) was accompanied by Colonel C. M. de Silva Rondon, a Brazilian army officer, during his 1913 trip through Brazil's interior. Rondon rose through the army's ranks to later become a general, and became well known for his natural history collections and notes on Brazil's tribal peoples. He also claimed to have measured a 38-foot anaconda killed by local people (Roosevelt, 1914:54). Here is Roosevelt's statement:

> During his trips Colonel Rondon had met with various experiences with wild creatures . . . Once while dynamiting a stream for fish for his starving party he partially stunned a giant anaconda, which he killed as it crept slowly off. He said that it was of a size that no other anaconda he had ever seen even approached, and that in his opinion such a brute if hungry would readily attack a full-grown man. Twice smaller anacondas had attacked his dogs; one was carried under water—for the anaconda is a water-loving serpent-but he rescued it.

Schomburgk (1931:80) made extensive collections of amphibians and reptiles in Guiana, and met an anaconda.

> Two of the lighter corials that had hurried ahead at the crossing of a Rapid had discovered a Commudi snake (*Boa draco gigas*) [= *Eunectes murinus gigas*]. It lay inert in a bush and had just cast its skin. As we approached Mr. Reiss shot at it, but the ball could not have wounded it mortally because it dragged itself slowly to the river. At this moment bold Hendrick sprang ashore, and with great skill threw a noose over its head, and was just in the act of hauling it when the snake turned round and made a movement as if to set on him; it was then that Hendrik's courage disappeared, for he jumped as hurriedly as possible over bush and rock into the water. All the Indians stood as if stunned, and could not be induced by anything to lay even a hand on the rope to drag the creature out of the bush, which made us almost lose the rope had not Mr. Cameron hit the animal in time with a ball at the back of the head, and had not Mr. Veith succeeded in throwing a second lasso over it, when we soon made it secure and brought it into the boat.

Charles Waterton [1909:218–221] encountered an anaconda while exploring South America.

> It must be observed, we were now about twenty yards from the snake's den. I now ranged the Negroes behind me, and told him who stood next to me to lay hold of the lance the moment I struck the snake, and that the other must attend my movements. It now only remained to take their cutlasses from them, for I was sure, if I did not disarm them, they would be tempted to strike the snake in time of danger, and thus for ever spoil his skin. On taking their cutlasses from them, if I might judge from their physiognomy, they seemed to consider it as a most intolerable act of tyranny in me. Probably nothing kept them from bolting, but the consolation that I was to be betwixt them and the snake. Indeed, my own heart, in spite of all I could do, beat quicker than usual; and I felt those sensations which one has on board a merchant-vessel in war time, when the captain orders all

hands on deck to prepare for action, while a strange vessel is coming down upon us under suspicious colours.

We went slowly in silence, without moving our arms or heads, in order to prevent all alarm as much as possible, lest the snake should glide off, or attack us in self-defence. I carried the lance perpendicular before me, with the point about a foot from the ground. The snake had not moved; and getting up to him, I struck him with the lance on the near side, just behind the neck, and pinned him to the ground. That moment, the Negro next to me seized the lance, and held it firm in its place, while I dashed head foremost into the den to grapple with the snake, and to get hold of his tail before he could do any mischief.

On pinning him to the ground with the lance, he gave a tremendous loud hiss, and the little dog ran away, howling as he went. We had a sharp fray in the den, the rotten sticks flying on all sides, and each party struggling for superiority. I called out to the second Negro to throw himself upon me, as I found I was not heavy enough. He did so, and the additional weight was of great service. I had now got firm hold of his tail; and after a violent struggle of two, he gave in, finding himself overpowered. This was the moment to secure him. So, while the first Negro continued to hold the lance firm to the ground, and the other was helping me, I contrived to unloose my braces, and with them tied up the snake's mouth.

The snake now finding himself in an unpleasant situation, tried to better himself, and set resolutely to work, but we overpowered him. We contrived to make him twist himself round the shaft of the lance, and then prepared to convey him out of the forest. I stood at his head and held it firm under my arm, one Negro supported the belly, and the other the tail. In this order we began to move slowly towards home, and reached it after resting ten times; for the snake was too heavy for us to support him without stopping to recruit our strength. As we proceeded onwards with him, he fought hard for freedom, but it was all in vain. The day was now too far spent to think of dissecting him. Had I killed him, a partial petrification would have taken place before morning. I had brought with me up into the forest a strong bag, large enough to contain any animal that I should want to dissect. I considered this the best mode of keeping live wild animals when I was pressed for daylight; for the bag yielding in every direction to their efforts, they would have nothing solid or fixed to work on, and thus would be prevented from making a hole through it. I say fixed, for after the mouth of the bag was closed, the bag itself was not fastened or tied to anything, but moved about wherever the animal inside it caused it to roll. After securing afresh the mouth of the coulacanara, so that he could not open it, he was forced into this bag, and left to his fate until morning.

. . . . At daybreak, I sent to borrow ten of the Negroes who were cutting wood at a distance; I could have done with half that number, but judged it most prudent to have a good force, in case he should try to escape from the house when we opened the bag. However, nothing serious occurred.

We untied the mouth of the bag, kept him down by main force, and then I cut his throat. He bled like an ox. By six o'clock the same evening, he was completely dissected. On examining his teeth, I observed that they were all bent like tenter-hooks, pointing down his throat, and not so large or strong as I expected to have found them; but they are exactly suited to what they are intended by nature to preform. The snake does not masticate his food, and thus the only service his teeth have to perform is to seize his prey, and hold it till he swallows it whole.

In general, the skins of snakes are sent to museums without the head: for when the Indians and Negroes kill a snake, they seldom fail to cut off the head, and then they run no risk from its teeth. When the skin is stuffed in the museum, a wooden head is substituted, armed with teeth which are large enough to suit a tiger's jaw: and this tends to mislead the spectator, and give him erroneous ideas.

The Indian Python, *Python molurus*

Riches (1930:828–829) described how the people of Nagpur, India catch pythons.

> On my return after an absence of two years I find that Sonia has grown more ambitious, although naturally such a conservative would not change his methods; he now flies at bigger game and pythons are included in his game register. I watched him catch one which measured 16 feet and which was exceptionally bulky. It was in scrub jungle travelling slowly when we located it; having sent a pal to its front end to attract its attention, Sonia literally dived into the scrub and quickly emerged dragging the snake backwards by its tail. It was then neatly persuaded to place its head in a wire noose, what time another was slipped along its body from the tail end.
>
> The usual method of catching pythons is to throw a long bamboo across them, and roll it along the body to the neck, when, provided the ends of the bamboo are held down, the snake is quite helpless and can be killed or tied up.

Fife-Cookson (1887:29) described finding an Indian python and the typical inoffensive behavior snakes usually take when encountered, even when mortally wounded (Figure 6–2). The unfortunate snake lost its life anyway because Fife-Cookson wanted its skin for a trophy. He wrote:

Figure 6–2. An encounter with a *Python molurus. From Fife-Cookson (1887:31).*

I was afraid of missing the head, which was rather a small mark to fire at, particularly as it was moving and I feared that to shoot the snake in the body would have no effect unless I could break the spine. I therefore fired at the neck, and succeeded in putting a solid bullet from my twenty bore into it. The serpent instantly stopped and coiled itself up, burying its head in the centre of its folds.

The Reticulated Python, *Python reticulata*

Searching for a large reticulated python, Raven (1946:40–41) trailed what he believed to be a huge snake, and related a second-hand story of an earlier encounter with this species.

One morning several days later a Javanese coolie, almost breathless, arrived in camp to say he had just seen the great python. I picked up my shotgun . . . and followed him down a little valley beside a stream that followed through the heavy

Figure 6–3. "My dogs were dispersed along the brink of a deep ravine, in which was an enormous boa constrictor (= *Python reticulata*). The monster raised his head to a height of five or six feet, directing it from one edge to the other of the ravine, and menacing his assailants with his forked tongue; but the dogs, more active than he was, easily avoided his attacks" (De La Gironiere, 1853:223–224). The author continued with a description of attempted capture of a boa constrictor (*Python reticulata*), with the snake escaping.

forest. He hurried along ahead of me for about half a mile, then stopped, and, as he looked at the narrow path, remarked in Malay that the python had gone. I could see the place where the snake had been on the path and told my companion we would follow its trail and kill it. He said that he had to go to work immediately or his boss would be very angry, and besides he was afraid of snakes.

I could not persuade him to stay, so as he went off I began cautiously to follow the trail. I had not gone more than a few yards before I realized that I was really on the trail of a giant. I was amazed at the apparent weight of the animal. Where it had moved sideways and pressed against little bushes they were bent flat, and where it had gone over a piece of dead wood, this was broken and pressed into the ground. Every moment I expected to see the fore part of the huge body rise up with gaping jaws, ready to strike at me, but nevertheless, I followed the trail for about 50 yards between rocks and over roots of trees, through twisted masses of lianas and rattans, where I occasionally had to use my machete.

Then the python had turned toward the stream, scraping the moss off the root of a tree as it had slid into the water. It had gone on downstream, sometimes sliding over rocks where I could easily see its marks, or over sand and gravel that looked as if a huge sack of grain had been dragged over them. Here, because the banks in some places were so high and steep, overgrown with ferns and begonias, and because in others the stream flowed under the bank and the projecting roots of great trees, I could no longer follow the trail and had to return to camp, down on my luck for having missed another giant python.

My friend, Mr. Lingard, of Borneo, a nephew of Conrad's Lord Jim, once told me of an experience he had with some Punan Dyaks and a python. The Dyaks . . . were paddlers on a trip up one of Borneo's beautiful rivers. . . . as they paddled along, a few feet from the bank, one of them in the middle of the canoe dropped his paddle, and with an exclamation leaned over the side and grabbed something. It was the tail of a python which had just been sliding off the bank into the water.

In the commotion that followed, the dugout was nearly overturned. The Dyaks kept their heads, however, although all of them, even the one pulling at the ser-

Figure 6–4. Alfred Russel Wallace (1869:228) had a reticulated python as a house guest on the island of Amboyna. He found a man to remove the snake, but not without a battle. Wallace considered the snake " . . . capable of doing much mischief and of swallowing a dog or a child."

pent's tail, were shouting like maniacs. Several had dropped their paddles and taken out their two-foot, machete-like knives, when out of the water darted the python's head. With a single blow one of them nearly severed it. They then got hold of the great body and made fast to it with rattans. All stopped paddling, and the canoe, tied to the huge, wriggling, bleeding python, drifted downstream. As the natives watched the dead body writhing in the water, they discovered that their victim had recently fed upon some large animal, for they could see the bulge in its sides. It was but a short distance to a bend in the river, where, owing to the low water, a large gravel shoal was exposed. There they encamped for the night and prepared the evening meal. Mr. Lingard said he was disgusted with those Dyaks, for they not only roasted and ate the python, which was about 20 feet in length, but also ate the two half-grown wild pigs they took from its stomach.

Ussher (1979:180–181) described a recent encounter with a 21.5 foot, 200 pound python in Brunei while visiting Brunei's rainforests.

We made our way carefully down a steep sided ridge until we reached the river and then turned south in order to follow it along to the camp. The water was very shallow and wading was not difficult. There were many pig tracks in the sand on either side of the river and so we both went slowly and carefully in case we should see one. After about 10 minutes of walking I rounded a bend in the river. The banks were very steep and ran down on to a grassy covered ledge right next to the water. It was on this ledge that an enormous python was lying, quite motionless, barely ten feet away from me. I stood quite still and indicated to Yusof what I had seen. Yusof stopped quickly, making a splashing noise in the water as he did so. The python obviously heard this and raised its head to see what was happening. We both stood very still while the python looked on, hardly daring to breathe; it then lowered its head back into its coils. We then crept very slowly to the opposite shore, climbed out onto the bank and up the steep side to a vantage point about 30 yards away. I thought the only way the museum was going to be able to record this magnificent specimen was for me to shoot it. It was certainly too large for two men to attempt to capture and the operation for even more men to have tried could have proved extremely dangerous. Time was short and it was too far away from camp to go and raise help before dark. I took careful aim at the python's head and fired. One bullet did the trick for it must have died instantly because there was hardly any movement from the snake after the bullet had struck. It simply uncoiled slowly and lay still. . . .

The retrieving party (8 men) returned to camp right on last light. Yusof had led the way back harnessed to the snake and pulling it most of the way. He was understandably very tired at the end!

The snake was seen to have a large bulge in its stomach which when dissected revealed a half digested barking deer, complete with antlers.

The snake was removed by the museum staff and flown out by helicopter to the Brueni museum at Bandar Seri Begawan, the next day.

Some of the meat was eaten by the expedition members but was found to be extremely tough and very tasteless.

The African Python, *Python sebae*

Africa has long attracted big game hunters and snakes have been hunted along with more traditional game (Figure 6–5). The following is a hunter's tale (Anon., 1856:97–100). Clearly, the snake was still alive when it was skinned.

Figure 6–5. An African python (*Python sebae*) meets its end. *From Hartwig (1878:628).*

Mr. Cumming, to whose exploits we have so frequently referred, gives the following account of a day's adventures, one of which was an amusing affair with a large python.

... As I was examining the spoor of the game by the fountain, I suddenly detected an enormous old rock-snake stealing in beside a mass of rock beside me. He was truly an enormous snake, and, having never before dealt with this species of game, I did not exactly know how to set about capturing him. Being very anxious to preserve his skin entire, and not wishing to have recourse to my rifle, I cut a stout and tough stick about eight feet long, and having lightened myself of my shooting belt, I commenced the attack. Seizing him by the tail, I tried to get him out of his place of refuge; but I hauled in vain; he only drew his large folds firmer together; I could not move him. At length I got a rheim round one of his folds about the middle of his body, and Kleinboy and I commenced hauling away in good earnest.

The snake, finding the ground too hot for him, relaxed his coils, and, suddenly bringing round his head to the front, he sprang out at us like an arrow, with his immense and hideous mouth opened to its largest dimensions, and before I could get out of the way he was clean out of his hole, and made a second spring, throwing himself forward about eight or ten feet, and snapping his horrid fangs within a foot of my legs. I sprang out of his way, and, getting hold of the green bough I had cut, returned to the charge. The snake was now gliding along at top speed; he knew the ground well, and was making for a mass of broken rocks, where he would have been beyond my reach, but before he could gain this place of refuge I caught him two or three tremendous whacks on the head. He, however, held on, and gained a pool of muddy water, which he was rapidly crossing, when I again belabored him, and at length reduced his pace to a stand. We then hanged him by the neck to a bough of a tree, and in about fifteen minutes he seemed dead, but he again became very troublesome during the operation of skinning, twisting his body in all manner of ways. This serpent measured fourteen feet.

A newspaper article in Malawi's *Daily Times* (Anon., 1981) titled *Man Stabs Python* chronicles the stabbing of a nine-foot-long python after a three hour grapple with Mr. J. M. Nkhata.

It was during the early hours of 1st March that Mr. Nkhata heard clucking and flapping noises coming from the direction of his chicken house.

Realizing that something was amiss, he hurriedly grabbed a spear and hurricane lamp and rushed to the source of the noise.

On taking a closer look, he discovered that one of the fowls had been swallowed by a python and the reptile was in the process of entangling another bird in its deadly coils.

Mr. Nkhata summoned enough courage and grabbed the trapped duck in an attempt to free it. At this juncture, the serpent started to inch its way towards the hand, so the fowl-owner tried to stab the snake.

After missing several times, Mr. Nkhata managed to inflict a deep wound in the animal's stomach, and while it was wriggling with pain he got hold of the three ducks and hurried them away.

But because they were frightened and also because of the darkness, he soon lost them and they returned to the "khola."

A determined Mr. Nkhata went back to the chicken house and this time was able to pierce the predator in several places rendering it unconscious.

In the morning, Mr. Nkhata returned to the khola only to find that the menacing reptile had crawled to the outside of the khola in its death throes.

According to one of the people who came in the morning hours to view the serpent, Mr. McLoud Mussa, the snake is said to have been hiding in a nearby anthill and its death had eased the people's minds since there will be no longer fear for their fowls as well as their dear lives.

Summary

Humans have been and continue to be major predators on snakes. This predation is not motivated by hunger, but, rather, by ignorance and fear, some of it perpetuated by religious teachings. The preceding accounts often inferred that the person who killed the snake was performing an heroic deed and was worthy of admiration. Not true, of course, but even as people are, in general, more environmentally sensitive than they were 10 and 20 years ago, killing a snake still does not carry with it the same stigma as, for example, killing a bald eagle or a baby seal. In reality, for many people the only requisite criterion for a snake of any species to meet in order to be killed is that it be alive.

CHAPTER 7

ATTACKS ON HUMANS

A magazine published for missionaries included these instructions for those among their numbers working in Africa; it gives an entirely new meaning to "missionary position" (from Rose, 1962:326–327):

> Remember not to run away, the python can move faster. The thing to do is to lie flat on the ground on your back with your feet together, arms to the sides and head well down. The python will then try to push its head under you, experimenting at every possible point. Keep calm, one wiggle and he will get under you, wrap his coils round you and crush you to death. After a time the python will get tired of this and will probably decide to swallow you without the usual preliminaries. He will very likely begin with one of your feet. Keep calm. You must let him swallow your foot. It is quite painless and will take a long time. If you lose your head and struggle he will quickly whip his coils around you. If you keep calm, he will go on swallowing. Wait patiently until he has swallowed about up to your knee. Then carefully take out your knife and insert it into the distended side of his mouth and with a quick rip and slit him up.

Humans rarely die from giant snake-related accidents. Nevertheless, giant snakes, venomous snakes, and, indeed, all snakes, are persecuted because most people can't tell one snake from another and, therefore, all are potentially life-threatening. This is a curious paradox, considering that annually many thousands of humans are killed by firearms or automobiles, and yet society has allowed these technologies to flourish while persecuting the mostly benign snakes. People who fear being killed by a giant snake are worrying for naught; human deaths from constricting snakes are rare indeed.

We suggest that, in Western culture, snakes are symbols for the dangerous and lethal aspects of nature to many people who, for the most part, should know better. Consider, for example, the following passage from Clark (1953:6–7) who, in discussing a remote area of Peru, relates a story about anacondas attacking humans. It is greatly exaggerated, and the quote speaks to this exaggeration in almost comic book fashion, but it also portrays a view of nature widely held in modern society. Remember that this is from a nonfiction book about the personal adventures of the author.

> Usually our men just disappear. We never hear from them again. Others often go insane. If they get out alive they are incompetent for any sort of work. We have just received a report from the mouth of the Morona River north of the Marañon. Juan Vargas is our mapper there. He has been found in the belly of a snake, the *yacu maman*, in his own screened launch. Our government launches have a heavy wire mesh carefully covering sides and roof so that the poison darts of the Indians will be caught in them. Vargas was sleeping on the boat. The crew were camped on a safe *playa* [river beach]. The anaconda, apparently hunting food, came out of the river and entered the boat through a hole torn that day in one corner. After killing and swallowing Vargas, it could not return through the hole, and was found in the engine room next morning.

"Is it possible to swallow a man whole?" I asked. "How about a man's shoulders passing the jaws? Most experts have doubted Indian claims that certain varieties of those snakes can swallow a deer weighing a hundred pounds."

Rosell laughed indulgently, though quietly, as befitting his position. "These snakes are capable of swallowing not only a 150-pound man, but a 500-pound animal such as a tapir. You see, they crush the larger bones, lather the head and unjoint their jaws. After swallowing its food, the snake's digestive juices are so strong that even large bones are dissolved. When hungry the snake will take any kind of living food-marine, crocodiles, land mammals and even himself."

Snakes may attack humans for three reasons. The first is simply to protect themselves because humans are major predators of snakes. Snakes, giants included, are often cryptic in their coloration and behavior, and humans can be close to a snake and be totally unaware of its presence. This can lead to the snake sensing a threat (e.g., being stepped upon) and being injured before the human even knows it is there. The second reason is for food. A hungry snake may perceive a human as a meal, but people are by no means typical prey for giant snakes. A snake's interest in eating a human may be triggered by the lingering odor of the snake's normal prey on a human, or by extreme hunger. The third reason is mistaking a human for more typical prey. Thus, a person with the scent of another animal on his or her skin is at much greater risk of being attacked. This can be a serious problem with people who keep large snakes and are unaware of the stimuli that trigger feeding behavior, or for a person walking with animals such as dogs or goats.

Humans have extremely plastic behavior, particularly when it comes to food. Snakes, on the other hand, are much more rigid in their feeding behavior and choices of food. The following accounts describe attacks motivated by self-defense and predation, as well as some that were errors in judgment on the part of the snake. It is not always possible to distinguish between them, and there may be other ways to interpret the events. Of course, some of these accounts are undoubtedly embellished, and a few are total fabrications.

Writing about the common anaconda, Quelch (1898:303) concluded that

> The fear of being seized by these reptiles, which deters so many timid people from bathing in the creeks and rivers, is no doubt natural enough, even if such seizures may only happen by mistake; but the chances of danger are so infinitesimal, that they are hardly worth regarding.

Savage's (1842:246) view on giant snake attacks in southern Africa is similar; he considers attacks upon man rare, and never occur except when the snake is in a state of extreme hunger. From West Africa, Starin and Burghardt (1992:60) commented " . . . it is remarkable how little danger there is from these large reptiles." And Sweeney (1961:44) discussed attacks on humans by African pythons:

> Under unusual circumstances a large specimen would be quite capable of killing a grown man, although as far as I am aware there is no case of an adult having been killed by this species. Many people, however, have been "attacked"; in such cases the human was always the aggressor, although perhaps quite unintentionally. Even to approach a python unknowingly may constitute "aggression" as far as the python is concerned. Nevertheless there are authentic cases of children being killed; whether by accident or design is a moot point, I imagine, quite a temptation to the animal which often attacks its prey from concealment.

Also a premeditated attack on a dog would be nothing unusual, such an attack might involve an attack on the owner of the dog.

As suggested by Auerbach (1987:153) in Botswana, one reason for so few attacks may be the damage humans have done to giant snake populations. While all of these comments are based on the anaconda and African python, similar situations exist in Southeast Asia (see Kopstein's comment below). Attacks on humans by giant snakes are so infrequent that when they do occur they make headlines worldwide. Unfortunately, many stories are second- or third-hand accounts and lack the details needed to classify the snake's motivation for making the attack. Bates's (1863:236) report of an incident with an anaconda in Brazil is a good example.

> At Ega a large Anaconda was once near making a meal of a young lad about ten years of age, belonging to one of my neighbors. The father and his son went one day in their montaria a few miles up the Teffé to gather wild fruit; landing on a sloping sandy shore, where the boy was left to mind the canoe whilst the man entered the forest. The beaches of the Teffé form groves of wild guava and myrtle trees, and during most months of the year are partly overflown by the river. Whilst the boy was playing in the water under the shade of these trees, a huge reptile of this species stealthily wound its coils around him, unperceived until it was too late to escape. His cries brought the father quickly to the rescue, who rushed forward, and seizing the anaconda boldly by the head, tore his jaw asunder.

From this description the child could have been playing and frightened the snake and it attacked because of the perceived threat, or, it could have been lying in ambush and the child presented a reasonable sized food item. There is simply no means of determining why the child was attacked.

Defensive Attacks

An incident that occurred in Nariva Swamp along Trinidad's east coast was reported by Kingsley (1890:277–278). The secondhand report of an attack on a woman by a huilla (= anaconda) seems to be defensive. The statement that the snake "held on stupidly" suggests the snake may have snagged several of its recurved teeth on the dress and could not release them easily.

> Four young ladies, whose names were mentioned to me, preferred, not wisely, a bathe in the still lagoon to one in the surf outside; and as they disported themselves, one of them felt herself seized from behind. Facing that one of her sisters was playing tricks, she called out to her to let her alone; and looking up, saw, to her astonishment, her three sisters sitting on the bank, and herself alone. She looked back, and shrieked for help; and only just in time; for the Huilla had her. The other three girls, tò their honour, dashed in to her assistance. The brute had luckily got hold, not of her poor little body, but of her bathing-dress, and held on stupidly. The girls pulled; the bathing dress, which was, luckily of thin cotton was torn off; the Huilla slid back again with it in his mouth into the dark labyrinth of the mangrove-roots; and the girl was saved.

Keays (1930:721–722) told the following story about a python attacking a fisherman. It seems probable that the snake was threatened by the man's foot and attacked in self-defense. The reported injuries sound severe considering the snake was only 9 feet long.

> . . . after adjusting his net, noticed something just under the surface of the water which in the dim light of the cave appeared to be a large fish that would not respond to the persuasion of his stick, he therefore thrust in his leg to investigate and was at once seized by the occupant of the hole who turned out to be a nine-foot python. The snake firstly threw one coil round the man's thigh and subsequently in the struggle succeeded in getting two more round his body raising its head and neck to the height of the man's shoulder. The terror stricken . . . cooly seized the neck of the snake and managed to hold it at arms length; then a violent struggle ensued for the next two minutes or so between man and snake. The cooly's shouts were luckily heard by another estate man who ran to his assistance. The rescuer was fortunately at the time carrying a sharp sickle the blade of which he managed to insert between one of the python's coils and the cooly's body and succeeded in cutting the snake in two. This took time however, and when freed from the severe constriction the cooly was found to be unconscious, but had not sustained any serious injury. He remained however paralysed for about three months and then made a gradual and steady recovery to complete health.

The following incident is clearly a case of a snake attempting to defend itself. Mayer (1920:854) related the story, which takes place in Malaya. The species involved is uncertain, but likely to be a reticulated python. The accompanying illustration shows a snake constricting a man while the snake is being caught. The story's validity is suspect because of the large number of people who watched the incident happen but were unable or unwilling to assist in releasing the man from the snake (Figure 7–1).

> The python was sleeping peacefully, digesting the pig. I called to the men and put them to work at staking the crate to the ground and securing it so that the snake could not lash it around. The crate was about eight feet long, six feet wide and two and one-half feet deep; just large enough to hold him and just small enough so that, once inside, he would not be able to get leverage and break it. Again I explained what each man was to do. Then I passed a rope through the crate, tying one end to a tree and preparing a running noose to be slipped around the snake's head when we were ready to draw him forward. Two more ropes were laid out, running from his tail. These we wrapped around the trees on each side of the tail, and I stationed men at the ends, showing them how they were to pay out the rope as the snake was drawn toward the crate, keeping it taut enough to prevent him from lashing.
>
> The python slept soundly through all these preparations. When we were ready, I gathered the men about me and cautioned them against becoming excited. I warned all those who had not been given work to do to stand back out of the way and not to approach unless we needed them.
>
> With bamboo poles we prodded the snake at the head and tail, standing by with the nooses, ready to slip them on when he stirred sufficiently. Before he realized what was happening, we had the head-noose over him. The instant he felt the rope tighten, he was awake!
>
> The natives holding the tail-ropes became excited and succeeded in getting only one of them in place. The python suddenly leaped forward, and, though he did not loosen the rope, whipped it out of the hands of the men and knocked several of them flat; then he caught one man, who had not been able to get out of the way, and wrapped the lower part of his body around him while five or six feet of

Figure 7–1. "The native screamed and the snake constricted suddenly, breaking nearly every bone in the man's body and crushing the life out of him." This illustration and caption accompanied Mayer's (1920) story about a man accidently killed while trying to capture a reticulated python that reportedly measured 32 feet.

his tail still lashed about with the rope. I yelled to the others to pull on the tail-rope, but the confusion was so great that they did not hear me. I went for the snake's neck, which is the most tender part of him, hoping to sink my fingers in on the nerve center and disable him for a moment until the men collected their senses and pulled the rope. By jumping forward, the snake had loosened the head-rope sufficiently to turn on me and sink his fangs into my forearm. I sprang back.

The man who was caught in the snake's coils screamed, and tried to beat off the tail as it was drawing in about him. Then the snake constricted suddenly, breaking nearly every bone in the man's body and crushing the life out of him instantly. Blood spouted from his mouth and ears, and he was thrown limply about as the snake lashed in the air.

I yelled to the men to pull the head-rope taut. Fortunately, the tail-rope had not become loose, and we caught it just as the snake tried to lurch forward again. We allowed him to move forward slowly, drawing his head toward the crate and, at the same time, holding his tail until we had him stretched out. By prodding his tail with sticks, we forced him to uncoil and to release the body of the native.

The head-noose had been slipped farther down than I wanted, and was giving his head too much play. Assuring the men that he could do no more harm, I took three of them with me and we grabbed the snake's neck. He tossed us about, and we had several minutes of exciting work before we got the head into the open end of the crate. When the rope was secured, we fastened another rope about the middle of him.

The snake lashed furiously, knocking several of the natives down. Stationing a crew of men at the tail-rope to slacken it as we moved forward, I took the others to the crate and set them at pulling on the middle rope. As we dragged the python forward, he coiled in the crate; then, when he was half in, we secured the middle rope and head-rope to trees, passed the tail-rope through the crate and dragged the tail in. There was great rejoicing when we closed the end of the crate and prepared to haul it back to Palembang. We had captured a prize specimen. Cross of Liverpool, to whom I sold him, told me that he measured thirty-two feet. I have never seen his equal in length and girth. But, huge as he was, he coiled up comfortably in his small quarters, promptly fell asleep and went on digesting his pig.

St. John (1863:259–260) mentions an incident involving *Python reticulata* that took place in July of 1861 on an expedition to Sarawak's Muka River. A mentally ill Malay suddenly sprang up in the boat, drew his sword, and killed two men and wounded several others, and then fled into the jungle. Ten days later he was found wandering on a beach, apparently unaware of his crime. St John told the following story which can be best described as self-defense by the snake.

> . . . one night, that threatened heavy rain, he crawled into a hollow tree to sleep. He was suddenly awakened by a choking sensation in his throat, and instinctively put up both his hands, and tore away what had seized him; it was a huge boa, which in the confined space could not coil around him. The Malay quickly got out of the serpent's lair, and fled, leaving his sword behind him. When found, there were the marks of the fangs on the sides of the torn wound, which was festering. The last news I heard of the man was that he was expected to die.

Minor incidents with pythons can be blown out of proportion by the press. The following newspaper account is difficult to categorize, but an 11-foot snake should not pose a threat to any healthy adult human who is capable of walking away from it! It certainly should not take 30 minutes to get out of the snake's way. The story comes from an AP wire story (Anon. 1992).

FARM WORKER BATTLES PYTHON AND WINS

Martizburg, South Africa (AP) - A farm worker battled an 11-foot python for a half-hour after it dropped on him from a tree, but the man finally squeezed, bit and beat the reptile to death, his employer said.

Edward Mkhize had gone to fetch cattle Wednesday when the snake fell from above and wrapped itself around him, Mkhize's employer, Suresh Maharaj, told local newspapers.

Man and snake fell to the ground in a tangle. Mkhize sank his teeth into the writhing serpent's throat, then twisted the thick body. The snake's strength finally gave out, and Mkhize smashed its head with a rock.

Maharaj said pythons had killed several calves and at least three people in the area recently.

Attitudes toward giant snakes were discussed by Branch (1984:237), and he quoted an article in the *Pretoria News*. Compare the newspaper article quoted here to the one above. The snake involved in this story is small, 2.2 meters and, as Branch points out, this snake may have been able to swallow a large rabbit. The similarities to the story above are incredible.

MAN'S STRUGGLE WITH PYTHON . . . A Durban gardener fought a life-and-death struggle with a huge python when it dropped on to him from a tree and tried to squeeze him to death . . . The man . . . was almost strangled as he desperately tried to remove the 2.2 m snake which had coiled around his neck and waist.

Snakes Make Mistakes

Wildlife photographers Joan and Alan Root (1971:370) described an attack on Joan by a *Python sebae*. Joan was standing waist deep in a pool when a python's head erupted from the water and struck her hand. The snake quickly retreated, but its teeth opened a nasty gash in her hand. The Roots' interpretation of the attack suggested the incident was a case of mistaken identity that was quickly corrected. Thus, snakes do make mistakes and at least some attacks appear to fall into this category.

In British Guiana (now Guyana), Quelch (1898:302) described an attack on a boy washing rice, and he suggested that this was due to the snake mistaking the boy for an animal drinking from the stream.

In this case a boy washing rice in a calabash by the waterside of one of the large creeks was seized by the hand by a medium-sized snake, and it would perhaps have terminated fatally but that the boy's father, who was chopping wood close by with a cutlass, at once despatched the reptile. From the circumstances of the case it is very likely that the attack was accidental. In the characteristically dark-coloured water of the creek it is hardly possible that the boy could have been seen by the snake. The probability is that the sound made by the calabash in the water was mistaken for that of some animal drinking, and the attack made accordingly. This seems more likely still from the fact that there was not the immediate coiling around the boy so characteristic of the attack of these creatures, and it is probable that if the boy had been able to keep still and allow of the withdrawal of the long curved teeth, the snake would have sunk again from sight.

William W. Lamar, a respected herpetologist who has spent years searching for snakes in South America, shared the following close encounter with us (pers. commun. to RWH, August 1995). While in Colombia in 1978, he and two companions were wading three-abreast in knee-deep water in a gallery forest stream in the afternoon; Bill was in the middle. "All of a sudden, an anaconda exploded out of the water," hit the man to Lamar's left and ripped his shirt off. Bill, almost reflexively, turned and shot the snake. They had to get out of the water because of the violent thrashing of the huge snake, which proved to be a 24-feet, 7-inch female that Lamar estimated to weigh between three and four hundred pounds. Lamar carefully examined the situation in which the attack occurred and concluded that it "was a case of mistaken identity." The anaconda had been lying in wait (ambush) along an obvious game trail and was, possibly, waiting for collared peccary (*Tayassu tajacu*) which were common in those situations. Lamar never considered that he or his companions were considered prey for the anaconda. Because of his experience and objectivity, we put considerable store in his interpretation of this event.

Attempts by Giant Snakes to Eat Humans

The earliest account we have been able to find which documents a human having been eaten by a snake is Bosman (1705:310). He described finding a human in an African python:

> About the same time another [*Python sebae*] was killed at Boutry, not much shorter than the former; in whole body a Negro was found.

M'Leod (1818:296–297), described an attack on a man which is, at best, a secondhand account.

> It may be mentioned, that, during a captivity of some months at Whidah, in the kingdom of Dahomey, on the coast of Africa, the author of this narrative had more opportunities of observing snakes. . . . Governor Abson, who had for thirty-seven years resided at Fort William (one of the African Company's settlements there,) described some desperate struggles which he had either seen, or had come to his knowledge, between the snakes and wild beasts, as well as the smaller cattle, in which the former were always victorious. A Negri herdsman belonging to Mr. Abson (who afterwards limped for many years about the fort) had been seized by one of these monsters by the thigh; but from his situation in a wood, the serpent, in attempting to throw himself around him, got entangled with a tree; and the man, being thus preserved from a state of compression which would have instantly rendered him quite powerless, had presence of mind enough to cut with a large knife, which he carried about with him, deep gashes in the neck and throat of his antagonist, thereby killing him, and disengaging himself from his alarming situation. He never afterwards, however, recovered the use of that limb, which had sustained considerable injury from his fangs, and the mere force of his jaws.

In the early part of the 19th Century, a sportsman fishing in what was then British Guiana (now Guyana) drew his canoe to the river's edge for a rest. He dangled a line in the water, had a loaded gun lying at his side, and was stretched out in the boat with one naked foot dangling over the side. The warm, humid air and lack of success at catching fish made the man drowsy and he fell asleep. He (Anon., in Gosse, 1850:170–174) described what happened when he awoke:

> I know not how long I may have slept, but I was roused from my slumber by a curious sensation, as if some animal were licking my foot. In that state of half stupor felt after immediately waking from sleep, I cast my eyes downward, and never till my dying day shall I forget the thrill of horror that passed through my frame on perceiving the neck and head of a monstrous serpent covering my foot with saliva, preparatory, as immediately flashed upon my mind, to commencing the process of swallowing it. I had faced death in many shapes—on the ocean—on the battle-field—but never till that moment had I conceived he could approach me in a guise so terrible. For a moment, and but for a moment, I was fascinated. But recollection of my state soon came to my aid, and I quickly withdrew my foot from the monster, which was all the while glaring upon me with its basilisk eyes, and at the same instant I instinctively grasped my gun, which was lying loaded beside me. The reptile, apparently disturbed by my motion, (I conceive it had previously, from my inertness, taken me for a dead carcass,) drew its head below the level of the canoe. I had just sufficient time to raise myself half up, pointing the muzzle of my piece in the direction of the serpent, when its neck and head again appeared moving backwards and forwards, as if in search of the object it had lost. The muzzle of my gun was within a yard or two of it; my finger was on the trigger; I fired, and it received the shot in its head. Rearing up part of the body into the air with a horrible hiss, which made my blood run cold-and, by its contortions, displaying to my sight great part of its enormous bulk, which had hitherto escaped my notice-it seemed ready to throw itself upon me, and to embrace me in its monstrous coils. Dropping my gun, by a single stroke of the paddles I made the canoe shoot up the stream out of its reach.

The story continued with a dramatic hunt, the snake was tracked down, killed, and said to have been measured and found to be 40 feet long. At face value the skeptic may brush the story off as a sportsman's tall tale but, at risk of reading too much into the story, part of it may be valid. In a previous chapter we established that giant snakes do not coat their prey with saliva before swallowing; instead, the saliva is laid down as the prey is swallowed. Nor do they always bite and constrict their prey before ingestion, particularly when the food is dead. It is entirely possible that the large anaconda had started to swallow the sportsman's foot and then backed-off, mistaking the sleeping man for carrion; and the sportsman mistook the release of his saliva-covered foot for the saliva-coating behavior commonly believed at the time to be part of snake feeding behavior. We suggest this because of an incident reported by herpetologist Clifford Pope (1961:45) who had a pet female Indian python that swallowed his son's toe. He wrote: " . . . the skin was barely penetrated, so delicately did she work."

Schomburgk (1922:370) provided a secondhand account of an anaconda attacking a human.

> Everybody here was still upset at the attack of an immense snake on two of the Mission inmates. An Indian had left here a few days before to go up the river with

his wife after wild fowl. A frightened duck had been shot and fallen onto the bank. As the hunter hastened after his bird he was suddenly seized by a huge Co-muti snake (*Boa murina*) [= *Eunectes murinus*]. In want of any weapon of defence, he having left his gun in the corial, he called to his wife to bring him his large knife. Hardly had the woman reached his side than she also was seized and encircled by the monster, a movement that fortunately afforded the Indian just sufficient space to free one arm, and inflict several wounds on the beast which, weakened by these, finally let go its hold and sought escape. This was the one and only instance which came to my knowledge of a *Boa murina* attacking man.

Secondhand accounts of anaconda attacks were told by Blomberg (1956:93), one of which ended with ingestion.

> We also hear gross exaggerations about how dangerous the anaconda is. Despite intensive research, I have only been able to find two definite cases of anacondas causing the death of human beings.
>
> One man was killed on the Napo River in Ecuador, when he went for a swim and was entwined by one of these snakes. He struggled in vain to get away but was drawn under water and carried off. He was later found farther downstream, dead and bearing distinct marks of the ghost-squeeze. Evidently the reptile had been unable to devour so large a victim.
>
> The other incident occurred at the mouth of the Yasuni River, a tributary of the Napo. Some children were bathing, and a boy of 13 suddenly disappeared. His friends were sure they saw bubbles rising from a spot near the shore, and one of the boys dived down to search. He came up pale with fright. He had felt around for his friend in the water and had touched something he was sure was an enormous snake—an anaconda! He had often been told that a gigantic anaconda haunted the river hereabouts. It was even said to have swallowed two persons. No doubt the same fate had now taken his friend. The dead boy's father was determined to take vengeance on the murderer and after a day and night of unwearied search, he discovered the reptile. It was lying with half its body on the shore, the other half in the water. It had vomited up the devoured boy. With five shots of his Winchester, the boy's father killed the snake. It was an enormous anaconda.

The most objective account of an anaconda attack comes first-hand from María del C. Muñoz (in litt. to RWH), an experienced Venezuelan field biologist who was involved at the time in a detailed ecological study of anacondas in the Venezuelan llanos. María and two male colleagues were tracking anacondas which had radio transmitters surgically implanted in their bodies. It was May 26, 1992 at 6:55 pm, and they were working in a caño (small river); the rainy season had started. She was in the water and had walked only about 20 meters when she picked-up the radio signal from the snake in an area of flooded savanna. She worked at localizing the radio signal and realized that the snake, a female the researchers had named Lina, was very close to her, but she was unable to see it. Three or four minutes later she still had not visually located the animal, a snake that was 5.02 meters in total length and weighed 50 kg (about 110 lbs.), in a canal that had water to a depth of only 25 cm. All of a sudden, she felt something "immense" move near her feet, and the snake ripped her pants at the level of the knee, but did not actually grab her flesh. It was Lina! Almost instantly, the big anaconda turned to attack again, raising her heavy body above the level of María's hip (about 1 meter); her immense mouth, full of sharp, recurved teeth, was gaped at about 180°. María is petite (1.56 meters in height and weighs 50 kg) and she did not want to get bitten by Lina. Never had she moved so quickly. After the two unsuccessful strikes, the snake did not pursue María. Only a month earlier, Lina had permitted María to approach within 1 meter of her head in order to examine a wound, but this time, in María's opinion, Lina was hungry and waiting in ambush for prey, and María was in the wrong place at the wrong time. Because of her small size, she was perceived as potential prey and, if Lina had been successful, María would have been a meal that would have equaled 100% of the snake's body weight. Although the attack was upsetting to María, she continued her studies of the common anaconda, and now knows more about them than just about anyone in the world.

Wall (1921:60) discussed humans as snake food and attributed the following incident to *Python molurus,* but it should be noted that *Python reticulata* also occurs in the area.

> One sometimes hears of humans being swallowed by pythons but though I have collected several instances of other large snakes overcoming men, I have no authentic instances of this snake doing so, but it is amply capable of overpowering the strongest man. A young European told me once in Hong Kong that he had witnessed, as a boy, with his brothers a large snake (almost certainly a *molurus*) swallow a Chinese baby on Stone Cutter's Island in the harbour. The mother left the child while engaged in some work, and the boys were afraid to encounter so formidable a snake. Major Sealy of the 4th Gurkhas tells me that a reliable old Gurkha Officer told him that once when officiating at a funeral pyre, a python emerged from the water near by, seized the corpse, and made off with it.

The Bombay *Courier* of August 31, 1799 carried the following story. Both *Python reticulata* and *Python molurus* occur in the Celebes (Sulawesi) and it is therefore difficult to assign this story to either species, although the size and probable abundance suggests *Python reticulata* is probably the species involved (Anon. 1799, in Gosse, 1850:182).

> A Malay prow was making for the port of Amboyna; but the pilot, finding she could not enter it before dark, brought her to anchor for the night, close under the island of Celebes. One of the crew went on shore in quest of betel-nuts in the woods, and on his return lay down, as it is supposed, to sleep on the beach. In the course of the night he was heard by his comrades to scream out for assistance. They immediately went on shore; but it was too late, for an immense snake of this species had crushed him to death. The attention of the monster being entirely occupied by his prey, the people went boldly up to it, cut off its head, and took both it and the body of the man on board their boat. The snake had seized the poor fellow by the right wrist, where the marks of the fangs were very distinct; and the mangled corpse bore evident signs of being crushed by the monster's twisting itself round the neck, head, breast, and thigh. The length of the snake was about thirty feet; its thickness equal to that of a moderate-sized man; and on extending its jaws, they were found wide enough to admit at once a body of the size of a man's "head."

The *Straits Times* (probably in November, 1880), a Malaysian newspaper reported a story from a sportsman hunting in the Campong Batta District (in Gould, 1884:177). The hunter happened upon a hut with an enormous python skin draped over its roof. A story accompanied the skin. One night the owner of the hut had awakened to the distress calls of his wife, believing thieves were invading his home he seized his parang (large knife) only to discover a large snake and

> . . . the whole of his wife's arm had been drawn down the monster's throat, whither the upper part of her body was slowly but surely following. Not daring to attack the monster at once for fear of causing his wife's death, the husband, with great presence of mind, seized two bags within reach, and commenced stuffing them into the corner of the snake's jaw, by means of which he succeeded in forcing them wider open and releasing his wife's arm.

The Malay managed to fatally injure the snake, but according to the story it left the hut only to die of its wounds in the man's plantain trees. The snake was in such agony that it thrashed about, damaging the trees. The man assured the informant that he had sold the meat to Chinese people for sixty dollars. If a true story, the snake involved was probably *Python reticulata*.

Rose (1955:80) quoted a story from a Calcutta newspaper about a man attacked and ingested by a python in Burma; the snake could have been either *molurus* or *reticulata*. The story is somewhat suspect because the man is said to have been swallowed feet first, an improbable behavior for a snake.

> Maung Chit Chine, a Burmese salesman for a firm of European jewellers, was shooting in Thaton district when he was attacked and swallowed by a large python. Another member of the party found Maung's hat near the python which was asleep. He killed the python, opened it and found Maung's body inside. He had been swallowed feet first.

Two incidents with Bornean reticulated pythons that appear to be attempts at feeding on humans were reported by Shelford (1917:89–90).

> Only two authenticated cases of men having been attacked by a *Python* have ever come to my notice. One of these was a Land-Dayak who was seized by the calf of the leg as he was passing a tree down from whose trunk hung a *Python*; a companion who was walking behind him chopped off the head of the snake, but the man still bore the scars of the *Python*'s bite some years after.

Two incidents of attack by *Python reticulata* were reported by Muthusamy and Gopalakrishnakone (1990:113). In one case, a man riding a bicycle dropped his flashlight near a creek. When he stopped to pick it up, he was attacked by a 14-15 foot python. The *P. reticulata* grabbed his hand, and the man pulled away, sustaining multiple lacerations on his hand. This appears to be an offensive attack; the snake was probably in ambush at the creek, and as the man stooped for the flashlight, the python made an unsuccessful strike. The second incident could be interpreted as an offensive attack or as a provoked defensive response. A man accidently ran his motorcycle over a *P. reticulata* about 15 feet long. When the man fell to the ground, the python grabbed his right forearm, the man pulled his arm away, the python grabbed his left forearm, and again the man was able to pull his arm away from the snake. He sustained multiple, deep lacerations on both forearms, exposing tendons.

The following is quoted by Shelford (1917:89–90) from the Sarawak *Gazette* of April 1891, p. 52:

At Judan, a village some six miles from Muka, a man and his son, aged from 10 to 12 years, were sleeping in their house, inside a mosquito curtain. They were on the floor near the wall. In the middle of the night the father was awakened by his son calling out, the lamp was out and the father passed his hand over his son but found nothing amiss, so he turned over and went to sleep again thinking the boy was dreaming. Shortly afterwards the child again called out saying that a crocodile was taking him. This time the father, thoroughly aroused, felt again and found that a snake had closed his jaws on the boy's head; he then prized open the reptile's mouth and released the head of his son, but the beast drew the whole of his body into the house and encircled the body of the father; he was rescued by the neighbors who were attracted by the cries for help of the terrified couple. The snake when killed was found to be about 15 feet long. The head and forehead of the boy are encircled with puncture wounds produced by the python's teeth.

Authors discussing humans being killed by giant snakes frequently mention a paper by Kopstein (1927:65–67) who reported three stories of snakes swallowing humans. Kopstein's account has been widely quoted by herpetologists as authentic instances of humans being eaten by reticulated pythons. However, the third story, reported by a newspaper, is partially improbable based upon the comment that the skeleton was badly broken. Kopstein was only relaying the information he received via two letters and a newspaper article, and while the comment about broken bones and a crushed skull raises some serious doubts about the credibility of the newspaper writer or story teller, it does not discount the authenticity of the other stories (translated for this work by Judith Hirt).

In the first issue of the fifteenth year of this magazine [*De Tropische Natur*], V.D.M.M. describes in a very interesting way *Python reticulatus,* known to old and young in Indonesia by the name of oelar swawah and oelar santja. Since this giant snake belongs together with the closely related *Python molurus* to the largest of its genus, it is in no way astonishing that people in that land of snake-stories can tell very numerous and adventuresome tales about it. It is generally assumed that once a python reaches a length of ten meters it is full-grown; nevertheless he was told stories of still more gigantic specimens. Is it therefore not easily conceivable that of those giants accused of having swallowed people—and that not only by the natives—one in ten may have been really guilty of it? An adult snake of four to five meters can work down a goat—so why shouldn't a specimen so much longer not be capable of, once in a while, by mistake or exception, swallowing a human!

Much could be said to question the truth of an incident reported that I want to translate here; such an event, however, remains extraordinary. I wanted to rescue the report from being forgotten, more so because there are so few reliable reports known about humans beings being swallowed by snakes. This incident, too, can finally not be considered proof, but I think that most will agree with me, that this report contains nothing that would warrant doubting the credibility of the event. When I once visited the Institute Pasteur in Bandoeng, I saw there the head of a very large *Python reticulatus* in a bottle; probably of an animal that had reached a length of about five meters. Mr. Papamarku, the then sub-director of the said institute was so kind as to let me know the story of the preserved item, and also made the relevant correspondence accessible to me. The two letters received read as follows:

Letter No. 1
BEO, July 19, 1921.

J.1. On the 13th of July, in the village of Bitoenoeris on the island of Salibathoe, a 14-year old boy was eaten by a snake. Since this was the first time here that a human has lost his life in such a way, and the snake is unknown here . . . let me know what should be done about this. The head of the snake has been sent to you by parcel post.
The commander of the Talaud-Islands
(w. g.) J. Pottinga

Letter No. 2
BEO, September 30, 1921.

In answer to your letter dated August 23, 1921 No. 774/X I [am honoured] to let you know that the affair came to pass as follows:
On the 13th of July the said boy went to the garden/field to fetch vegetables; it was at that time around five o'clock in evening, but he didn't return home. They looked for him right away, but couldn't find him that night nor the next day. On the 15th of July men went on the search again, until a man from Bitoenoeris saw a place close to the village where some vegetables lay on the ground. About two meters farther from the path they found traces of blood, and those who were willing to go another 10 meters farther saw a giant snake asleep under a tree. They thought immediately of the missing boy, and the snake was clubbed to death in less than no time.
Oleh, Captain-Laoet of Bitoenoeris, Pontolomioe, medic of Liroeng, and C. Tamawiwy of Liroeng were called, and when these people arrived, the snake was cut open and they found the boy inside in the following position: The legs were crossed with the left hand stuck between them, the right arm was wound around and behind the head, everything was completely smeared with dirt and blood, the dead body was covered with dirty slime.
Even though I have not seen it myself, because I arrived too late in Liroeng, I personally stand for the trustworthiness/credibility of the afore-mentioned persons as well as of the inhabitants of Bitoenoeris.
(w.g.) J. Pottinga
Even without having seen the head of the snake, it should have been obvious that the criminal cannot have been anything other than a *Python reticulatus*. A second snake that could be considered is *Python molurus,* but it is not found east or north of the Celebes, whereas the former species occurs from Indochina-Malaysia-Indonesia, to Timor, Tenimber, and Halmahera, and onward from there all the way to the Philippines. There are no other giant snakes in that part of the archipelago, so there can be no doubt about the species.
Even though such incidents are strange and rare, they can be slowly, over time, comprehended. Such a great snake should not experience difficulties in swallowing an adult person; the resistance of an unarmed/unarmoured person against an animal eight to ten meters long would be rather insufficient. As soon as the snake has bitten once in one way or another, the reflexive constriction of the victim generally follows immediately thereafter. And from there it is only a small step to swallowing the slaughter-victim. Disappearances of people through giant snakes thus find an explanation in the reflexive action. Those reports have always been received with some reservations, and can only be accepted as credible when the circumstances and the trustworthiness of those giving the report justify it. Tasikmaalaja.

Dr. F. Kopstein

P.S.—Some time after the writing of the above, I found the following story in the Batavian newspaper of December 6, 1926: "Some days ago in the vicinity of Pandjang (Oosthaven) one of the villagers out to gather wood in the forest was suddenly grabbed by the legs by a five to six meter-long python. In less than no time the beast had wound itself around its victim and cracked its bones. His companion, who saw the spectacle from some distance, went to the nearest village for help. When they returned, the victim was already dead, and the snake was occupied with dragging him out of the bush. For this purpose the animal had wrapped its tail-end around the slaughtered victim's neck and thus dragged it over the ground.

As soon as the beast noticed the people, it let go of its prey and disappeared with great speed into the bushes, so that pursuit was impossible.

The body of the slaughtered victim was totally damaged; everything up to the skull was cracked and broken.

Frank Buck (1939:199), apparently not shy about self-aggrandizement and certainly not a slave to facts, shared this story with his readers.

And once I was forced to kill a python [probably *Python reticulata,* but the story seems to lack veracity regardless of the species involved] according to the old jungle rule of self-preservation. It happened that I was releasing a [small animal] from a native trap. When the tiny animal had scampered back into the forest, I decided to break up the trap. As I reached for it, something struck my arm like a hammer blow. I felt a strong grip on my forearm, and then saw the head of an immense python.

The jaws were firmly clamped on my arm. Through the intense pain I realized that once he got his coils around my body he could crush out my life in a minute. I called for Ali, who quickly started hacking at the python's neck with his parang [large knife] as a coil of the snake's body went round my arm. The pressure on my arm was tremendous—it seemed that any moment the terrible strain must snap the bone. Somehow, with the superhuman effort men manage under stress, I loosed my revolver from its holster with my free hand. I had to be careful not to shoot into my arm, but I quickly brought up the gun and put three rapid shots into the back of the snake's head. There was a slackening of pressure on my arm; a great wave of relief swept through my body as the python slid to the ground and I stood free.

Buck (1932:125–129), who, based on his books, seems capable of sensationalizing anything, felt that it was "very unusual for [a python, *P. reticulata* or *P. molurus*] to single out a man for attack." He went on to explain that it took nearly 20 years before he encountered a verifiable case of a human being swallowed by a python. The event apparently occurred in Burma (Myanmar), and a 135 pound Burmese male was the victim. Since the python was found to be 28 feet [in length], it was undoubtedly *P. reticulata.* Buck felt this was the first verifiable record of an adult human having fallen prey to a python, although he acknowledged that there "has been many a case of a python swallowing a child . . . " The man had been hunting with a group of friends, and eventually his companions realized that something was amiss when he did not respond to their shouts. They

. . . took up the search for their companion. Not much time had elapsed when a member of the part let out a blood-chilling scream. His friends, who were just behind him . . . saw at a glance what had caused their comrade to cry out. On the ground, a few feet away, was a huge python. Its tremendous bulge plainly indicated that it had just gorged itself.

It wasn't difficult to guess what had happened. The jungle monster (it later developed that it measured twenty-eight feet) had devoured their friend.

One of the group raised his rifle and was about to pump lead into the giant constrictor.

'No!' shrieked one of his companions. 'Suppose a bullet enters the body of our friend inside the python's skin. It would amount to killing him all over again and we should never be forgiven.'

A hardier and less superstitious member of the group raised his rifle and fired. Two other members of the party followed suit. The great reptile—too sluggish to escape or defend itself—proved easy prey and soon succumbed. In fact, the aroused Burmese almost shot the creature's head off.

The dead snake was transported to the local hospital where it was cut open, "disclosing the crushed and broken body . . . He had been swallowed feet first, the hospital officials reported."

From the Philippines comes another account of predation by *Python reticulata* on a human (Buck, 1932:103–106). In Cotabato Province, Buck encountered an old Moro gentleman who kept a 25-foot python as a pet. When it was only about 12–13 feet long, it was allowed to roam free and it kept the premises free of rats. While Buck was visiting the old man, he received word that his beloved pet had escaped (Figure 7–2).

Figure 7–2. Swallowed Alive—An illustration of the story told by Frank Buck (1932: 103–106). Based upon what is known about snake feeding behavior, and contrary to the title, the person ingested was undoubtedly not alive when swallowed. Issued as a trading card by Topps Gum Company, in 1938 and 1950. *Courtesy of The Topps Company, Inc.*

The old man stopped his wailing long enough to explain that normally the python (which he referred to as 'my god') would not have taken advantage of the opportunity to escape. But the creature was hungry. 'I had been looking for a stray dog to feed him,' explained the old boy. 'But I could not find one. I did not want to feed him one of my goats unless I had to.' . . .

A search was initiated for the missing python, and the old man encouraged everyone in their efforts. Just before search efforts were about to end, a soldier located the fugitive. The python, which Buck estimated to weigh in excess of 300 pounds, had obviously just consumed a meal.

> Interested to know what the snake had devoured, I ran my hands over the bulge. I could feel a round knobby something that suggested a human head! Working both hands feverishly a little below this point, I found myself tracing the outline of human shoulders! There was no longer any doubt in my mind. There was human body inside that reptiles—probably that of a child.
> When I communicated my belief to the old man he showed no concern, his joy over the finding of his 'god' representing his one and only emotion.

The old man called a meeting of his family which consisted of six wives and 21 children. The meeting was held beside the python's cage. It was determined that the only son of his "number one" wife was missing, and he was the favorite child of the old man.

> . . . When the head-man officially decided that his pet son was no more I expected him to set up a terrific wailing. Instead he entered the cage, and, stroking the sluggish python where the boy's head bulged out, said, 'My Taqua [the boy's name] will sure go to heaven; he is inside god.' With this he consoled [his weeping wife], even rebuking her for failing to share his view of the matter.

Buck (1932:131–133) also recounted a story involving a newborn baby and an averted tragedy (Figure 7–3). It occurred in Perak on the Malay peninsula. An Englishwoman was newly arrived in the country. She had just given birth and was confined to bed. While dozing one afternoon she awoke with a start and, looking up, saw a 20-foot *Python reticulata* gliding into the room through a doorway opening on the veranda and heading straight for the crib in which her baby lay. Her attempts to scream for help were ineffective, and

> " . . . It was not until the snake started moving up on of the crib's supports that the woman found her voice. She let out a blood-curdling shriek and, as she did, the constrictor turned and eyed her coldly [we're glad this is an objective account]. Again the woman screamed . . .
> The gardener [who had been just outside the house] arrived as the python, turning his head away from the woman, again centered his attention on the crib. By now the great snake's head was almost on a level with the top of the crib. In a fraction of a second he would be within striking distance. Putting everything he had behind the blow, the [gardener] swung his *parang* [large knife] and dealt the constrictor a terrible blow behind the head. . . . the [gardener] having landed one deadly blow that did plenty of damage, kept hacking away until he severed the snake's head . . .
> This was one case where cold steel proved itself superior to coiled lightening.

Figure 7–3. A Child Saved By The Knife—An illustration of the story told by Frank Buck (1932:131–132). Issued as a trading card by Topps Gum Company, in 1938 and 1950. *Courtesy of The Topps Company, Inc.*

Reticulated python attacks on humans in southeast Asia were discussed by Hoogerwerf (1970:483) and he included the incidents reported by Kopstein above, and the following:

> In May 1938 a mandur (foreman) was attacked at Kisaran (North Sumatra) by a python that dropped on him from a tree, but he was freed, still alive but unconscious, with internal injuries. In September 1937 15 men were required in Singapore to release an adult male from the clutches of a 7.5 metre python.

An unusual attack by a reticulated python on a man riding in a boat is described by Mjoberg (1930:73–74). The incident occurred on Borneo.

> On another occasion a huge python put up his head unexpectedly at the side of my boat, and raised his body with the intention of attacking the nearest oarsman. The rower, in company with all the others, threw himself over the other side of the boat. I shot the snake with my fowling-piece, and he soon disappeared for ever.
>
> It is certainly very rare for *Python*-snakes to attack human beings, and I myself would never have believed it if I had not seen it with my own eyes. Still, it only happens in extreme cases, when all other food has failed. In the districts where the attack was made on us, practically all the wild boars had disappeared, having evidently wandered off in another direction, possibly because that year there had been a shortage of acorns on the wild oak-trees.
>
> Hunger, as we all know, is a very strong incentive, and perhaps this was the reason of the enterprising spirit shown by the *Python*-snakes in the wilds which we have just described.

A more recent death attributed to *Python reticulata* was reported in several newspaper articles (Anon. 1995; Emmanuel and Sittamparam, 1995).

> A 29-year-old rubber tapper Ee Heng Chuan was attacked, killed, and almost ingested by a large (25 cm diameter, 140 kg, 7 m) reticulated python in Segamat, Malaysia. Chuan's house was in a remote location and the backyard was densely vegetated. He left the house about 2230 hours to start an electrical generator, when he did not return to the house his mother sent his older brother to look for him. The brother found him in the coils of the snake, and the snake had swallowed his head. Puncture marks on his legs suggested the snake seized him, probably before he realized the snake was present. A China Press photographer was first on the scene, and he photographed the snake constricting the man, and with the man's head in his mouth. Clearly, this was an attempt by this species to feed on a human.

Pythons (*Python sebae*) in East Africa were responsible for two deaths reported by Loveridge (1931:9–10). Both are secondhand accounts. Again, these incidents have been widely cited by other herpetologists.

> Ukerewe Island [in Lake Victoria] is somewhat famous for its big pythons; the large dimensions which they reach may be attributed to the beliefs of the Wakerewe who object to the killing of these snakes, for they hold that death or misfortune will befall the slayer or his relatives as a consequence of his actions.
>
> A few months prior to my arrival on Ukerewe Mr. W. Scupham, District Officer of Mwanza had visited the island and shot a python there. He had planned to return to Mwanza the same evening but the engine of his motor launch broke down and, having neither oars nor sail, he and his men drifted about all night till the currents brought them back to Ukerewe Island in the morning. "There you are" said Chief Gabriel, "that comes from killing pythons." A few weeks later a further communication from Gabriel reported that a python had caught and killed a woman on the island. I was asked by Scupham to investigate the report. Curiously enough on the very evening of my arrival at Murutunguru, Père Conrads of the Catholic Mission of Marienhof, himself a well-known naturalist, showed me the head of this snake and communicated to me the details of how it had killed the woman.
>
> The woman had been engaged in washing clothes beside a stream and spreading them out upon the ground nearby. She was not very well, having only eight days previously given birth to a baby which had died. A native coming to the ford observed the clothes spread about but no sign of the owner; he called but received no reply. Thinking this strange he began a search in the vicinity and came upon the woman lying dead in the coils of a huge python. Returning to the village he summoned the men who, overcoming their usual reluctance, killed the reptile with four spear thrusts and two knifings. The snake was measured and found to be four and a half meters, with a midbody diameter of forty centimetres.
>
> The natives stated that thirty years ago a youth or big boy (*kijana kubwa*) was killed by a python on the island. This is the only fatal case in the recollection of the old men who said that though many persons have been caught by pythons, they invariably escape by exerting their strength. An educated Mkerewe told me that so great was the aversion to killing a python that should one of his fellow tribesmen find his own child dead in the coils of one of these snakes he would not kill the snake for he would argue, "The child is dead anyway, why should I die also for killing the reptile." Tangible evidence of their dread of dead pythons was observed when one of our specimens was being skinned by the side of the main road; several

natives were seen to retrace their steps on catching sight of it afar off and then they made an extensive detour rather than pass within a hundred feet of the remains.

Branch and Haacke (1980:305–306) documented a fatal attack by an African python with more details and objectivity than have been provided in other incidents.

The incident occurred at about 5:30 p.m. on Thursday 22 November 1979, on the farm Grootfontein (28°17'E, 24°05'S, No. 31 Waterberg district), east of the Dorset police station, Northern Transvaal, South Africa. Two young Tswana herd boys were chasing cattle along a pathway, when the leading boy (Johannes Makau, 13 years old, 1.3 m high, 45 kg, and in general good health) was grabbed on the right calf by a large python that lay in long grass by the side of the path. The other boy ran to a nearby kraal, situated 0.5 km away to get help. When he returned 20 minutes later with two elders, the victim was completely entwined by the python. One of the elders (55 years old) tried to attack the snake with a pickaxe, but reported that the snake grabbed the handle of the tool in its mouth, and in trying to wrench it free he dislocated his shoulder, causing him to drop the weapon. However, when hit by stones the python released its victim and re-treated. The victim at this stage was already dead, and the body was taken back to the kraal. The police at Vaalwater were informed of the attack by telephone, and arrived approximately 2 hours after the incident. The circumstances of the attack were recorded, and the body, which at this stage had been cleaned was taken away by ambulance for autopsy at the Nylstroom mortuary. The coroner's report states that "death resulted from suffocation and internal injuries". The African elder whose shoulder had been dislocated was also taken for treatment. He reported that when recovered the victim's head was covered in saliva.

Attempts were made to locate the python responsible for the attack, but it was not until Saturday, 24 November 1979 that the snake was found by Mr. Louis van Wyk, principal of the Vaalwater school, and Police Sergeant Zagrys van Em-menis. Its tracks were followed approximately 0.5 km, and the snake was found coiled under an overhanging rock.

Commendably it was captured alive, and handed over to the Transvaal De-partment of Nature Conservation, who subsequently released it on the Farm Wit-bank (27°43'E, 23°58'S), No. 31 Waterberg district, which is part of the Mogol River Nature Reserve in the northern Transvaal. The snake was approximately 4.5 m long, of unknown sex and in good condition.

The weather at the time of the attack, was warm with intermittent sun and ap-proximately 50% cloud cover, but no rain. The area is covered in relatively thick rooibos scrub, with many emergent rock koppies. Pythons are very common in the region, but usually of smaller size (2,5–3 m). Predation by pythons on small game has been observed by the local farmers on a number of occasions, but no previous attacks on stock or humans had occurred. . . .

. . . It is often stated that although these snakes may kill adult humans, they could not swallow them due to the great width of the shoulder region. However, in the case of the African rock python this may not be so. The shoulders of an adult man when collapsed forward may measure only 35–40 cm wide, and could probably be engulfed by pythons in excess of 5 m. . . .

. . . The case reported here, however, is almost certainly a true feeding attack, and indeed there is every indication that the snake would have continued swallowing the boy had it not been disturbed. Pythons are known to catch ante-lope, etc., by lying in ambush by the sides of game paths. The close proximity of the cattle being herded by the victim, and his sudden arrival as he ran along the path, probably initiated an instinctive feeding reflex in the python.

Unsubstantiated stories of human deaths caused by snakes and human attitudes towards the snakes were discussed by Branch (1984:237).

> In 1951, a Ugandan newspaper stated that a Lango youth had been attacked and swallowed, but that the snake (whose size was not given) was forced to disgorge the body. In 1973 a Mozambican newspaper reported the death of a Portuguese solider, who vanished whilst on guard duty, and whose body was later recovered from the stomach of a large python. About the same time a similar incident is said to have occurred in Angola. Few details are available, and it may even have been the same case mistakenly reported initially from Mozambique - Portuguese soldiers were on active service in both countries at the time. Photographs were taken by an unknown photographer of a large python, killed near the town of Henrique de Carvalho (now known as Saurimo), the capital of Lundo District in north-east Angola. It was bloated with its prey and when opened was found to contain the corpse of a black man. The actual size of the python is unknown, but it appears from the photographs . . . . to have been between five and six metres long. This incident confirms that pythons of this size can swallow humans. However, in this particular instance the snake may not have killed the person; it may simply have scavenged a casualty of the bush-war that raged in the area at the time.
>
> . . . In 1961, a Nyasa man working at the Alpine Mine in the eastern Transvaal tried to catch a large python in the hills above the bushveld mine. He took on more than he could handle, and in the ensuing struggle the python constricted him and both fell . . . He died the following day and an autopsy revealed a ruptured spleen and kidney.
>
> A python's mouth is almost as dangerous as its coils. No venomous fangs are present, but it contains over 50 long, needle-sharp teeth, and makes a formidable weapon. In a large python these teeth may be 10 mm long. A full strike is like a hammer-blow, and the curved teeth penetrate deeply, causing long, ragged wounds. A colleague of mine required 57 stitches after being on the receiving end of a defensive strike.

Stories of attacks may get confused, or duplicated, and one attack reported in different places may become accepted as two separate occurrences. Roger Caras (1975) referenced a 1973 Mozambique newspaper article describing an incident where a python was reportedly found to contain the body of a Portuguese solider. Haacke (1981:16) wrote about a similar incident that happened about the same time in Angola, or were they the same event? Haacke suggested they may be (Figures 7–4, 7–5).

> . . . at the same time a similar incident happened in Angola. Recently, Mr. Rod Douglas, now living in Johannesburg, showed me two photographs, he lost a third of a series, which he bought from the local photographer of the town then called Henrique de Caralho, the capital of the Lundo district in northeastern Angola. These photos had been taken a few days before he bought them during April or May 1973 when a large python from that area which had been killed, containing a large prey item was opened. These photos, which were part of a series of three, showed how in the presence of a doctor (?, man in white coat) the snake was opened and the corpse of a black man is exposed. According to the other figures in the photograph the victim appears to have been a person of average adult Portuguese size. Unfortunately there is no information whether the snake actually killed the person or swallowed a corpse which it encountered, nor are any other particulars available. Mr. Douglas who was doing geological fieldwork in the area at the time has no further information.

Figure 7–4. Portugese soldiers examining the remains of a large African python which contained the remains of a human. The human body is still encased by the python's digestive tract. Photographed during April or May 1973 near Saurimo (Henrique de Carvalho) in northeastern Angola. Photographer unknown. *Courtesy of W. Branch of the Port Elizabeth Museum.*

It is a strange coincidence that two then Portuguese colonies had a practically identical incident happening roughly at the same time. The only difference appears to be the reported involvement of a solider in the one case while, according to Mr. Douglas, in the Angola case an ordinary black man was the victim. Since python attacks are rather rare, it is hard to believe that a similar incident occurred on opposite sides of Africa under such similar conditions, where a large python was found to have swallowed an adult man without any witnesses. There is a slight chance that in fact the Angola incident was the same case as the one reported to have happened in Mozambique.

Haacke (1982:9–10) discussed a case of a snake attacking a human which received a high profile in the world press. The tabloid account of this story follows for a slightly different perspective.

BOY BITES ATTACKING PYTHON TO DEATH

In two recent reports on fatal attacks by *Python sebae* (Branch and Haacke, 1981 and Haacke, 1982) on human beings the potential danger of large individ-

Figure 7–5. The man on the left may be a doctor doing a postmortem on the corpse of a man found inside of the snake killed in Figure 7–4. Photographer unknown. *Courtesy of W. Branch of the Port Elizabeth Museum.*

uals of this snake was illustrated. However, the above headlines, which appeared on street posters of the 'city late' edition of the 'Pretoria News' of October 12, 1982 as well as similar reports of the same incident in other newspapers, show that would-be predators do not always have it all their way.

The actual heading in the newspaper read 'Boy (14) bites attacking 5 meter python to death' and part of the report was as follows: "A young herdboy gripped in the coils of a giant five metre python, ravenous after winter hibernation, bit out the monsters throat to escape, police at Richmond said today. Detective Sergeant Chris Quentin of Richmond CID said, the herdboy, who left without giving his name, arrived at the police station last week with his family carrying the giant python in an egg crate which normally holds 35 dozen eggs. It was still bulging over the top—it took two men to carry it."

During a telephone conversation detective-sergeant Quentin from Richmond, which is south of Pietermaritzburg and west of Durban in Natal, had the following to add. Since publication of the newspaper reports he had talked to the herd-boy again. His name is Petrus Mthebmu from the Gengeshe area near Richmond. According to him, while herding goats this snake attacked him and as it was winding itself around from the right the head came over his left shoulder. He then pushed his small knobkierrie with his right hand into the mouth of the snake, which apparently held onto it. During a struggle lasting about 20 minutes he managed to bite the throat of the snake until it finally released him.

When Petrus and his family reported the case to the police several wounds on the throat of the then dead snake were noticed which could have been caused by human bites and might have caused its death.

At the time the snake was stepped off and marks were made on the ground at the police station indicating the length of the snake. On the next day the distance between the two marks was taped as 16'2", the equivalent of 4,95 m. Since nobody was killed and the killing of a protected snake was supposedly in self-defence, the police had no further interest in the case. Petrus Mthembu and family then claimed the dead snake, to skin it and sell fat, meat etc. for 'medicine'.

The magazine *Scope* of November 26, 1982 gave its own dramatized version of the story apparently based on a personal interview. It differed in a number of points from the original report as well as the information provided by detective-sergeant Quentin. The journalist reports Petrus Mthembu as small for an 18 year old and that the snake was only three meters in length. When first grabbing him, it apparently bit his trousers, missing his leg. The ensuing battle lasted 15 minutes and the victim broke his two upper front teeth while "chewing" on the snake's throat. Whatever happened - he finished off the snake by hitting it with his knobkierrie!"

P. Mthembu (*National Enquirer,* 1982) told his own story to a tabloid reporter (Figure 7–6).

This was not the only time a person saved himself from a giant snake by biting it. Rose (1955:79–80) reported another incident from South Africa.

. . . near Potgietersrust, a piccanin, out on the veld with his dog, was seized by a large python, which wrapped him in its coils and bit him several times. Unable to do anything else, his arms being held, the terrified youngster retaliated by biting the snake. Disconcerted by this unexpected defense, it released him and he

Teen Tells of Terrifying Life & Death Battle

In a bizarre escape from death, South African teenager Petros Mthembu freed himself from the crushing coils of a 13½-foot python by biting the giant snake's spinal cord in half! "Petros used his head — if he hadn't, he would have been dead for sure," said Detective Sgt. Chris Quintin of the South African Police, who examined the snake after the 18-year-old's amazing feat October 12. Here, in his own words, is Petros' astounding story of courage.

I Killed a Huge, Deadly Snake — With My Teeth

By PETROS MTHEMBU

I was dying. I could feel my life's breath being crushed from my body. A giant snake had me wrapped in its coils — and there was no way out.

I was staring straight into its cold, deadly eyes as it opened its hinged jaw. I knew the python was preparing to try to swallow me.

I sent up a desperate prayer: "Please, God, don't let me finish my life as a snake's breakfast!"

The big brown snake had thrown itself out of the bush at me as I was going to round up some goats near my home in Natal, South Africa. I had fallen backward trying to avoid it — and in an instant the snake was upon me, wrapping its thick coils all around me.

"God help me!" I prayed. In my right hand I held a knobbed stick I use in herding goats. I thrust it at the snake's mouth — but the vicious creature locked its jaws on the knob and tightened its coils on me.

It was getting harder for me to breathe. With all my strength I tugged at the stick. Suddenly it came free — but it flew out of my hand and fell out of reach.

By now the snake's coils completely covered me from my feet up to my shoulders.

FATAL BITE: Petros shows how he bit into the python's neck.

It Held Me in Its Coils . . . I Could See Into The Gaping Mouth

Then, to my utter horror, the snake's head appeared before my blurred vision. I could see right into its gaping mouth.

In desperation I sank my teeth into its cold flesh. The snake hissed furiously. I knew now what I had to do. I had to gnaw through several inches of snake flesh — and then bite through its spinal cord!

I tore away a chunk of flesh with my teeth and spat it out. My mouth was filled with the disgusting taste of raw flesh. I forced myself to take bite after bite. Suddenly the snake jerked away from my mouth. Its jaws gaped wide again.

"I won't die like this!" I vowed. And with all my remaining strength I bit into the awful creature's neck. This time I felt bone between my teeth. I felt my teeth chipping as they met bone. But it worked — my teeth knifed through its vertebrae.

The snake shuddered, a mighty shiver I could feel right down my body . . . then I felt the coils relaxing their deadly grip.

My whole body was badly bruised, and my two front teeth were chipped. I stag-

TROPHY: Petros shows off the skin of python that attacked him.

gered home with the snake draped around my neck. We skinned the python and ate the meat. I still have the snake skin — I plan to keep it to remind me of God's goodness in sparing my life.

Figure 7–6. From the *National Enquirer* (October 12, 1982).

fled home. Returning with his parents, they found that the python had made up for its disappointment by devouring the dog.

Attempts by snakes to feed on humans have been discussed for four of the legless giants, but we have not yet implicated the scrub python in any of these accounts. This may be due to the relatively slender body of the snake which makes taking a bulky human difficult. Rose (1955:78), however, discussed an incident in northern Australia where a woman reached for her 3-month-old baby only to feel the baby's feet being pulled away from her, and then touched the scaly skin of a python. The woman's screams brought her husband, and the baby was rescued from the snake with only superficial facial wounds. For some reason Rose attributed this encounter to the diamond python, *Morelia spilota,* which rarely exceeds 3 meters. Why he did not attribute it to the larger *Morelia amethistina* is not clear.

Accidents with Captive Giants

One of the most unusual attacks reportedly made by captive giant snakes is that described by Carl Hagenbeck (1910:181–182), an animal dealer who had large quantities of giant snakes pass through his business on their way to zoos. In this story four large snakes attacked his son simultaneously, an event that seems unlikely. He wrote:

> A very serious adventure, in which the reptiles appeared in all their native savagery, occurred at Stellingen in the early summer of 1904. We were preparing to pack up four great specimens of the species *Python reticulatus,* varying in length from twenty to twenty-six feet, to be sent to the St. Louis Exhibition. My son Heinrich, having made all the necessary preparations, went to open the door of the cage, but no sooner had he opened it than the four reptiles, as though by a prearranged plan, flew at him with wide-open jaws. One of them very nearly succeeded in coiling itself round him in spite of his efforts, and if it had succeeded his death would have been a certainty. But he defended himself vigorously, and I myself and a keeper running to his aid, helped him with all our strength in his struggle against the monster. But it was some minutes before we finally succeeded in freeing him. . . .

People keeping giant snakes as pets may become lulled into believing their snake is "tame." Evidence suggests this attitude is dangerous and that giant snakes that are normally docile can severely injure and even kill their owners or members of their families. Events like this are rare, but they do occur, and ignorance about snake behavior and carelessness are invariably the reasons for these tragedies.

Accidents with large, captive boids have been summarized by de Vosjoli (1993: 38–39) and categorized into (1) misinterpreted constriction, where a person places a large snake around his or her neck or shoulders, and the snake tightens its coils to maintain its balance; (2) defensive constriction during restraint, where the snake constricts because it feels threatened; and (3) feeding accidents where the snake strikes when the cage is opened due to conditioning, or where the snake mistakes the keeper for the food item, due to odor or movement. Some incidents are best regarded as simple accidents. The incident described by Mole (1924:238), who reported a man killed while playing with an anaconda, is a classic example of the first category.

Though quiet and secretive in their habits, anacondas, when disturbed, are quite fierce. They are wonderfully strong. One was observed to leave the river at Cunapo and to steal quietly toward the place where a man was cutting grass. Whether it intended an attack it is impossible to say, for the Negro was warned in time. There is no doubt, however, that a sixteen-footer, if it threw its coils round a man could kill him instantaneously by a single contraction of its muscles. An American collector, Mr. S. M. Klages informed me that in Venezuela he saw a young Indian done to death in this manner. The snake had been caught, and the unfortunate native was playing with it and had placed it on his shoulders.

At the Transvaal Snake Park, one of FitzSimons's (1930:18–19) employees was attacked by a captive African python in a classic example of a category 2 incident. He wrote:

One of our keepers was a careless fellow, very self-confident. Despite advice, he entered the python cage with his shirt sleeves rolled up to the elbow, and boldly strode toward a big python with the intention of gripping it by the neck.

All we saw was a red and white flash, before the gaping jaws of the python closed, hard and strong over the man's forearm. Simultaneously three coils were thrown round his right leg, and he was battling for life. Only too well he knew that if the snake succeeded in getting a coil round his chest his ribs would be crushed, and the splintered ends would pierce heart and lungs like so many sharp daggers.

To save the man we were obliged to sever the python's backbone at the neck.

A newspaper story (Anon., 1984) documents a tragic incident involving an 11-month-old human infant. On August 6, 1984, in Ottumwa, Iowa, a pet, 10-foot *Python molurus,* housed on the second floor of a private residence, pushed its way out of its cardboard box cage, made its way to the first floor and the crib of the sleeping infant. Speculation about the snake seeking the warmth of the crib, and the infant's movements threatening the snake make this a possible category two incident, but the events are not well documented in the article.

A similar incident occurred in Reno, Nevada, in 1982. The gruesome details of a child's death in the coils of a pet reticulated python were documented by McCarty et al. (1989:240–242). One of the interesting conclusions that came from this incident was that the authors stated, "Accounts of bone-crushing force while constricting appear to be exaggerations . . . " thereby supporting the view we have taken here: contrary to many literature accounts, constriction does not normally break bones. Similar to the Ottumwa incident, this does not fit easily into any of the accident categories listed above.

The father of a 21-month-old male child reported that he had awakened in the early morning hours and first entered the kitchen of his residence where he observed disruption of articles upon the kitchen counter. Further inspection led to a glass aquarium on the floor where an 8-ft (2.4-m) pet python (*P. reticulatus*) was normally kept. The wooden top of the aquarium was ajar and the snake was absent. The father ran to the child's bedroom where he found the child unresponsive, lying prone in bed and cool to the touch. The child was clad in a diaper and a long-sleeved shirt. The snake was resting on a cribside bookshelf approximately 4 ft (1.2 m) from the bed.

The reptile had been in the household for approximately three weeks before this incident, having been moved into the home by its owner who resided in the basement of the residence. The snake had been a pet for three years and was normally fed rats or mice at intervals of twice per month. No feeding had occurred for the prior seventeen days.

. . . The child was a well nourished, well-developed, male weighing 10 kg and measuring 86 cm long at the time of death. Head circumference was 49 cm and chest circumference measured 48 cm.

. . . Over the chin, nose, and mouth region extending to the right face were multiple puncture wounds varying from 1 to 2 mm in diameter. Individually these punctures were accompanied by surrounding ecchymosis and fresh hemorrhage. The puncture wounds were arranged in linear and semi-parallel fashion with groups of approximately six punctures in each row. . . . Approximately 4 mm of unbroken skin separated each individual puncture site. Underlying fascia was punctured only to a depth of approximately 3 mm.

Palpable on the lateral right forehead and superior to the right ear was a raised area of ecchymosis without disruption of the external skin. Superficial hemorrhage within the galea beneath the raised ecchymosis was noted upon reflection of the scalp. No skull fracture was present. A superficial recent cerebral contusion 1 cm in diameter was seen on the right frontal lobe of the brain. No other significant lesions were identified.

. . . The immediate cause of this child's death was listed as asphyxia caused by constriction. The multiple puncture wounds are consistent in size, spacing, and with the dental arcade of the reptile. The bites are considered indicative of the habit of constricting snakes to secure their prey by biting while subsequently constricting the prey by wrapping it in coils. The frequency at which large constricting snakes are involved in human deaths is rare.

A 15-foot Indian python that was kept in a school and was handled by hundreds of children attacked a school employee when she opened the cage door to change the water. This appears to be an example of a snake behaviorally conditioned to being fed in its cage and when the door was opened the snake was expecting food and struck at and constricted the person (Eig, 1990:19).

Attempted feeding may also be the best way to describe the following incident, and it is similar to the Ottumwa and Reno incidents in many ways. This event was remarkable for several reasons. First, the 336 cm, 24 kg, captive-raised snake killed a healthy 43 kg human, thus prey mass was 179% greater than predator mass. The second remarkable aspect of this incident is that the victim was sleeping when attacked, but then apparently awoke and attempted to remove the snake from his body (based upon tooth marks on the fingers). The snake apparently had free run of the house. Chiszar et al. (1993:261–262) documented this fatal attack of a captive *Python molurus* on a Colorado teenager. The authors worked with the Commerce City, Colorado, Police Department to acquire the detailed information regarding the incident.

The victim was a 15-year old male, 152 cm tall, weighing 43 kg. While in bed, naked except for briefs, be was bitten on the right instep, with maxillary and palatine-pterygoid tooth marks clearly visible on the dorsal surface of the foot and dentary tooth marks clearly visible on its plantar surface. . . . The snake had apparently loosened and regained its grip on the instep because two superimposed sets of tooth impressions were present on the plantar surface. Numerous tooth

Killer snake to be spared

UPI Telephoto

St. Louis Zoo director Charles Hoessle [left] and other zoo workers Thursday hold the 16-foot, 100-pound Burmese python that Wednesday killed its owner, Robert Vierling of Winchester, Mo. Police said an autosy showed that Vierling, 42, had been crushed to death. Vierling's wife, Christina, said her husband had complete trust in the snake and often played with it on the bed. The snake was found loose in their bedroom. Hoessle said the reptile will not be destroyed but will be used for breeding.

Figure 7–7. Newspaper wire story and photo carried April 28, 1983. See also Figure 7–8.

impressions were present on the fingers of both hands, but only on their palmar surfaces, indicating that the hands had tried to pry open the snake's jaws from around the instep. . . . The fingers and the foot bled profusely. Autopsy photographs revealed scleral ecchymotic hemorrhage, and venous congestion in the cerebrum (petechial and ecchymotic hemorrhage both present), all beings signs of agonal breathing consistent with a diagnosis of suffocation as a cause of death. No attempt was made during autopsy to distinguish between suffocation and circulatory arrest . . . as causes of death; however, in subsequent correspondence the pathologist hypothesized that circulatory arrest would more likely be the cause of death of smaller prey, whereas suffocation would be more likely with larger victims. Although blood was present on the victim's face, hands, arms and legs, there was no blood present on the neck or on the middle of the torso, suggesting that the snake's coils had been wrapped around this area. Bruising of the victim's skin, consistent with this hypothesis, was visible in the photographs. There was no evidence that the snake had attempted to swallow any part of the victim.

According to an Associated Press story (Anon. 1996), in October 1996, a 19-year-old male was killed by a 13-foot Burmese python. The victim had purchased a live chicken to feed the snake and it is believed that the odor of the chicken was on the man as he handled the python. The snake mistook the man as the food and killed him. Apparently the victim and his brother "hoped to make careers out of caring for big snakes . . . " This is a classic example of a type 3 incident, and another example of irresponsible behavior. Handling a large hungry snake immediately after handling

Python crushes owner to death

WINCHESTER, Mo. (AP)—A West St. Louis County man was crushed to death in his bedroom by his pet python Wednesday, authorities said.

Ballwin Police Chief Donald "Red" Loehr said the body of Robert J. Vierling, 42, was found Wednesday morning by his wife, Christine. She believed he had suffered a heart attack, but an autopsy showed he had been crushed to death. The snake was found loose in the room of their Winchester home.

Mrs. Vierling said her husband had complete trust in the 16-foot reptile and often played with the 100-pound Burmese python on the bed.

The snake was taken to the St. Louis Zoo for safekeeping.

Zoo Director Charles H. Hoessle said pythons have been known to crush humans, but such attacks are rare.

"When it does happen," Hoessle said, "it usually makes the news coast-to-coast."

Vierling's neighbors, who described the victim as "an animal lover," said the car salesman often let the snake roam loose in his backyard during warm weather, but was careful not to let it escape.

Figure 7–8. Newspaper wire story carried April 28, 1983.

potential snake food is a serious error. The food for the captive python should have been brought to its enclosure; the snake should not have been taken to the food.

There seems little doubt that small children are at much greater risk from large snakes than are adults. Awareness of this fact is important for people who keep large snakes and children. Clearly, children should not be left unattended in the presence of free-roaming snakes, nor should snakes be placed on children.

Death by Anaconda and Murder by Python?

Charlevaix, in the *History of Paraguay* (in Bourke, 1884:203), postulated human sacrifices to large anacondas. This seems improbable. Snakes are finicky eaters and none of them are "programmed" to recognize humans as food. Thus, a person placed in a cage with an anaconda, or other large snake, is more likely to first die of dehydration, stress, or starvation than of being constricted. On the other side of the argument, a corpse scented with fish, bird, or mammal odor may potentially be consumed.

Alvarez, during his attempt to reach Peru from Paraguay, is reported to have seen "the temple and residence of a monstrous serpent, whom the inhabitants had chosen for their divinity, and fed with human flesh. He was as thick as an ox and seven-and-twenty feet long, with a very large head and very fierce though small eyes. His jaws, when extended, displayed two ranks of crooked fangs. The whole body, except the tail, which was smooth, was covered with round scales of a great thickness. The Spaniards, though they could not be persuaded by the Indians that this monster delivered oracles, were exceedingly terrified at first sight of him, and their terror was greatly increased when on one of them having fired a blunder-buss at him he gave a roar like that of a lion, and with a stroke of his tail shook the whole tower.

Statements like this are difficult to interpret; they may have some basis in fact, or they may be totally fabricated and politically motivated to justify the exploitation of the "savage" aboriginal people living in the area.

Using giant snakes as scapegoats for murder is a plot that has not, as yet, been exploited by the movie industry. However, a 1933 Paramount Production (now available through MCA Universal Home Video) entitled *Murders in the Zoo* (starring Charlie Ruggles, Lionel Atwill, Randolph Scott, and Gail Patrick) comes close. The villain, played by Atwill, meets his end in the coils of a *Python reticulata*. The scene is done quite nicely and the entire movie is great fun. Shelford (1917:90–91), however, described such an incident that apparently occurred on Borneo.

A third instance of a python attacking a man appeared at the time to be authentic, but since my return to England I have had reason to doubt it. The story is this: Two Malays who had been trading amongst the Dayaks of the Samarahan River reported to headquarters in Kuching that, one evening whilst camping on the river-bank, a companion went down to the river to bathe; shortly afterwards they heard his shrieks for assistance, and running to the rescue, found him in the coils of a huge python; they attacked the python with their chopping knives and eventually succeeded in freeing their friend, but the snake escaped and its victim, all his ribs and one arm being broken, shortly expired; in a tropical climate a corpse cannot be kept for long, so they buried him. Their story was accepted in good faith by the authorities. The late Colonel Bingham, a well-known naturalist who had a wide experience as a forest officer in Burma, to whom I detailed this story, told me that two similar reports were made to district magistrates in Burma to account for the disappearance of two natives. In each case the magistrates, suspecting foul play, caused the bodies to be exhumed, and it was found that the unfortunate men had been murdered; their bodies had been entwined with coils of rattan which were hauled tighter and tighter by the murderers until life was extinct. The murderers contemplating an investigation into their crime, had chosen this method of committing it in the erroneous belief that the weals and bruises made by the rattan thongs simulated the marks made by a crushing snake, and that consequently the authorities could be gulled into believing that the murdered men had met their death in encounters with pythons. With this gruesome evidence before one, it is permissible to regard the Sarawak Malay's story with considerable doubt.

Some Tall Tales

The supposed ability of snakes to hypnotize prey was discussed in the chapter on food. This legendary power of serpents is most likely based upon two biological facts. The first is the unblinking gaze of snakes due to their lack of eyelids, and the second is that many species of animals have a freeze response when confronted by a predator. In this story the snake uses some imagined form of telepathy to hypnotize and lure a man. Lange (1912:218–225) fully accepts the reality of the story he told about an anaconda's apparent attempt to lure a man within striking distance.

> Jose Oerreira, a rubber worker, had left headquarters after having delivered his weekly report on the rubber extracted, and was paddling his canoe at a good rate down the stream, expecting to reach his hut before midnight. Arriving at a recess in the banks formed by the confluence of a small creek called Igarapé do Inferno, or the Creek of Hell, he thought that he heard the noise of some game, probably a deer or tapir, drinking, and he silently ran his canoe to the shore, where he fastened it to a branch, at the same time holding his rifle in readiness. Finally, as he saw nothing, he returned to the canoe and continued his way down-stream.
>
> Hardly more than ten yards from the spot, he stopped again and listened. He heard only the distant howling of a monkey. This he was used to on his nightly trips. No! there was something else! He could not say it was a sound. It was a strange something that called him back to the bank that he had left but a few minutes before. He fastened his canoe again to the same branch and crept up to the same place, feeling very uneasy and uncomfortable, but seeing nothing that could alarm him—nothing that he could draw the bead of his rifle on. Yet, something there was! For the second time he left, without being able to account for the mysterious force that lured him to this gloomy, moon-lit place on the dark treacherous bank. In setting out in the stream again he decided to fight off the uncanny, unexplainable feeling that had called him back, but scarcely a stone's throw from the bank he had the same desire to return—a desire that he had never before experienced. He went again, and looked, and meditated over the thing that he did not understand.
>
> He had not drunk *cachassa* that day and was consequently quite sober; he had not had fever for two weeks and was in good health physically as well as mentally; he had never so much indulged in the dissipations of civilization that his nerves had been affected; he had lived all his life in these surroundings and knew no fear of man or beast. And now, this splendid type of manhood, free and unbound in his thoughts and unprejudiced by superstition, broke down completely and hid his face in his hands, sobbing like a child in a dark room afraid of ghosts. He had been called to this spot three times without knowing the cause, and now the mysterious force attracting him, as a magnet does a piece of iron, he was unable to move. Helpless as a child he awaited his fate.
>
> Luckily three workers from headquarters happened to pass on their way to their homes, which lay not far above the "Creek of Hell," and when they heard sobbing from the bank they called out.
>
> The hypnotised *seringueiro* managed to state that he had three times been forced, by some strange power, to the spot where he now was, unable to get away, and that he was deadly frightened. The rubber-workers, with rifles cocked, approached in their canoe, fully prepared to meet a jaguar, but when only a few yards from their comrade they saw directly under the root where the man was sitting the head of a monstrous boa-constrictor, its eyes fastened on its prey. Though it was only a few feet from him, he had been unable to see it.
>
> One of the men took good aim and fired, crushing the head of the snake, and breaking the spell, but the intended victim was completely played out and had to lie down in the bottom of the canoe, shivering as if with ague.
>
> The others took pains to measure the length of the snake before leaving. It was 79 palmas or 52 feet 8 inches. In circumference it measured 11 palmas, corresponding to a diameter of 28 inches. Its mouth, they said, was two palmas or sixteen inches, but how they mean this to be understood I do not know.

A tall anaconda tale from Trinidad was reported by Ditmars and Bridges (1935: 223). These authors did not consider this to be a serious story.

> At that point the professor's narrative leaped high into the air and he told us his snake stories. Once he killed a water comoudi—an anaconda—that was thirty-four feet long. That was a moderate enough estimate and did little credit to the professor's powers of exaggeration, for anacondas actually have been known to reach a length of twenty-five feet. However, there were some special features about this particular anaconda. The creature seized him while he was hiding on the river bank calling a big alligator. It coiled thrice around his waist, and then like lightening it whipped him up into a tree and pinned him against a limb eight feet from the ground. The snake was just opening its mouth to devour him, and presumably the limb of the tree, when the professor drew one arm free, snatched at the knife that hung on his belt, and slashed the snake in two. Then he pinned the ragged end of the reptile to the limb with his knife and slid down the carcass to safety on the ground.

Some stories seem to have been fabricated to keep laborers alert and to prevent them from wandering off. Such is an anonymous story retold by Gosse (1850:183). He also included a drawing that appeared in the *Oriental Annual* (no date) by a Mr. Daniell (Figure 7-9). The story was not a direct quote and it is unclear whether or not the story appeared with the drawing in the publication. The snake involved may be *Python molurus*, but the locality is close to the western edge of the range of *P. reticulata* in northeast India.

Figure 7–9. The Sunderbunds, an extensive swamp along the coasts of India and Bangladesh facing the Bay of Bengal, was the setting for a story about a python attacking a Lascar while he slept in a boat. The species involved is probably *Python reticulata. From Gosse (1850:183).*

A few years ago the captain of a country ship, while passing the Sunderbunds, sent a boat into one of the creeks to obtain some fresh fruits, which are cultivated by the few miserable inhabitants of that inhospitable region. Having reached the shore, the crew moored the boat under a bank and left one of their party to take care of her. During their absence, the Lascar who remained in charge of it, overcome by heat, lay down under the seats, and fell asleep. Whilst he was in this state of unconsciousness an enormous boa constrictor [= *Python*] emerged from the jungle, reached the boat, had already coiled its huge body round the sleeper, and was in the act of crushing him to death, when his companions fortunately returned; and attacking the monster, severed a portion of the tail, which so disabled it that it no longer retained the power to do mischief. The snake was then easily despatched, and was found to measure sixty-two feet and some inches in length.

Another example of a story with the original intent to deter certain human behavior rather than document a human being eaten by *Python reticulata* in the Philippines is that told by La Gironiere (1853:225):

This man having committed some offense, ran away, and sought refuge in a cavern. His father, who alone knew the place of his concealment, visited him occasionally to supply him with food. One day he found, in place of his son, an enormous boa [= python] sleeping. He killed it, and found his son in its stomach. The poor wretch had been surprised in the night, crushed to death, and swallowed.

A quite unbelievable tabloid story about an African python swallowing a child who is then rescued by his father is most likely a total fabrication considering what is currently known about python feeding behavior (Anon., 1986.)

A 25-foot python swallows African toddler Tim Heptinstall whole, but here's the clincher: The boy's dad actually freed him from the serpent's belly—with an Axe!

Heptinstall, 2½, was hospitalized for multiple injuries after the nightmarish ordeal. And while doctors near his home in Choma, Zambia, reported his condition as touch and go, they agree it was a miracle he was still alive.

According to the Zambian press the snake swallowed the boy feet first and by the time his father found him, only his face was showing from the python's throat. 'He has broken arms, fractured ribs and internal bruising but he will live,' said Dr. Gregory Ogden, chief medical officer at the Life Regional Clinic. Brian Heptinstall said his son was attacked while playing near a creek in a heavily wooded area behind their home.

"The snakes are an ever-present danger here I had warned him and warned him about playing by that creek," said Heptinstall. "But he slipped away and was gone for an hour or more before I realized he was missing."

"Thank God I knew exactly where to look for him. If I hadn't, he would be dead."

Heptinstall said he raced to the creek and almost turned away when he saw the snake coiled and writhing on the bank. Then he heard a muffled scream. "At first I couldn't tell where it came from," he said. "Then I heard another scream and spotted what looked like flesh in the python's mouth—Tim! At a time like that you don't think—you act—and I lunged at the snake." But the python—which weighed an estimated 280 pounds—was too strong. In desperation, Heptinstall ran back to his house and got his ax. Directing the blade just below the bulge in the snake's body, he hacked and hacked until he sliced it in two, exposing the boy's shoes.

"The python went limp," he said, "and I pulled my son from its throat just like you'd pull a knife from its sheath."

Figure 7–10. There is substantial evidence that large snakes may occasionally hunt from trees. Thus, they may occasionally attack humans from arboreal perches. This illustration appeared in Anon. (1856:91) but it has no accompanying story, or explanation of its origin.

Summary

Attacks on humans by giant snakes in the wild are rare, and accounts of attacks frequently lack detail or contain information that is inconsistent with what we know about giant snake behavior. There is ample anecdotal evidence that anacondas occasionally kill and ingest humans in the wild to assume that it does happen from time to time. And reliable documentation exists to verify that humans are occasionally killed and ingested by free-ranging *Python molurus*, *Python reticulata*, and *Python sebae*. In general, humans as prey items for large snakes are not the ideal: walking upright they probably appear formidable, and even if successfully killed the shape of the head (round; not tapered as in most animals) and the shoulders present obstacles to successful ingestion. It is clear that, while adult humans are sometimes attacked by giant snakes, it is children (i.e., smaller prey items) that are almost invariably killed and ingested.

While the accounts we have presented here make interesting reading, there is scarcely more evidence of predation on humans by wild giant snakes than there was in 1961 when Clifford Pope published his book on giant snakes. However, since 1961, more giant snakes—probably tens of thousands—have been kept in

Figure 7–11. "In moments the dragon [= snake] got hold of Kamram. Kamram looked at Murad helpless and shouted, 'Help me! He is crushing my bones. Get me out of his grip or I will die.' Murad cleverly tried to attack dragon's eyes and dragon's grip around Kamram loosened." Mr. Rehan and Mr. U. Mehta translated the Pakistani text. From a Pakistani comic book, ca 1960. *Courtesy of Sherman A. Minton.*

captivity and it is clear that, as captives, the four largest are responsible for a few human deaths in the United States and other countries. In all cases that we have reviewed, the deaths were the result of carelessness on the part of the owners or snake handlers.

CHAPTER 8

EXPLOITATION, POPULATIONS, AND CONSERVATION

> Nearly everyone has an opinion about snakes, and the usual result of those opinions is unfortunate for the crawling reptiles. Thus snakes are sensitive barometers of environmental attitudes. Snakes are among my favorite animals. I continue to wish more people would appreciate them. Not as pets or members of the household but as important components of our natural environments. People are gaining a greater awareness of and concern about the welfare of natural environments and wildlife. This emerging philosophy should include our snakes. (Gibbons, 1993:79)

The human population on Earth is fast approaching, if it has not already exceeded, five billion. That is five billion people demanding food, shelter, drinking water, and the other resources needed not only for survival but, optimally, a comfortable lifestyle. That lifestyle requires a large input of energy and the source of that energy is the environment. Those of us living in temperate North American and European cities tend to forget that large animals were, and are, valuable resources to people who live off the land in both temperate and tropical climates. Giant snakes are no exception and, wherever they are found, people exploit them in one way or another. In fact, many of us who live in the developed temperate cities exploit them to a much greater degree than we may realize.

Giant Snakes as Symbols

Not surprisingly, snakes as powerful symbols in human cultures are common. They have a distinctive limbless body yet are capable of graceful, fluid movement; staring, unblinking eyes; secretive behavior which allows them to appear and disappear silently and mysteriously; and venomous (and, to a lesser degree, giant) species have life-ending power. All of these characteristics provide snakes with a mysterious aura and one certainly capable of evoking tales of supernatural powers (not only in so-called primitive cultures, but in the 20th century United States of America as well). In a survey of cults, Cesaresco (1909:111) found serpents to be the most common subjects of animal cults. Here we cursorily examine the roles giant snakes have played in human culture as symbols, and the existing evidence suggests that, aside from the obvious impact a giant may have as a predator of humans, they have been extremely important in other facets of the people's lives with whom they live.

For example, rainbow serpent beliefs are a collection of folklore stories wherein the mythical serpents are guardians of some valuable resource and they exist in the folklore of many tribal cultures throughout the world. Hambly (1931:37–42) summarized African rainbow serpent beliefs, where the rainbow snake almost always guards water, forests, grain, or women. It often has control of rain and may be directly associated with rainbows. Evidence for these mythical animals originating from a specific species is usually lacking, but on the basis of size alone it is tempting to attribute the mythical beasts to the giant snake species living within the geographic area of the particular culture. In Australia, a mythical rainbow serpent named Ngaloit has sharp teeth and whiskers and lives at Fish Creek, guarding its waterhole from children who came to bathe there. Ngaloit punished children who entered the water by releasing small snakes from his body which then enter the navels of the children and kill them (Morris and Morris, 1965:19). Similarly, in Abyssinia, a snake monster guarded a beautiful girl and only after a traveler had learned the secret of how to kill the snake could he enter the girl's house and marry her (Hambly, 1931:41). Likewise, where the borders of Guyana, Venezuela, and Brazil meet, the flat-topped Mt. Roraima is said to be guarded by a large eagle and camoodie snake (= anaconda) that would show their displeasure by causing more rain to fall, should men start camp fires in the area (Roth, 1915:239). There are hundreds of folktales in cultures throughout the world, and it is not difficult to imagine how each of these stories functions in a society. While each may represent a single, isolated piece of folklore, it seems probable they are vestiges of more widespread snake-associated belief systems which have evolved as the cultures evolved.

Beliefs from the Western Hemisphere

There is some evidence that the tribal peoples of the Amazon worshipped, or at least revered, the anaconda. In de Vega's (1966 4:222–223 translation) *Royal Commentaries of the Incas and General History of Peru,* he wrote:

> In these provinces of the Antis they commonly worshipped as gods tigers [jaguars] and great serpents called amaru [anacondas]. These are much thicker than a man's thigh and twenty-five or thirty feet long. . . . The Indians worshipped them all for their monstrous size. They are stupid and do no harm. They say that a witch put a spell on them to prevent them from doing harm: before they were very fierce. They worshipped the tiger for his ferocity and courage. They say that the serpents and tigers were the natives of those parts, and as lords of it, deserved to be worshipped . . .

In Brazil, along the Rio Xingu, aboriginal tribes frequently decorate the walls of their communal houses with symbolic animal figures. Karsten (1926:234–236) discussed anaconda symbols and a snake dance, suggesting *Eunectes murinus* was involved in holding the spirits of their ancestors. Among the beliefs of the Carib Indians of the Guianas, an anaconda seduces a Warrau woman and she gives birth to his offspring. The woman's brothers were so disturbed by this that they captured the father and the offspring, took them deep into the forest, and cut them into many pieces. Later, it was discovered that each piece grew into a Carib Indian, thus the Carib nation was born (Roth, 1915:143–144).

Beliefs from the Eastern Hemisphere

To understand the role of snakes in modern western culture it is necessary to digress momentarily from the giants. Judeo-Christian traditions view snakes as mysterious creatures, symbols of evil to be feared, despised, and eradicated. This is of interest since it is in sharp contrast to most non-Judeo-Christian cultures which regard snakes as powerful, positive, life-affirming symbols of sexuality, fertility, and immortality. The problem of image for the snake appears to have occurred as the Hebrews moved into Canaan and subjugated its people. The principal divinity of the people of Canaan was a goddess, and associated with the goddess was the serpent, a symbol of the mystery of life. The Hebrews, a culture with a male-god belief system, rejected the goddess of their enemies. Thus, there was a historical rejection of the mother goddess as implied in the story of the Garden of Eden (Campbell, 1988:48). Therefore the mythological temptation of man by the serpent via a human female in the Old Testament (Genesis 2, 16) was politically correct at the time. It is this story that is often acknowledged to be the root of the fear and distrust (the proverbial "snake in the grass") of snakes in Western culture.

The Biblical story of the snake tempting Eve and Adam is only one, albeit incomplete, version of a widespread story-type anthropologists refer to as the "Origin of Death Story," or the "Story of the Perverted Messenger" (LaBarre, 1969:55). Snake symbolism in origin of death stories extends in an arc from northwest India through the Middle East into Egypt, and it later spread to pre-Hellenic Greece. From Egypt it may have been dispersed southward through Africa (although Hambly [1931:75] doubts Egyptian snake worship influenced the sub-Saharan serpent cults), and it spread eastward into southeast Asia.

The Garden of Eden story contains two trees, the tree of life (immortality) and the forbidden tree of knowledge (morality). When the serpent deceived Eve and humans lost their immortality, the serpent eats of the tree of life and gains immortality; to the lay mind, real snakes may seem to exhibit this immortality by shedding their skins. The Garden of Eden scenario is only one version of the origin of death story in which God sends a message promising immortality (tree of life) to humans via an animal messenger (the serpent), and the message is altered by accident or intention with the messenger keeping the secret for himself and lying to man. God then curses or punishes the messenger, but humans are left mortal beings, subject to death, while the messenger gains immortality. LaBarre (1969:58) commented on this confusing situation:

> ... the story of the Fall of Man in the third chapter of Genesis is an abridged version of the myth which is more complete and understandable in its African forms. Indeed, it is otherwise unclear why God should be angry that man became *moral* (having knowledge of good and evil) through the good offices of the serpent; it is, rather, that a benevolent God would be angered because the snake and not, as intended, man, became *immortal*. And man, likewise was punished because he disobediently ate the fruit of the wrong tree. Thus God, giving man immortality through the Second Adam, Christ, was only bestowing what he had always intended. The snake, or man's sinful nature, merely delayed dispensation.

Since the serpent is accepted as a symbol of life in so many cultures, its negative image in Judeo-Christian cultures is a refusal to affirm life. Campbell (1988:47) wrote:

> In the biblical tradition we have inherited, life is corrupt, and every natural impulse is sinful unless it has been circumcised or baptized. The serpent was the one who brought sin into the world. And the woman was the one who handed the apple to man. This identification of the woman with sin, of the serpent with sin, and thus life with sin, is the twist that has been given to the whole story in the biblical myth and doctrine of the Fall.

Nature is now viewed as evil and in need of being brought under human control. Astoundingly then, the explanation for the negative image of snakes, the sexist attitudes of the Judeo-Christian tradition, and the view that nature should be subjugated by humans all have a common origin.

African cultures have retained the origin of death stories in more easily understandable forms, and in all of these cultures snakes symbolize a phallus. It is the result of naïve body image thinking, from a nonscientific perspective, and many cultures in both hemispheres have artistic snake symbols with beards, other hair, or feathers, which add to the sexuality of the symbols. Furthermore, in many cultures mythical snakes make water, rain, seduce women, are repositories for souls or seeds, and other overt or subtle characteristics of a phallus (LaBarre, 1969:65, 89).

Giant snakes provide a superstimulus for symbolism of this nature. Shape, large size, large numbers of eggs, and the extended periods of time (hours) snakes spend *in copula,* predispose them as excellent symbols of sexuality and fertility. Additionally, snakes shed their skin, an activity that predisposes them for a rebirthing or immortality symbol. Circumcision rites predate civilization, and appear to be modeled after the snake shedding its skin. Skin shedding gave immortality to the snake, therefore removal (shedding) of the foreskin conveyed immortality to the nonscientific mind (LaBarre, 1969). Cultures as distant as Southeast Asia and Africa revere the python as a positive, life affirming symbol.

In the late 1930s shaman Sam Bram of the Jarai hill tribe of central Vietnam let it be known that a beautiful Jarai woman living in the Ayun Valley gave birth to a python-god that could talk like a man. Bram led a nativistic movement using the python-god as a rallying symbol while the French and Vietnamese confiscated tribal lands. He was arrested and sentenced to a life term in prison in 1938, but was released by the Japanese in 1945. Here is an example of a python being a powerful symbol in a nonviolent message that emphasized ethnic idenity. Hickey (1982:345–358) documented this affair and, while he does not provide the details, he does suggest that the python has long been an important positive symbol to these forest-dwelling peoples.

Substantial documentation exists for python worship and python cults in West Africa, particularly Dahomey, and also in Uganda. The following information is based upon numerous authors covering 300 years (Bosman, 1705; M'Leod, 1818; Duncan, 1847; Burton, 1864; Ellis 1890; Rattray, 1923; Hambly, 1931; Talbot, 1967).

The symbolic powers of the python were requested in times of stress: war, drought, and pestilence. People participating in the python religions made offerings of money, silk, cattle, food, drink, and European-made goods in hopes of gaining the giants' favor. It was also believed that contact with a python could cause madness in attractive, young women who encountered a python. The madness could be cured by sending them to a boarding school-like environment where they were trained in the python cult's protocol. Accounts suggest that two thousand young women were involved in the cult at any given time in the 1600 and 1700s. Should the women become pregnant while being educated, the python-god was, of course, the father. The education of these women and the cure for madness was paid for by their families, who gave the python priests money.

Reverence for the giant snakes was imposed by the cult, and any contact with a snake had to be mediated by a priest or other cult official. Injuring or killing a snake prior to 1700 could result in death. One English ship captain and his men landed in Whydah, and moved into a house where they found, and promptly killed, a python. The local people were so incensed by this that they attacked and killed the Englishmen, and burned their house. Trade with Europeans was slowed by this incident, but when the Europeans returned to trade, the people of Whydah were wise enough to inform the foreigners of the python's god-status. However, harsh punishment for anyone injuring a python continued well into the 19th century.

Secret fesitvals to the pythons were held in Whydah in an attempt to drive out sickness. On the eve of the festival's procession the priests and python wives would go through the town and warn the inhabitants, white and black, to close their doors and abstain from looking out their windows into the streets under penalty of death. Apparently some Europeans violated the decree, were betrayed by their servants, and fell victim to poison. On the day of the procession the python priests and wives went through the town and killed every dog, hog, and fowl they encountered because these creatures annoyed Dañh-gbi, the python-god. At nightfall the procession participants would parade through the town stark naked, carrying a python on a platform, beating drums and blowing horns. This was followed by an orgy at the python-temple (Figure 8–1).

Public processions were held three or four times a year and all members of the town were encouraged to participate. These often involved animal sacrifices and were held at times of civil and economic distress.

It is clear that the python in West African and Ugandan cultures is a symbol for prosperity. Women desiring children, farmers hoping for abundant harvests, and hunters and fishermen hoping for success all acknowledged the python in some form. Specific themes of reincarnation and fecundity are tied to African snake beliefs. The association of snakes with conception, phallicism, and fecundity is most prevalent within cultures that worship pythons, although these beliefs also occur in areas where other snakes are revered.

Giant Snakes Used for Rodent Control

There are a few tantalizing comments in the literature which suggest reticulated and African pythons have been purposefully used to control rodents. This would be a use which would be consistent with maintaining the populations of giant snakes and demonstrates a certain level of sophistication in thinking about human ecological problems.

In the Malayan peninsula, Cantor (1847:57) gave a second-hand report suggesting people use *Python reticulata* for rodent control; he wrote:

> Dr. Montgomerie has seen in George Town, Pinang, a young one which the inhabitants suffered to retain unmolested possession of the rice stores in order to secure them against the ravages of rats.

On Borneo, St. John (1863:260) also suggested *P. reticulata* was used to control rodents; he wrote:

> Many persons are very partial to small boas, as wherever they take up their abode all rats disappear; therefore they are seldom disturbed when found in granaries or the roofs of houses. . . .

Figure 8–1. The temple for python worship in Dahomey. From Hambly (1932: plate 3). *Courtesy, The Field Museum, Chicago.*

In a discussion of the Philippines, Worcester (1898:514) stated that small specimens of *P. reticulata* were sold for their rat-catching proclivities. Similarly, an anonymous observer (1903:149) wrote:

> It is not uncommon to see small specimens offered for sale in the larger towns, where they are put in storehouses and over the ceilings of rooms in dwellings in order that they may keep down the pest of rats.

African pythons have also been considered useful for rodent control. A UPI newspaper article (Anon.) in August of 1980 from Pretoria, South Africa documented the situation (Figure 8-2).

Branch (1988b:64) noted that, although efforts to conserve the African python in Natal were brought about by concerned farmers, not all farmers are so enlightened

S. African army
plans snake attack

PRETORIA, South Africa [UPI]—A South African army recruiting campaign is under way—not for soldiers but for pythons.

A statement released Wednesday by defense headquarters appealed for citizens to donate pet pythons to the army because South Africa is losing its war against an infestation of rock rabbits on the Botswana-Zimbabwe border.

The rock rabbits have virtually taken over the area, invading mess halls and camp sites. Rock rabbits are the favorite food of pythons, an army spokesman said, and the snakes can get into places where soldiers cannot go to flush out the invaders.

THE ARMY NEEDS at least 100 snakes. It was decided not to use poisons because of the abundant wildlife in the region.

The army asked anyone owning a "problem python" to contact headquarters in Pretoria and hand it over—out of patriotism.

But the rock rabbits probably have time on their side. The army appeal included the warning that "it is illegal to keep pythons without a permit and those wishing to catch pythons in order to donate them to the defense force should first obtain the necessary permit and papers."

Figure 8–2. A UPI wire story carried August 15, 1980.

and many have little tolerance or understanding of the role natural predators play in pest control. Often these people are short-sighted and do not view stock losses to snakes as being off-set by their value as agents of pest control.

Giant Snakes as Food

While many of us may grimace at the thought of eating snakes, they are eaten by people in many cultures, and they provide those people with an excellent source of protein. Giant snakes may be favored food items because of their size, for even neonate anacondas and hatchling pythons are large enough to provide substantial protein and calories.

Eating snakes has been recorded by many explorers. Francisco Pizarro and his men are said to have eaten large snakes while they were stranded at Gorgona (de Vega, 1966:653). However, adventure writers often use this odd menu item as a way to elicit strong emotional responses from their readers rather than to objectively document the eating habits of a tribal people, or predation on reptiles by humans. Fountain's (1904:98) passage regarding the common anaconda is an example:

> They immediately set to work to make fires, in the way so common to savages, by the friction of two pieces of half rotten and dried wood, and roasted large chunks of the snake's flesh, which they devoured. . . .

Later he (Fountain, 1914:248) wrote about the taste of anaconda meat and his dislike for it.

> During the month, also, we killed no fewer than five or six anacondas, each of them approximately twenty feet in length. The Indians and the Negro feasted on the flesh of these: but George and I were not yet sufficiently starved to stomach such food. I did, indeed, taste anaconda flesh, and found it coarse and stringy, and almost flavourless. What taste there was in it was decidedly fishy.

Lopez (1984:117) reports that in Venezuela the Yanamamos Indians eat the meat of *Eunectes murinus,* preparing it by roasting it wrapped in leaves.

The anaconda is also an apparently common choice on restaurant menus in French Guiana (Gasc and Rodrigues, 1980), and the appearance of Indian python on menus for humans is widespread; Wall (1912:466) observed:

> All through the East certain natives regard the flesh of this snake very highly, and I can quite believe that it may be excellent. . . . In Southern China I know it is eaten as a great delicacy. In Burma the Karens and Burmese both regard it as excellent fare, and no python met by them is likely to be spared for this reason. In Travancore Colonel Dawson tells me the hillmen eat the snake and its eggs too. In *Land and Water* (August 10th, 1867) a correspondent says that a gipsy tribe in the Dun eat pythons, and Mr. Mackinnon tells me that there is a tribe called Myhras inhabiting the Dun that are ophiophagous. Many Indian people are snake-eaters, and as such are not likely to disdain the flesh of the python. Such are the Santhals, who occupy a strip of country between the Ganges and the River Baitarani, the Oraons or Dhangars, and Kols of Chota Nagpur, the Garos of the Garo Hills, Assam, the Nats, a nomadic gipsy caste, the Chentsus of the Nallamalley Hills, the Kanjars of the United Provinces, and according to a Mr. Edwin, who wrote to a London paper in 1768, the Ceylonese too, and doubtless there are many others.

In a review of snakes in the diet of humans, Irvine (1954:183–186) reported the export of the Indian python to China where it is eaten, and noted that it could be seen in Hong Kong shops. He described python meat as good, and its price higher than that of beef, adding that *Python reticulata* is also eaten in Malaya, China, and elsewhere in Southeast Asia. Raven (1946:38) related the following:

> I had the pleasure of meeting a Norwegian explorer, the late Dr. Carl Lumholtz, who was also planning an expedition to Borneo, and in the course of our conversation he told me there would be times when I would have difficulty in obtaining fresh meat for food. At such times, he said, if I could get a python I would find its flesh very good, though best of all, he thought, was the liver. This had been his experience, gained years before, when he had visited the tropical part of North Queensland, Australia. . . . I found that the Dyaks who inhabit the interior of Borneo make a practice of eating the flesh of the python and appear to like it.

Python sebae is consumed by many cultures in Africa, and hunters follow python tracks to a burrow or other hide where they set snares to trap the snake as it emerges from hiding (Schmidt, 1924; Angel, 1950; Broadley, 1983). Those cultures that worship snakes, or use snakes as totems or fetishes may avoid using snakes for food, but cultures lacking snake-eating taboos can be expected to exploit them. In Cape Palmas, West Africa (probably Liberia), Savage (1842:243–244) described a python that was skinned, and wrote:

... the flesh when denuded, was of the most delicate white. It was divided among them [native people], and not a particle, whether of skin or any other was lost. All was carried home, cooked, and eaten. From the skin was made a soup. I was extremely disgusted at the sight of a man carrying off in his hand, with an air of great satisfaction, a string of intestines.

Broadley (1983:68) commented on African python steaks grilled in red-hot coals, describing it as "not unlike codfish in colour and texture, is most palatable, tender and of good flavour." Cardinall (1927:91) described a large python that was killed and prepared as food on Africa's Gold Coast:

... other men accompanied him to the scene. They had waited for the python to grow more or less quiet and had then carried it to me, first cutting off the tail, so to avert any evil the snake might magically work. It was skinned for me and the men ate the meat. Minus the head and tail it measured twenty-one feet nine inches.

A side note to the human consumption of snake meat is that snakes are frequently hosts to pentastomids. These parasites are worm-like in shape, but are actually degenerated arachnids making them more closely related to mites and ticks than to any group of worms; they often have two hosts in their life cycle, a snake and a mammal. Pentastomid adults live in the lungs and respiratory passages of snakes and they release eggs and larvae which infect other organs and may escape the snakes body. Humans eating poorly cooked snake meat, or cleaning cages where an infected snake lives, run the risk of contracting this deadly parasite (Frye, 1981:219).

Giant Snakes as a Source of Traditional Medicine

In an attempt to understand the connection between healing and serpents, Arturo Castiglioni (1942:1160) of Yale University's School of Medicine, wrote:

Love had its origin in fear; worship in menace; and faith in the healing power, in the constant danger of death. . . . Wherever we find serpent worship. . . . the serpent is always the teacher of wisdom, the benevolent oracle of future events, and above all the bringer of health to whom the prayers of all suffers are directed in the hope of recovery.

It is not surprising, therefore, that wherever giant snakes are found, people have relied upon them as sources of traditional medicines. Karsten (1926:287–288) suggested the Jibaro Indians in Ecuador use parts of the anaconda to make a poison; to the best of our knowledge, however, these giant snakes do not contain any venoms or toxins. The use of anaconda eyes in sexual rituals also appears to be unique. Karsten wrote,

when they have killed an anaconda, [Jibaros] are in the habit of taking out the eyes, which are dried in the sun, and thereafter pounded into a powder and mixed with *achiote* (*Bixa orellana*). The Jibaro men, when they want to attract a woman, paint themselves in the face with this dye, the painting being supposed to exert an irresistible influence upon the female sex.

Often these traditional medicines are composed of the fat, oils, and gallbladders of giant snakes. Anaconda oil and fat are used to treat rheumatic and arthritic pains by people in Guyana (Quelch, 1898:305). In the Orient, python fat is also regarded as a cure for rheumatism, and the uric acid excrement is used for a variety of health complaints (Shelford, 1917:87). The fat and skin of African pythons is regarded as "muti" or medicine by numerous tribal peoples (Broadley, 1983; FitzSimons, 1930; Pienaar, 1966). The African python's gall bladder and vertebrae are also used by Zulu diviners in a variety of rituals (Berglund, 1989). Arthur Loveridge (1953:210), one-time curator of herpetology at Harvard's Museum of Comparative Zoology, encountered an old woman in central Africa wearing a necklace of python (*Python sebae*) vertebrae.

> She had no intention of disposing of the necklace as she wore it to strengthen her throat-and she coughed realistically to illustrate her meaning. Afterward she withdrew to remove a belt of snake vertebrae worn beneath her wrap for the purpose of strengthening the old woman's stomach (digestion).

Gallbladders of animals have taken on the myth of holding life forces, power, and medical importance in many cultures. Traditional Oriental medicines often include the use of snake gallbladders. Skeat (1900:302) reports that the gallbladder of the python, *uler sawah,* is in great demand among native practitioners. This python is purported to have two of these organs, one of which is called *lampedu idup,* or the live gallbladder, and it is believed that if this organ is dissected out and kept, it will develop into a serpent twice the size of that from which it was taken. In a similar vein, on Borneo, Shelford (1917:87) found the Dayaks believed that if the terminal bone of the vertebral column of a python is planted in the ground a new snake will grow from it. Natal's Zulus believed that killing and eating the gallbladder of a man who had killed a python would convey youthful vigor and a long life. FitzSimons (1930:82–89) apparently lost a friend to this custom. In Botswana, Auerbach (1987:153) reported the spurs (vestigial limbs) of the python are coveted charms and are used as ingredients and indicators in various cultural rituals. He also described a Pedi custom for a widow: a band of python skin worn around the head would cause her to forget her sorrow.

Sympathetic magic underlies the folklore belief reported by Newman (1963:12) for the Nyasas of Africa. Apparently they equate the ease of a snake regurgitating a meal with an easy childbirth, and found a way to transfer the ease of the process to a woman in a difficult labor.

> A Python [*Python sebae*] found in the act of swallowing a duiker is watched until it has finished its meal. A stick of any kind and size, green or dry, is then taken and rubbed gently across the snake's back. This should have the effect of making the snake disgorge its meal. Having done this, the Python presumably slithers away, leaving you with a valuable stick, and also some venison!
> The stick is kept until one of the women at the kraal is having a difficult and prolonged labour. The magic wand is now rubbed gently across the mother-to-be's stomach, this will end her pains, and the baby will be born within half an hour. The stick is put away until needed again and its magical qualities last indefinitely.
> You must use the same end of the stick for rubbing the mother as was used on the Python. You can lend it to anyone and it will work, but only for the use stated. It will not cure constipation or any other stomach ailments.

In Sri Lanka, Wall (1912:466) reported python fat was used for cuts, abrasions, and sprains, and in India's Travancore it was also used topically for fractures, bruises and rheumatism, while it was used internally for leprosy. The gallbladder is also prized in Burma (Wall and Evans, 1900:191; Wall, 1912:466). Widespread use of snake lipids in traditional medicines may suggest some actual benefits, and it may contain some active molecules which actually reduce pain that could be absorbed through the skin. However, African python fat is believed medicinal by the Zulus because the snake is considered a symbol of oneness or togetherness, and it is thought that rubbing python fat on an injury or painful area causes the pain to stay in one part of the body (Berglund, 1989:355). It seems probable that this kind of thinking is more responsible for the belief in medicinal properties of snake fat than some unknown chemically active property of the fat.

However, before we totally discount the healing power of snakes to cultural beliefs and folklore it should be noted that snakes may actually have molecules capable of healing humans. Angeletti et al. (1992) discovered that the saliva and oral tissues of the nonvenomous, widespread European colubrid *Elaphe quatuorlineata*, contains an epidermal growth factor and its receptor molecules. They suggest that Greco-Roman priests used this snake in a healing ritual where they placed the mouth of the snake on skin lesions to heal them.

Giant Snakes as a Source of Entertainment and as Pets

As we have shown, human fascination with snakes is ancient and it is not surprising, then, that snakes play a role in modern entertainment, and that role is one which is directly linked to ancient symbolism. Humans tend to create symbols and then react to the symbols as if they were actual stimuli. For some, snakes represent the dangerous aspects of nature and the snake charmers of Asia play on these fears as well as curiosity, as Wall (1912:455) so aptly describes:

> Its size, beauty, and placid disposition make it a welcome addition to the snake charmer's stock-in-trade, so that scarcely a member of the fraternity is without one. It is therefore in India a very familiar creature to everyone. The juggler produces his specimen with some ostentation from a bag or basket, seeking to impress the on-lookers, and he trades upon the public's natural fears, for if one comes forward too close to inspect the creature, it is more than likely that the owner affects the greatest alarm for his safety, as though to foster the belief already prevalent in the assembled throng that it is to him, and him only that the snake is a peacefully inclined and harmless creature.

Human curiosity about snakes is legendary. In 19th century England, giant snakes were a major draw for carnivals, circuses, and sideshows. British showman George Wombell purchased two large reticulated pythons for 75 pounds in 1805 and recovered his investment within three weeks (Morris and Morris, 1965:148). Exhibits of this type were on prominent display as evidenced by handbills (Figures 8–3, 8–4).

A newspaper article (from an unknown source, in the rare book collection of The Field Museum Library, Chicago) apparently discussed the same exhibit, although the source of the snakes do not match. If the poster is correct and the snakes were from

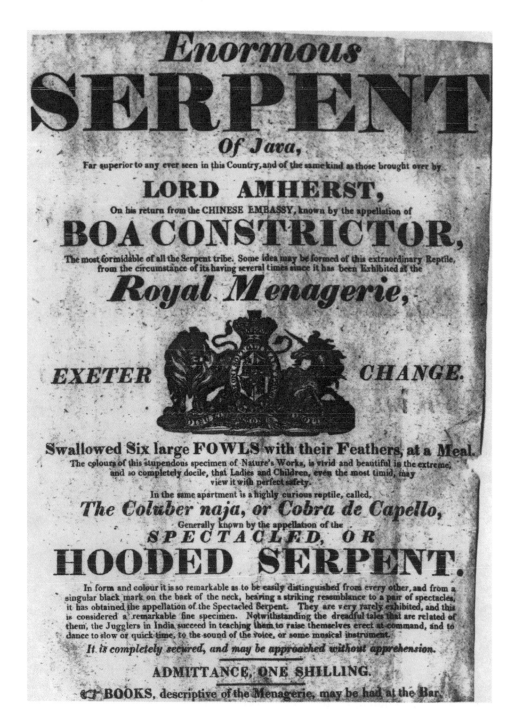

Figure 8–3. Old handbill. *Courtesy, The Field Museum Library, Chicago.*

The Original
LIVERPOOL
MUSEUM,

NOW EXHIBITING AT

28, Old Bond-street,

Contains more than 5000 beautiful Specimens of
QUADRUPEDS, BIRDS, REPTILES, FISHES, INSECTS,
MINERALS, FOSSILS AND SHELLS;

ALSO AN ASSEMBLAGE OF

CURIOSITIES,
FROM THE VARIOUS PARTS OF THE WORLD:
INCLUDING

Specimens of uncivilized Art and Ingenuity, brought from the Islands of the Pacific, and
other remote parts.

Relics of Ancient Armour,
COMPRISING CURIOUS SWORDS, SPEARS, HELMETS, BREAST PLATES, AND A SUIT OF CHAIN ARMOUR.

A CHINESE TEMPLE, of elaborate Workmanship.
A PAGODA, WROUGHT IN MOTHER OF PEARL, &c. &c. &c.

Among the QUADRUPEDS are

THE GREAT ANT-EATER,
SEVEN FEET LONG, A RARE & PERFECT SPECIMEN.——THE
LIONESS,
A NOBLE ANIMAL, ADMIRABLY PRESERVED.
THE PECCARY,
AND SEVERAL SPECIMENS OF THE OPOSSUM TRIBE.

THE BIRDS
Include every variety, from the MAJESTIC EAGLE and GIGANTIC CRANE, down to the diminutive but elegant
HUMMING BIRD, all grouped and arranged in a way adapted to display their respective habits and splendid plumage.

THE REPTILES
Exhibit the great BOA CONSTRICTOR and AUSTRALIAN SERPENT, in the act of destroying their prey, and include
most of the LIZARD SPECIES, with the interesting CHAMELEON.

THE FISHES AND INSECTS
COMPRISE NUMEROUS SPECIMENS, RARE, CURIOUS AND BEAUTIFUL.——AMONG THE

Minerals and Shells
ARE MANY SPECIMENS, NOT OFTEN FOUND IN THE CABINETS OF THE COLLECTORS.

This Exhibition has long existed in Liverpool, and acquired a popularity there which justifies the Proprietor in the expectation
that it will prove equally attractive and interesting in the Metropolis.

J. PIGOT AND SON, PRINTERS.

Figure 8–4. Old handbill. *Courtesy, The Field Museum Library, Chicago.*

Java, they were undoubtedly *Python reticulata;* if from Ceylon (Sri Lanka) they were undoubtedly *Python molurus.* The article or announcement discussed the cobra display, and then said:

> . . . Also a Pair of Real BOA CONSTRICTOR SERPENTS, which are considered beautiful specimens of that extraordinary reptile, indigenous to the island of Ceylon, and known to the natives as the Strangling Serpent, very destructive and terrific, and, when arrived at maturity, of the immense length of 50 feet, so carnivorous as to feed on tigers, horses, and buffaloes, and in pursuit of prey, adds undaunted courage to patient subtlety. The above surprising specimens may well deserve the attention of the Naturalist, and must be seen to be duly admired. N.B. These reptiles are well secured, so that the most timid may approach them with safety. —Admittance 1s.

To others, snakes still represent sexuality and fertility, even in modern cultures. Consider the comment by Richardson (1972:160) about exotic dancers using giant snakes.

> Many a young Indian python or boa belonging to a stage performer, belly-dancer or stripteaser, has never known a proper cage, being carted round the globe in a canvas bag and exercised on the chair backs in theatrical digs. And yet they seem to do well enough. There is no limit to the indignities to which an innocent snake will submit at the hands of a naked showgirl, allowing her to pop its head halfway down her throat, or between her legs, while she writhes about in a pseudo-erotic frenzy . . .

Giant Snakes as Captives

Snakes in zoos can also be considered entertainment, but they also serve to educate. As more people educate themselves in the ways of snakes and the role snakes play in ecosystems, the ancient symbolisms and fears can be replaced with an appreciation and knowledge that snakes are remarkably adapted predators with interesting life histories and function as important components of ecosystems. The association of snakes with evil and humans' loss of immortality needs to be replaced with valid knowledge of snakes as animals, a transformation that can best be accomplished by positive snake-human interactions. Thus, while zoos stimulate interest in snakes in general, and venomous and giant snakes in particular, getting to know serpents on intimate terms only occurs when humans keep them as pets, and they (including giant species) have become popular pets.

Many pet shops in the United States and Europe sell hatchling pythons and, much less frequently, neonate anacondas. Indian and reticulated pythons are particularly popular. Groombridge and Luxmoore (1991:110) and Luxmoore et al. (1988) reported that more than 25 thousand *Python molurus* were exported from Thailand, Malaysia, and Vietnam in 1985. In the same year, more than 15 thousand *Python reticulata* were exported from Thailand, Malaysia and Indonesia. Most of these snakes were imported by the United States with fewer numbers going to Germany, the United Kingdom, Switzerland, Japan, and other countries. During 1985, only 959 live *Python sebae* and 310 live *Eunectes murinus* were exported to the United States, Germany, the Netherlands, and a few other countries.

Figure 8–5. The reticulated python pictured is said to be 23 feet long. Its owner lived in Fort Wayne, Indiana and sent the snake to the Toledo Zoo each winter to prevent it from contracting a respiratory illness. The photograph is from *The Indianapolis News*, November 22, 1965, page 33.

These numbers may seem large, but, as we will see, the pet trade in giant snakes is insignificant when compared to the skin trade. Observations of the giant snakes sold in pet shops and through animal dealers support the idea that most of the giant snakes removed from the wild for the pet trade are usually hatchlings and neonates, an age class that probably suffers a high mortality in the wild. Removing these in small numbers has, in all likelihood, a minimal impact on the wild populations.

Many snakes in the pet trade do not come from wild populations, but from captive populations. Color and pattern mutants have attracted the attentions of snake keepers and the general public. This first occurred with the North American corn snake, *Elaphe gutatta* (Bechtel, 1995), but has now spread to the giant snakes. It seems highly probable that the Indian python is destined to become the koi of the giant snake world. Clark (1996:56–67) documented the history of captive reproduction of many python color and pattern morphs, noting that at least one of these mu-

Owners of dogs, cats warned don't try to pet missing python

Webster Groves, Mo. (UPI) — John Kountz Jr. has filed a missing python report with police.

Kountz, 19, said his 7-foot Burmese python, Bernice, escaped Thursday from her plywood-and-glass cage in his home. He said the snake may be somewhere inside the house, probably in the attic. but he has notified police anyway.

"It was my carelessness," said Kountz, explaining that he did not properly latch the cage.

Kountz said the snake normally eats once a month and was fed three rabbits just a week ago.

"It's not anything you can get attached to," Kountz said of his pet, "You can't call it by its name and see it respond."

But nonetheless, he said, "I like to hold it and feel it."

Kountz, who bought the snake 10 months ago when it was only 4 feet long, said Bernice is brown or copper with a gold, brown and black pattern similar to military camouflage.

Kountz warned neighborhood residents not to pet the python, especially if they have recently touched a dog or cat.

"If it gets the smell of an animal, that's the only time she'll bite," Kountz said of Bernice.

Couple Retrieves Half-Swallowed Dog From Snake's Mouth

Durban, South Africa (UPI) — A suburban couple thought their maid was joking when she told them a snake is eating the dog."

Mr. and Mrs. Vaughan Cochrane had a quick change of mind, however, when they reached the backyard and found their Pekinese half-swallowed by a nine-foot python.

Mrs. Cochrane said her husband jumped on the snake's back while she pried open the jaws and the maid extracted the whining pet.

He was still alive when we removed him, but soon afterwards he rolled his eyes and died," she said.

While they were trying to revive the dog, the snake, which is native to South Africa, slithered away.

Mrs. Cochrane said Friday that they reported the incident to authorities, who warned them against harming the snake if they see it again as it is on the protected-wildlife list.

Figure 8–6. Escaped pet pythons are bad publicity for responsible snake enthusiasts.

Truly a pesky critter

FORT LAUDERDALE, Fla — David Spalding first spotted the monster snake in his backyard a month ago, calmly feasting on a raccoon. After calling a park service and a museum — to no avail — he found Todd Hardwick, who runs "Pesky Critters," a firm that traps nuisance animals. Thursday, the 20-foot, 250-pound reticulated python was captured in a crawl space under Spalding's living room. Hardwick (second from right) said, "People say they've seen it eat 30-pound raccoons like they were marshmallows." He added that he believes the snake is the largest ever captured in South Florida, where many exotic pets are illegally released into the wild.

Figure 8–6, *Continued*.

tant strains sells for $7,500 each and that his snake breeding facility was burglarized in 1994. Responsible captive breeding projects such as Clark's have interesting implications: (1) they generate good will and educate the general public about snakes, (2) they reduce the drain on wild populations, and (3) they increase knowledge about variation and heredity in the species under propagation.

As more people keep giant snakes as pets, ancient fears have surfaced in the uneducated. Stories of escaped giant boids terrorizing quiet neighborhoods have stimulated many city councils, village boards, and state governments to enact policies and legislation preventing people from keeping large snakes, or in some cases, any snake. Although we do not advocate keeping venomous species or huge giants, such blanket legislation is an unreasonable overreaction to fear of snakes and irresponsible pet owners. Dogs represent a much more dangerous category of pets than nonvenomous snakes ever will.

Newspaper articles document many escaped pet giant snakes. Often these articles are accompanied by photos of four or five people holding the snake. In Menomonie, Wisconsin, Marvin Smith and his wife were terrorized not by a live snake, but by tracks 10-feet long and 8 inches wide found around their property and presumably made by a snake investigating buildings on the property. In Richland Hills, Texas, Jana Klarich had her day ruined when she found a 10-foot python on her porch. In Walker, Michigan, a couple riding their bicycles ran across "Big Sid," a 20-foot-long, 140-pound, escaped reticulated python. One undated article (probably about

1950) chronicles herpetologists Wilfred T. Neill and Ross Allen searching for a "30-foot boa constrictor" in a swamp near Jacksonville, Florida. They captured a 10-foot, 45-pound snake that the article suggests was a descendent from the 30-footer that escaped from a circus train 53 years before. As improbable as this is, it does make for an interesting story.

In an essay titled "Beware of Flying Reptiles," humorist Dave Barry (1995:36) noted a recent lawsuit filed by a Texas couple and their 5-year old daughter against Continental Airlines because they were not aware that the passenger seated in front of them had a python tucked into a gym bag under his seat. Clearly, this situation is almost as bad as the infamous "toilet snake" problem which features escaped boids rising from bathroom fixtures and intimidating homeowners as they move from toilet to toilet via the city plumbing systems (Barry, 1992; Vettel, 1986). Thus, as snakes become more popular as pets, a few careless snake keepers have given all snake keepers a bad name in the media.

Snakes are not affectionate like the more commonly kept domesticated felines and canines. Since they show little overt appreciation to their owners, what do snake fanciers get for their efforts? We suggest that keeping snakes and other wild animals is one way humans reinforce their link to nature, wilderness, and their biological heritage. Individual motivation for keeping snakes in general and large boids in particular undoubtedly ranges from those seeking attention or wanting to present a "macho" image within their social group, to those having a genuine interest in snake biology.

Giant Snakes as a Source of Leather and Related Products

Before discussing the trade in giant snake skins, it is interesting to note that, at the start of the 19th century, Alexander von Humboldt and Aimé Bonpland observed that people living along the Río Guárico, near Calabozo, in the Venezuelan llanos, killed anacondas for their long tendons. The snakes were apparently captured and killed while they estivated during the dry season. Humboldt (1885, 2:133) wrote:

> Boas are killed, and immersed in the streams, to obtain, by means of putrefaction, the tendinous parts of the dorsal muscles, of which excellent guitar-strings are made at Calabozo, preferable to those furnished by the intestines of the aloute [= howler] monkeys.

In Ceylon, Wall (1912:466) noted python skin was used in art, and observed it used for purses, belts, and letter cases. However, he noted it rarely appeared in large, commercially produced items due to the difficulty in procuring skins in quantity. Nearly all large specimens were skinned by those who killed them, and the skins were retained as trophies which could frequently be seen adorning the walls of houses.

Extensive commercial use of lizard and snake skins is a relatively recent phenomenon which started in the 1920s, and by the 1930s involved India, Sri Lanka (then known as Ceylon), Indonesia, Thailand, the Philippines and Brazil in a well-organized commercial collection of lizard and snake hides. Leather from these animals was originally used in customized, high priced shoes, but methods of tanning and finishing skins improved and the demand increased. Soon hand bags, shoes, and belts made of lizard and snake skins were being mass produced. Because squamate skin was available in a variety of patterns and tones, wore well, and could be finished in a variety of colors, the products appealed to a variety of fashion markets. Customs statistics do not differentiate between lizard and snake skins in Singapore and Indonesia until 1958 and 1968, respectively, and Thailand did not start distinguishing between skins until 1970. The Singapore/Indonesian exports rose from about 10 tons in 1958 to more than 200 tons in 1984. Thailand exports peaked in 1986 at 170 tons (Groombridge and Luxmoore, 1991:99; Anon. 1933:1). The species of snakes involved in this trade are unknown, but Groombridge and Luxmoore (1991: 100) obtained the opinion from dealers in Singapore that almost all were pythons until the 1980s. However, Lloyd et al. (1933:Table A) listed 39 snake species used in the skin trade which included: the Asian rat snake, *Ptyas mucosus;* the dogfaced water snake, *Cerberus rhynchops;* the Javan file snake, *Acrochordus javanicus;* and the common Asiatic cobra, *Naja naja;* all are species that are still exploited today. Therefore, the annual 20–60 tons of snake skin exported from Indonesia may have represented as many as 80–240 thousand air-dried python skins, assuming an average weight of 250 grams per skin, and only pythons were involved in the trade.

We used the import data reported in Luxmoore et al. (1988) for the number of skins of each of four giant species reported to CITIES (The Convention on International Trade in Endangered Species of Wild Fauna and Flora). These authors also provided export data, but because the exported skins were fewer than the imported skins, and because the countries of export are often questionable (i.e., the species do not occur naturally in those countries) the import data are here presumed to be more accurate for determining the number of skins and the total length of skins in trade.

Snake skins in trade can be reported as the number of skins, the length of skins, square meters of skin, or weight of skins. This makes determination of the precise number of individual snakes exceedingly difficult, but rough estimates are possible. Thus we have restricted the data we present here to the number of individual skins, and we have converted the linear metric units to individual snakes by using the mean length of skins in trade for each species given by Fuchs (1975). We are somewhat suspicious of the lengths suggested by Fuchs since they tend to be small: 2.1 m for *Eunectes murinus,* 1.7 m for *Python molurus,* 1.8 m for *Python reticulata;* Luxmoore et al. (1988) assumed a length of 1.7 m for *Python sebae* because it is believed to be similar in size to *Python molurus.* Therefore, our numbers should be conservative. But Groombridge and Luxmoore (1991:111) present data for *Python molurus* skins based upon a sample size of 6,964 which had a mean length of 3.22 m, almost twice the length of the mean given by Fuchs (1975). If Fuchs's numbers are correct, it suggests that most of the snakes collected for the skin trade are relatively small animals.

Eunectes murinus

The United States and Italy were the major importers of *Eunectes murinus* skins during the study period. Luxmoore et al. (1988) point out that the vast majority of skins reported originated in Paraguay, a country that has only a small area within the known range of *Eunectes murinus.* In other words, most of these skins probably originated in Brazil, and were illegally transported across the border to Paraguay from which they were then exported. Some of these skins were also said to have originated in Argentina, again a country that is not known to have wild population of

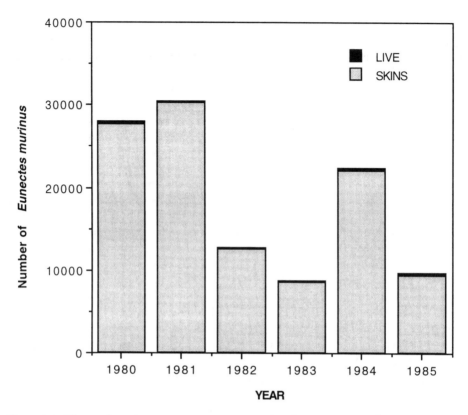

Figure 8–7. The number of *Eunectes murinus* reported to the IUCN/CITES from 1980 to 1985 as live animals and skins and imported into 17 countries. The graph is based upon data presented by Luxmoore et al. (1988).

Eunectes murinus, and Luxmoore et al. (1988) suggest some of these may be misidentified skins of a smaller species of anaconda, *Eunectes notaeus.* Colombia, Bolivia, and Guyana were also major sources of skins. Panama supplied almost 25% of the world's anaconda skins in 1983, yet this is another country that has no known wild population of anacondas within its borders.

During the 6-year period, 73,680 individual skins were reported to CITES and an additional 210,438 meters of anaconda skins (=100,209 individuals when divided by 2.1 m per individual). The total is 173,889 snakes, or an average of 28,981 snakes per year for the 6-year study period. The number of live animals imported is small, ranging from 176–359 per year and totaling 1,712 animals for 6 years (Figure 8–7).

Python molurus

The major importer was the United States, but the United Kingdom, Germany, Japan, Switzerland and the Netherlands also created a significant demand. Almost all

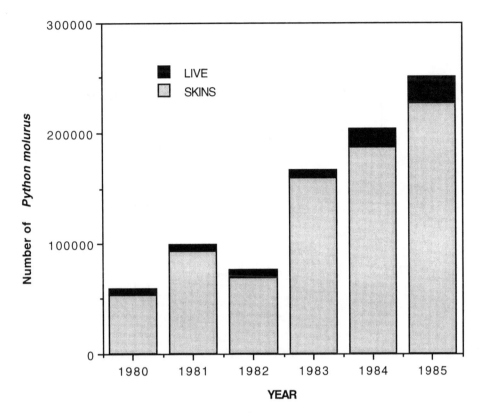

Figure 8–8.The number of live *Python molurus* and *Python molurus* skins reported to the IUCN/CITES from 1980 to 1985 and imported into 32 countries. The graph is based upon data presented by Luxmoore et al. (1988).

of the skins reported came from Thailand, with Vietnam and Indonesia being the next largest exporters. In Figure 8–8, note the steady increase in trade from 1980 through 1985. During the 6-year period, a total of 433,353 individual skins was reported, plus 602,463 m of skin (= 354,390 individuals, using 1.7 m as the average length of skin in trade), and 67,270 live specimens for a total of 855,013 *Python molurus* being taken out of the wild over a 6-year period, or averaging 131,291 per year. Note in Figure 8–8 that the imports of live *Python molurus,* presumably for the pet trade, make up a relatively small fraction of the total imports per year. The total number of live snakes imported is 67,270 animals, or an average of 11,212 per year.

Python reticulata

The major importers of *Python reticulata* skin were the United States, United Kingdom, Italy, and Germany. The major exporters were Indonesia, Thailand, and Malaysia. There is an overall increase of imports of these snakes during the 6-year

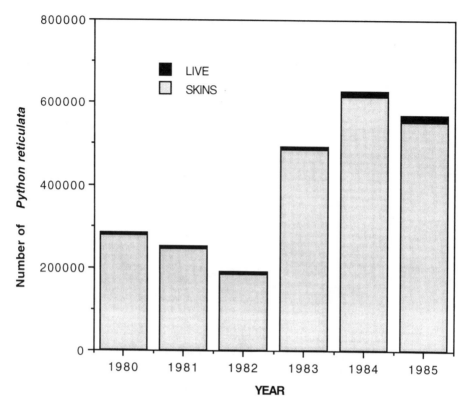

Figure 8–9. The number of skins and live *Python reticulata* reported to the IUCN/CITES from 1980 to 1985 and imported to 46 countries. The graph is based upon data presented by Luxmoore et al. (1988).

study period (Figure 8–9). A total of 1,413,417 individual animals was reported, with an additional 1,499,860 m of skin (= 83,3256 individual snakes when divided by 1.8 m). Add to this 52,364 live snakes. Thus, the total estimated number of reticulated pythons taken from natural populations during the 6-year period equals an incredible 2,299,037, and averages 383,173 per year. The import of live snakes, again presumably for the pet trade, makes up a tiny fraction of the total number of snakes taken from wild populations.

Python sebae

The major importing countries were Italy and Germany. The major exporters are Sudan, Nigeria, Ghana, and Togo. Total imports of skins for six years equals 26,418 animals, live pythons adds another 2791, for a total of 29,209 *Python sebae* imported over a period of six years (Figure 8–10). This averages 4,868 animals per year. Luxmoore et al. (1988:279) concluded, "This volume of trade seems unlikely to pose

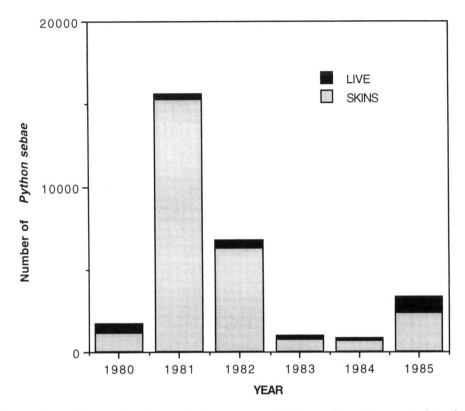

Figure 8–10. The number of live *Python sebae* and *Python sebae* skins reported to the IUCN/CITES from 1980 to 1985 and imported into 38 countries. The data are taken from Luxmoore et al. (1988) and do not include any data where individuals are estimated based upon total skin lengths reported in meters, unless they did the conversions.

a threat to the species as a whole, but, although it may well be adversely affecting local populations, adequate population data are not available to evaluate this possibility."

Following is a summary of total numbers of live snakes and skins of snakes imported during a 6-year period (1980–1985) and reported to CITES.

Eunectes murinus	173,889
Python molurus	855,013
Python reticulata	2,299,037
Python sebae	29,209
TOTAL	3,357,148

The above summary and Figure 8–11 clearly illustrate that *Python reticulata* is the most heavily exploited species of giant snake, followed distantly by *Python molurus*. *Eunectes murinus* and *Python sebae* are the least exploited of the four giants. Figure 8–12 is a summary of the exploitation of all four of the giant snakes for each of the years reported by Luxmoore et al. (1988). It illustrates that these ranked positions hold true for each of the years between 1980 and 1985, even though the percentages may change. These statistics clearly raise the question, can giant snakes, particularly *Python reticulata*, survive this level of exploitation?

Giant Snake Skin Trade in 1985

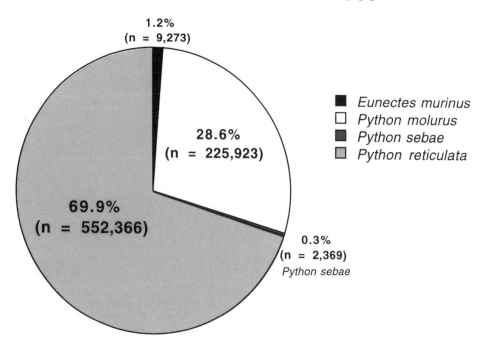

Figure 8–11. The relative proportions of each of the four species of giant snakes in trade in 1985. Note that *Python reticulata* is the most heavily exploited species.

More recent data regarding exports of giant snakes were provided by the IUCN and CITES (Figures 8–13 through 8–19). Although the data are not the same in terms of what they represent (i.e., we did not have to do any extrapolations to get the numbers for the more recent data), it is possible to make some valid comparisons and identify new or continuing trends. (1) *Python reticulata* continues to be the most heavily exploited of the giants, but the numbers have decreased somewhat (whether because of reduced exploitation or because fewer snakes were encountered is not known); (2) *P. molurus* numbers have decreased, and, as for *P. reticulata*, we do not know why; (3) exploitation of *P. sebae* has increased dramatically; and (4) *Eunectes murinus* is still the least exploited of the giants, but trade in live anacondas has increased.

An Equatorial Belt?

Clifford Pope (1961:241) made what first appears to be a rash statement in his book *Giant Snakes*,

> . . . it is readily calculated that the earth could have each year a handsome new equatorial belt of snake hide. This I wish to emphasize, would not have to include hides of any venomous species.

The Earth's equatorial circumference, according to our almanac, is 24,901.55 miles or 40,822.2 km. Is it possible that humans use almost 25,000 miles of snake skins per year? And, what proportion of these hides come from giant snakes?

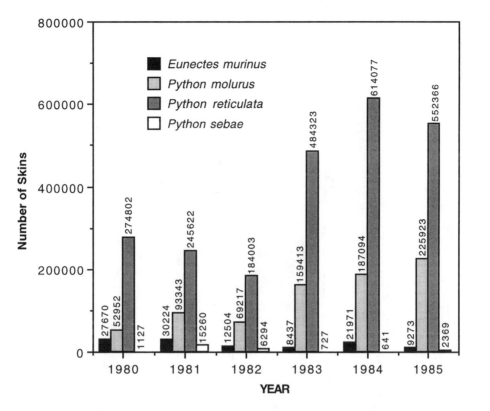

Figure 8–12. The number of skins in trade from the four giant species between 1980–1985.

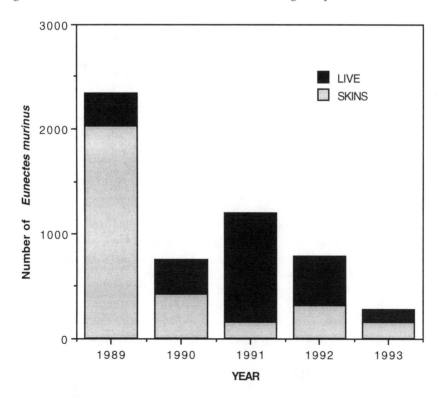

Figure 8–13. The number of *Eunectes murinus* exported that were reported to CITES between 1989–1993. Compare this to Figure 8–7 and the implication is that exploitation of the anaconda has been dramatically reduced.

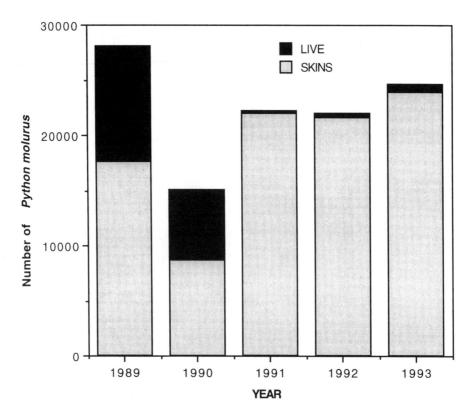

Figure 8–14. The number of *Python molurus* exported that were reported to CITES between 1989–1993. Compare this to Figure 8–8 and the data suggest that exploitation has remained relatively high since 1983.

As previously noted, data regarding snake skins were reported to CITES as (a) number of skins (b) total metric length of skins (c) mass (kg) of skins, and (d) square metric units of skins. Only data reported by number of skins and total metric length of skins was usable for calculating the number of individual snakes taken from the wild, thus making our numbers very conservative.

We converted the data from total individual skins to metric lengths by multiplying the number of skins in trade by the mean length of the skins in trade, and by adding the total number of skins for each species it was possible to obtain an estimate for the total number of kilometers of snake skins these reptiles contributed to the leather trade. Calculating the numbers for 1985, the leather industry used 1,449,475 meters, or about 1450 kilometers, or 884.5 miles of giant snake skins. Note that this is for one year in the middle of the last decade, not for a span of six years, or for a decade. This number is extremely conservative because it is based on the number of individual snakes and metric lengths of skins reported to CITES, and does not include snake skins listed by mass or by square metric units. Furthermore, it does not include snake skins collected and retained within the country of origin, and it assumes the numbers reported to CITES are accurate. It could easily be half, or less than half, of the actual number of giant snakes used for leather goods.

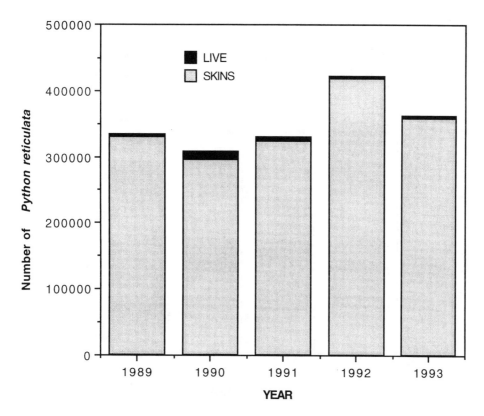

Figure 8–15. The number of *Python reticulata* exported that were reported to CITES between 1989–1993. Compare this to Figure 8–9 and the data suggest that exploitation of this snake has been well over 200,000 animals per year since 1980, peaking in 1984.

While this number does not come close to Pope's (1961) prediction of a leather belt 25,000 miles long, it does represent only four species, and the dozens of other species which are exploited may in fact bring the number closer to Pope's 25,000 mile prediction. Is the last giant snake on the planet destined to end its life so someone can have a pair of python cowboy boots?

Populations, Abundance, and Status

There is minimal hard evidence that giant snakes were once more abundant than they are today, at least in some parts of the world. Groombridge and Luxmoore (1991:17) noted the lack of published numbers, densities, and population trends for southeast Asian pythons; they acknowledge the difficulties in establishing and monitoring snake populations on a long-term basis due to their secretive and elusive nature, and the fact that their activity is often linked to specific weather conditions. Nonetheless, they suggest that statements about abundance made by a variety of authors are valuable. These statements are always anecdotal and based upon an author's often subjective opinion about the frequency with which they encountered snakes. Few studies have been done on the

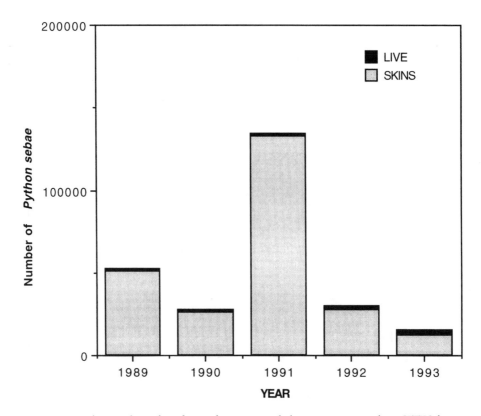

Figure 8–16. The number of *Python sebae* exported that were reported to CITES between 1989–1993. When these data are compared to those for 1980–1985 (Figure 8–10) it suggests that exploitation of the African python has dramatically increased since 1980–1985.

abundance of any tropical snakes and those that have (see Murphy et al. 1994 for a review) suggest that field work produces one to three individual snakes per day, while field work in temperate climates can generate many more individual specimens per unit of effort per day (by a factor of at least 10). Here we examine comments that have been made in the literature regarding the abundance of giant snakes.

Eunectes murinus. During his exploration of the Orinoco at the turn of the 19th century, von Humboldt (1885:342) wrote that they saw anacondas almost from the first day they embarked on their journey. Quelch (1898:300) considered the anaconda common enough in the Guianas to be a serious nuisance to people who kept poultry. Andre (1904:178), discussing the anaconda, stated "These water snakes appear to be common enough on the Caura and its tributaries . . . " Fountain (1904:27), however, considered it scarce; and Mozans (1910:75) wrote:

> One of the officers of the steamer told us that he had been sailing up and down the Orinoco for twenty years and had never seen one of these boas before. And more wonderful still, it was the first and last we ourselves saw, although we subsequently traveled many thousands of miles on tropical rivers along which such serpents have their habitat.

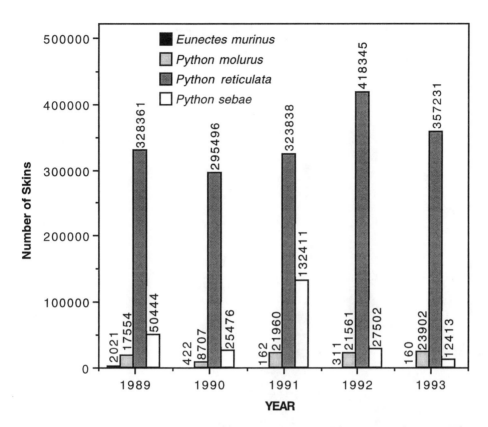

Figure 8–17. The number of skins exported reported to CITES between 1989–1993. When compared with Figure 8–12 for the 1980–1985 study period it is clear that the number of skins taken is variable, but shows an overall increase in exploitation of all species except the anaconda, *Eunectes murinus*.

Python molurus. Knowledge of this species' populations was summarized by Groombridge and Luxmoore (1991:31–98) and the following information is based upon their account, unless otherwise noted. In Bangladesh this species is considered uncommon, except for the Sunderbans. The moist deciduous forests of the central part of the country are considered devoid of pythons, and habitat loss and exploitation for skins are considered the reasons for the decline. In Bhutan and Brunei there appears to be little information regarding this species. In Cambodia it may be hunted for local use, but there has been no significant export of skins since the early 1970s. China's populations have been exploited, and it is believed to be rare, with the possible exception of Hainan. Hong Kong's population is considered sporadic in occurrence and uncommon; one CITES report from 1985 estimated 50 to 200 individuals. Hong Kong imports considerable numbers of hides for processing, but the natural population on this island has probably been reduced by exploitation and habitat degradation. India's populations of *Python molurus* are widely distributed but heavily exploited and may be locally extirpated. Whitaker (1993:87–89) considered cutting scrub forests for charcoal and converting the land to agriculture a more serious threat than the skin trade.

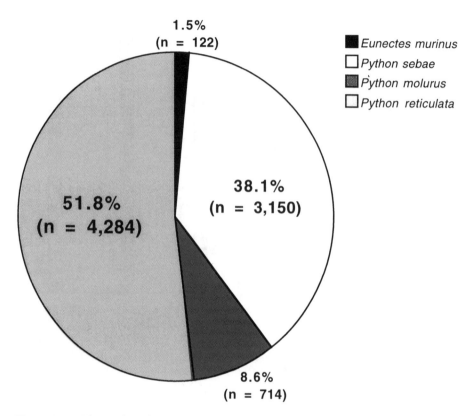

Figure 8–18. The trade in live giant snakes in 1993. Most of these animals are probably juveniles, and the numbers removed from the wild are relatively small.

While few population studies have been carried out on giant snakes, a study done at Keoladeo National Park in Rajasthan (Bhupathy and Vijayan, 1988) reported 144 *Python molurus* in the park during the winter of 1985–86, and 111 snakes in the winter of 1986–87. The park is only 29 km² (8.5 km² of the area is aquatic habitats); terrestrial habitat, therefore, makes up 20.5 km². Thus there was an esimated 3.8–4.96 snakes per km². Interestingly, during their study period, 10 snakes (6.9%) were found dead during the first winter, and 5 (4.5%) were found dead during the second winter. They also found dens (or python points) which had been dug out by humans, and 6 other snakes were unaccounted for. Of the 15 dead snakes, 8 (53%) had hoof marks, and 2 (13%) had puncture wounds, presumably from porcupine quills. The authors reported that hoof marks and punctures were also observed on live snakes.

Indonesia's *Python molurus* population is smaller and more geographically restricted than the *Python reticulata* population. And, the Indonesian Ministry of Agriculture listed *P. molurus* as a protected species in 1978. In Laos, *Python molurus*

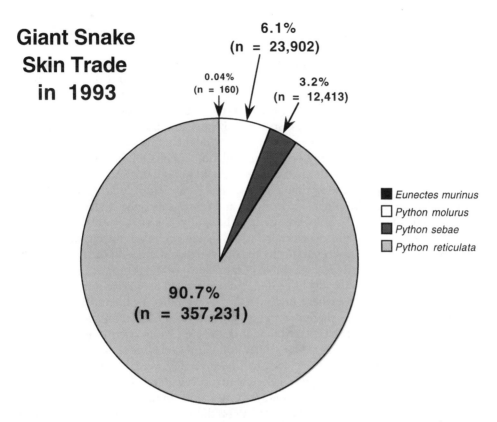

Giant Snake Skin Trade in 1993

6.1%
(n = 23,902)

0.04%
(n = 160)

3.2%
(n = 12,413)

90.7%
(n = 357,231)

■ *Eunectes murinus*
□ *Python molurus*
■ *Python sebae*
▨ *Python reticulata*

Figure 8–19. The trade in giant snake skins in 1993. When compared to Figure 8–11 this suggests fewer animals taken for the leather industry in 1993. But, was this due to conservation measures or because snakes became more difficult for hunters to find?

was historically considered common, but is believed to have declined due to local use and export trade (Groombridge and Luxmoore, 1991:65). In Myanmar (Burma), pythons are believed to be common, although no distinction is made between *Python molurus* and *Python reticulata*. Nepal regards *Python molurus* as an endangered species, but only anecdotal information is available on its status. Sri Lanka lacks a trade in *Python* skins and, while the species may be used locally for food, habitat destruction may be the major cause of its decline in this island nation. *Python molurus* was hunted for its skin throughout its range in Thailand, but this activity was stopped or slowed in the early 1990s. An increase in snake skin trade from Malaysia occurred in 1986 and 1987 and this may have resulted from an increase of illegal hides entering Malaysia from Thailand.

Python reticulata. While exploring Borneo, Swedish explorer Mjöberg (1930:73) commented on this python's abundance: "Certain districts in Borneo swarm with *Python*-snakes, which may attain the respectable length of eight and a half yards." Flower (1899:654) stated that it is fairly numerous in suitable places in the Malayan Peninsula, and that it is very numerous in the city and suburbs of Bangkok; Ridley's (1899:196) statements agree with those above. The island nation of Singapore apparently has a viable population of reticulated pythons; Lim and Lim (1992:48) stated that they are fairly common and are sometimes kept in Chinese temples as sacred animals.

Comments on this species' populations and exploitation were summarized by Groombridge and Luxmoore (1991:31–98) and the following information is from this source unless otherwise noted. Bangladesh's population appears to be confined to two small areas of rainforest in the east and southeast regions of the country. There is apparently no trade in this species in Brunei, and no data are available from Cambodia. In India, this species occurs in the Andaman and Nicobar islands, with unconfirmed reports from the northeast mainland, and it is unlikely to be exploited there because of its restricted range. However, in Indonesia this species is heavily exploited and the bulk of the available python skins come from Indonesian *P. reticulata*. Snakes are caught in nets set in rivers and streams at right angles to the bank and occasionally baited hooks are used; additionally, the snakes are collected opportunistically by agricultural workers. Most snakes are taken during the wet season (twice the number collected during the dry season), skinned in the field, and the skins are nailed to boards and air-dried. Because most of the people of Indonesia are Muslims, snake meat is usually not eaten, but some tribal peoples in northern Sumatra, Kalimantan, and elsewhere undoubtedly eat pythons. Gallbladders are in demand in China, and are therefore frequently extracted, dried, and sold. Groombridge and Luxmoore (1991) talked to hide dealers in various parts of Indonesia and received a variety of responses. One dealer in Jakarta said large skins were more difficult to obtain, two others said hides had been readily available over the past 20 years, and a fourth said there was a decline in hide availability due to competition. Two dealers in southern Sumatra reported fewer skins in the past 20 years, another said there were fewer, but five of six men could collect 20–30 snakes in a 2-week hunting trip. In northern Sumatra, one dealer reported buying 50,000 m of python skins in 1979, and twice that amount in 1989, and suggested one man could collect 20–30 pythons in 1 week. In Kalimantan, one hide buyer reported more python skins were available than were a decade ago and that hunters do not have to travel far from the rivers to find snakes. *Python reticulata* is said to be "not uncommon" in Laos, and they appear exploited only on a local level. In peninsular Malaysia a system of licensing is used, with each M$15 permit issued being valid for 50 skins.

The difficulty in finding reticulated pythons in primary rainforests is illustrated by data collected by Robert Inger at three sites in Sarawak (east Malaysia) where the herpetofauna was being intensively studied. These sites were worked for 366, 128 and 160 days and the number of *P. reticulata* seen at each was 8, 10, and 4 respectively (Groombridge and Luxmoores, 1991:67). In the Philippines, *P. reticulata* is exploited locally with small quantities of skins being exported. *Python reticulata* was exploited in Thailand throughout much of its range and the problem exacerbated by land cleared for agriculture, and farmers killing snakes when they found them. Reticulated pythons are now protected in Thailand. A small quantity of *P. reticulata* skins comes from Vietnam, and this country is expected to increase its export of pythons to China.

Python sebae. In West Africa, Mary Kingsley (1897:547) noted African pythons were abundant enough to be a nuisance to poultry keepers. "The common run of pythons is 10–15 feet, or rather I should say this is about the sized one you find with painful frequency in your chicken-house." Pitman (1938:52–53) considered it common in the Sudan's Blue and White Nile drainage basins, ubiquitous in Uganda, and abundant on the islands in Lake Victoria. Sweeney (1961:44) considered it common in the vicinity of lakes, rivers, and marshes in Nyasaland. Bruton and Haacke (1980:263) considered the African python common in areas of permanent water in Maputaland. Alexander (1990:32) reported it extirpated from the municipality of Durban, where it had once been present.

The only quantitative assessment of population density of *P. sebae* comes from The Gambia, where a population density of 0.6–0.75 pythons over 2.0 meters per hectare was determined (Starin and Burghardt, 1992).

There is an absence of baseline data to document that giant snake populations have a surplus of animals that could be harvested by humans without endangering the populations. Regardless, humans do exploit giant snakes and these uses may stress local populations and pose a serious threat to the survival of the giants.

Conservation of the Anaconda

The most ambitious, long-term, field-oriented research project with any of the giant snakes is currently underway in Venezuela. It is a project that was thoughtfully conceived and it is, at the time of this writing (January 1996), entering its fifth year. Sponsored in part by CITES, but largely by the Wildlife Conservation Society (formerly the New York Zoological Society), it has already produced exciting results (Thorbjarnarson, 1995), indicating that the facts about the common anaconda's natural history are every bit as exciting as the imaginative (but somewhat wanting for accuracy) tales of South American travelers over the past 300 years. Certainly one of the goals of "Proyecto Anaconda" in Venezuela is determining whether or not the snakes can be harvested on a sustainable yield basis. Ultimately, the project will provide guidelines for managing the species, including the feasibility of captive-rearing in order to meet commercial demands.

Nature reserves now occur in every country in South America found within the range of *Eunectes murinus*. Hopefully, these reserves will ensure the future of this amazing snake.

Conservation of the Indian Python

Many countries have legislation to protect wildlife, but when it comes to snakes the laws are frequently not enforced. Also, laws protecting snakes are only useful when they are capable of being enforced, and in many parts of the range of this snake that is not the case.

The initiation of a restocking program in 1982 for *Python molurus* was discussed by Whitaker (1993:89), but was not maintained. He commented that populations were well-protected at some wildlife sanctuaries, while protection was lax at others. A captive reproduction program should be relatively easy to accomplish with *P. molurus,* and, if combined with a public awareness campaign and habitat protection, the future of this species in India, and other countries, could be secure.

An incident in Nepal's Chitwann National Park is unusual in that an injured snake was attempted to be rehabilitated. It was documented by Dhungel (1983:7–8) and it illustrates some of the problems associated with snake conservation. More than 60,000 people enter the park during a 15-day period to cut thatch grass for their roofs. A few of these people encountered a 4.7 m (15 ft), 115 pound, gravid female

P. molurus which resulted in the snake being badly injured. The Park staff, and the staff of the Smithsonian Tiger Ecology Project, noticed the disturbance and stopped the people from killing the python. The snake was immediately transported to the Tiger Ecology Camp at Sauraha where the author treated her wounds and gave her penicillin orally. After 2 days, the snake was able to bask outside in the sun for about 3 hours before returning to the house where she was being kept. After a week she became more active, her external wound had begun to heal, and bleeding had stopped.

While the python was in captivity she was visited by about 400 people each day for several days. After a few weeks she became dull and listless and despite consultation with the local veterinarian, she died after 5 weeks. The author, curious to know the cause of death, performed an autopsy. He noticed four deep wounds in the lung which he suspected to be the cause of death. Dhungel concluded, "My experience in handling this animal prompted me to observe that a wounded animal whose instinct tells it that is being helped, will not attack its rescuer and exhibit docile behaviour."

Conservation of the Reticulated Python

This is clearly the most heavily exploited species and, while it is protected in India and Thailand, it is being taken in huge numbers (0.7 million taken from the wild in 1988 was estimated by Groombridge and Luxmoore, 1991:3]) from Indonesia, although a permit system is in place. Again, *Python reticulata* is hunted in Malaysia, a hunting license is required, there is a bag limit of 50 specimens, and under the 1972 Protection of Wild Life Act, immature animals may not be shot, or otherwise killed, or removed. The fact that humans have been able to remove literally millions of these large animals from their habitats over the last decade (a time period that is probably equal to about 1.5–2.0 generations of the snakes) suggests to us that they are, or were, abundant and their large size makes them extremely susceptible to human predation.

Conservation of the African Python

Based only on the numbers in trade, *Python sebae* is probably faring much better than *Python molurus*. Branch (1988b:64), however, considered the species vulnerable, noting that it is well-established in preserves, but that it is easily exterminated because of its large size. It may also be threatened by habitat alteration, and he cites massive land clearing for sugar cane farming in Natal as being a reason for local extinction. He wrote:

> Although efforts to protect the African rock python in South Africa were first motivated by concerned farmers in Natal . . . not all farmers are so enlightened. Many farmers have little tolerance or understanding of the role natural predators (eg, eagles and snakes, etc.) in the control of 'pests' such as dassies, cane rats, jackal, etc. The death of a few stock animals is viewed as direct loss, that is not obviously off-set by unseen predation on 'pests'. In the northern Cape, pythons also cause the loss of precious water due to their habit of basking in cattle water troughs and opening the ball-cock valve (Burdett, pers. comm.). They are there-

fore destroyed or removed as 'problem animals', whereas it would be more sensible to 'python-proof' the ball cock.

Comrie-Greig (1984:237) had earlier reported the results of a survey of 150 farmers in Natal. Eighty-four responded and 53 (63%) believed the python should be protected. Cane rat distribution was found to coincide remarkably well with python distribution, suggesting the snake is probably a major predator on this pest species.

Currently, the African python is well-protected under general legislation in the Cape Province (Ordinance 19 of 1974) and Transvaal (Ordinance 12 of 1983), and is a specified protected indigenous reptile in Natal (Ordinance 15 of 1974). In addition, it is listed on Appendix 2 of CITES (under all Boidae). However, increased educational programs are needed for farmers to maintain awareness of the importance of this snake in controlling pests.

Branch noted that a limited attempt has been made to reintroduce pythons into the Andries Vosloo Kudu Reserve, an area of dense Fish River Scrub near Grahamstown, which is within the known distribution of the Eastern Cape population that became extinct earlier this century. Thirty-four pythons were released in the area between April 1980 and January 1987 and, since their release, pythons have been sighted within the reserve. But a number of adults have also been killed on nearby farms, one following a series of stock losses. A sighting of a hatchling python within the reserve in January 1985 suggested that reproduction has been successful.

Summary

Giant snakes have been of value to humans as a source of inspiration for varied cultural belief systems, agents of rodent control, food, skins, and traditional medicines. The number of snakes killed for the skin trade indicates that populations of giant snakes, particularly the reticulated python, may be much denser than expected, and that humans are currently exploiting them at a rate that exceeds one-half million per year (Figure 8-20). Other giant snake species are not exploited at this rate, possibly because they have smaller population sizes, are fortunate in having a distribution that includes governments which have been

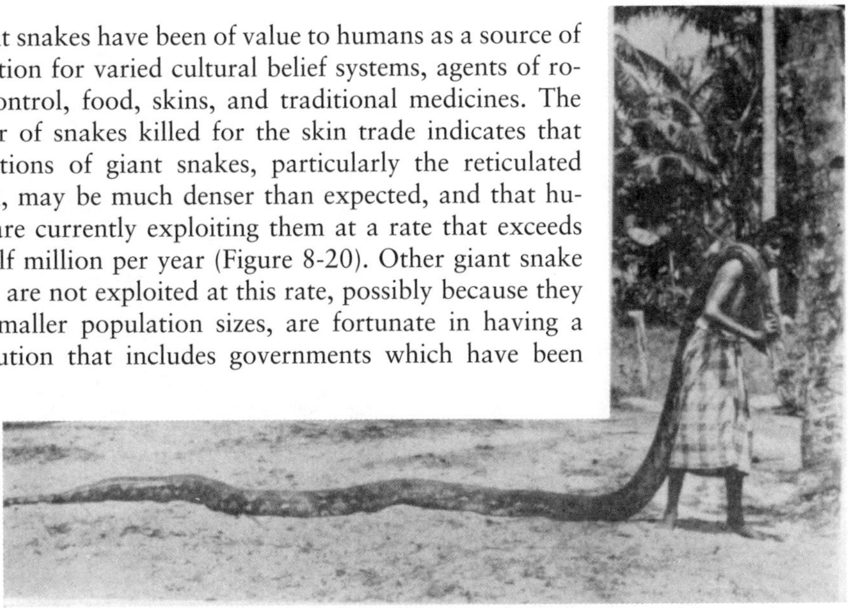

Figure 8–20. The end of a large reticulated python on Sumatra. *Courtesy, The Field Museum, Neg# 69925, Chicago.*

somewhat successful in protecting them, or live with cultures that revere them. Another possibility is that reticulated pythons actually thrive in human-modified environments and that domesticated animals actually increase their food supply—after all, this species does appear to be particularly adept at colonizing islands and surviving in urban habitats (traits not as evident in the other giants). The lack of baseline data to establish densities for each species in various habitats needs to be corrected with thorough studies before these snakes are dangerously reduced or completely gone from most of their current distributions. Including snakes, specifically the giants, in the emerging environmental ethic that Gibbons refers to in the quote at the beginning of this chapter appears to us to be particularly important. The apparent abundance of these animals in some habitats suggests they could be keystone species in their ecosystems.

LITERATURE CITED

Acharjyo, L. N. and C. G. Mishra. 1976. Aspects of reproduction and growth of the Indian python, *Python molurus molurus* in captivity. British J. Herpetol., 5:562–65.

Acharjyo L. N. and C. R. Mishra. 1980. Growth rate of Indian *Python molurus molurus* (Serpentes Boidae) in captivity with special reference to age at first egg-laying. J. Bombay Nat. Hist. Soc. 77: 344–350

Alexander, G. 1990. Reptiles and amphibians of Durban. Durban Museum Novites 15:1–41.

Allen, R. 1963. The anacondas. Ross Allen's Reptile Institute Bulletin No. 14.

Amaral, A. do. 1948. Serpentes gigantes. Bol. Mus. Paraense Emilio Goeldi 10: 211–237.

Amaral, A. do. 1976. Brazilian Snakes: A Color Iconography. Univ. São Paulo.

Anderson, C. W. 1906. A Descriptive Catalogue of the Tertiary Vertebrates of the Fayum, Egypt. London: British Museum (Natural History).

Andre, E. 1904. A Naturalist in the Guianas. London: Smith, Elder and Company.

Angel, F. 1950. Vie et Moeurs des Serpenetes. Paris: Payot.

Angeletti, L. R., U. Agrimi, C. Curia, D. French, and R. Mariani-Costantini. 1992. Healing rituals and sacred serpents. The Lancet 340:223–225.

Anonymous. 1856. Thrilling Stories of the Forest and Frontier. By An Old Hunter. Philadelphia: H. C. Peck and Theo. Bliss. 295 pp.

Anonymous. 1866?. Cassell's Popular Natural History. Volume 4. London: Cassell, Petter, & Galpin, La Belle Sauvage Yard, Ludgate Hill, E. C.

Anonymous. 1903. Official Handbook. Description of the Philippines. Part 1. Compiled in the Bureau of Insular Affairs, War Department, Washington, DC. Manila: Bureau of Public Printing.

Anonymous. 1924. Boa constrictor vs. Alligator. J. Bombay Nat. Hist. Soc., 30: 704.

Anonymous. 1930. Annual Report of the Director to the Board of Trustees For the Year 1929. Field Museum of Natural History Report Series, Publication 271.

Anonymous. 1933. Reptilian leather. Industrial Bulletin of Arthur D. Little, Inc. (81):1–4

Anonymous. 1938?. Vagabondage through the United States of Brazil. by Sinbad - the Vagabond Sailor. [typescript in K. P. Schmidt Library]

Anonymous. 1980. S. African army plans snake attack. UPI, Chicago Tribune, 15 August 1980.

Anonymous. 1981. Man stabs python to death. Daily Times (Malawi), 10 March 1981. Reprinted in the J. Herpetol. Assoc. Africa 1981(25):15. [see Haacke, 1981]

Anonymous. 1983. Python crushes owner to death. AP, Chicago Sun-Times, 28 April 1983.

Anonymous. 1984. Snake kills infant; tragedy continues. Chicago Tribune, 28 August 1984.

Anonymous. 1986. A 25-foot python swallowed African toddler. Weekly World News, 11 February 1986.

Anonymous. 1988. World's largest python in Nicobar. *News Today,* December 27, 1988. Reprinted in Hamadryad 13(2):9.

Anonymous. 1992. Farm worker battles python and wins. Joliet Herald News/ AP, September 18, 1992.

Anonymous. 1995. Pythons are endowed with strong senses. New Straits Times, September 6, 1995.

Anonymous. 1996. Pet snake suffocates owner. Milwaukee Journal Sentinel, October 11, 1996.

Arnold, S. J. 1993. Foraging theory and prey-size-predator-size relations in snakes. Pages 87–115. In: Snakes: Ecology and Behavior, R. A. Seigel and J. T. Collins (eds.). New York: McGraw-Hill.

Auerbach, R. D. 1987. The Amphibians and Reptiles of Botswana. Mokwepa Consultants.

Auffenberg, W. 1981. The Behavioral Ecol-

ogy of the Komodo Monitor. Gainesville: Univ. of Florida Press, 406 pp.

Auffenberg, W. 1994. The Bengal Monitor.
Gainesville: Univ. Press of Florida, 560
pp.

Aymar, B. (ed.) 1945. Treasury of Snake
Lore. New York: Greenberg.

Bacon, P. R. 1978. Flora and Fauna of the
Caribbean. Port of Spain: Key Publications. 319 pp.

Bancroft, E. 1769 (1971 reprint). An Essay
on the Natural History of Guiana. New
York: Aron Press and The New York
Times. 402 pp.

Barbour, T. 1926. Reptiles and Amphibians:
Their Habits and Adaptations. Boston:
Houghton Mifflin, 129 pp.

Barker, D. G. and T. M. Barker. 1994.
Pythons of the World, Vol. 1, Australia.
Lakeside, California: The Herpetocul-
ture Library, Advanced Vivarium Systems. 171 pp.

Barker, D. G., J. B. Murphy, and K. W.
Smith. 1979. Social behavior in a captive
group of Indian pythons, *Python molurus* (Serpentes, Boidae) with formation
of a linear social hierarchy. Copeia
(3):466–471.

Barnett, 1993. The amethystine python
(*Morelia amethystina*). Captive keeping,
reproduction and growth. Monitor,
Bull. Victoria Herpetol. Soc. 4(3):77–
128.

Barrett, R. 1970. The pit organs of snakes.
Pages 277–300. In: Biology of the Reptilia, Volume 2, Morphology B. C. Gans,
and T. S. Parsons (eds.). New York: Aca-
demic Press.

Barrie, J. 1990. Skull elements and additional remains of the Pliestocene boid
snake *Wonambi naracoortensis*. Mem.
Qd. Mus. 28(1):139–151.

Barry, D. 1992. Notes on Western Civilization: Toilet-snake case winds its way
through courts. Chicago Tribune Magazine. 1992:41–42.

Barry, D. 1995. Beware of flying reptiles.
Chicago Tribune Magazine. 17 Decem-
ber:36

Barton, A. J. and W. B. Allen, Jr. 1961. Observations of the feeding, shedding and
growth of captive snakes (Boidae). Zoologica, 46(2):83–87.

Bates, H. W. 1863. The Naturalist on the
River Amazons. London: J. Murray.

Beccari, O. 1904. Wanderings in the Great
Forests of Borneo: Travels and Researches
of a Naturalist in Sarawak. Translated by
E. H. Giglioli and revised and edited by F.
H. H. Guillemard. London: Archibald
Constable.

Bechtel, B. 1995. Reptile and Amphibian
Variants Color, Patterns, and Scales.
Malabar, Florida: Krieger. 206 pp.

Beebe, W. 1946. Field notes on the snakes
of Kartabo, British Guiana, and Carip-
ito, Venezuela. Zoologica, 31 (part 1):
11–52.

Begbie, A. 1907. The food of the pythons.
J. Bombay Nat. Hist. Soc. 17:1021.

Belluomini, H. E., A. F. Maranhào Nina,
and A. R. Hoge. 1959 [1960]. Con-
tribuiçào a biologia de gênero *Eunectes*
Wagler, 1830 (Serp. Boidae). Mem. Inst.
Butantan 29:165–174.

Belluomini H. E. and A. R. Hoge. 1958.
Operaçào cesariana realizada em *Eunectes murinus* (Linnaeus 1758) (Serpentes). Mem. Inst. Butantan 28:187–
194.

Belluomini H. E. and T. Veinert. 1967.
Notes on breeding anacondas, *Eunestes
murinus*, at São Paulo Zoo. Internat.
Zoo Yearbook, 7:181–182.

Belluomini, H. E., T. Veinert., F. Dissmann,
A. R. Hoge, and A. M. Penha. 1977. No-
tas biológicas a respeito de gênero *Eunectes* Wagler, 1830 "Sucuris." [Ser-
pentes: Boinae]. Mem. Inst. Butantan
40–41:79–115.

Benedict, F. C. 1932. The physiology of
large reptiles with special reference to
heat production of snakes, tortoises.
lizards and alligators. Washington,
D.C.: Carnegie Institute.

Berglund, A.-I. 1989. Zulu Thought-Pat-
terns and Symbolism. Bloomington: Indiana University Press. 402 pp.

Bhupathy, S. and M. N. Haque. 1985. Association of rock python (*Python molurus*) with porcupine (*Hystrix indica*). J.
Bombay Nat. Hist. Soc. 83:449–450.

Bhupathy, S. and V. S. Vijayan. 1989. Status, distribution and general ecology of
the Indian python, *Python molurus
molurus* Linn. in Keoladeo National

Park, Bharatpur, Rajasthan. J. Bombay Nat. Hist. Soc. 86:381–387.

Black, C. P., G. F. Birchard, G. W. Schuett, and V. D. Black. 1983. Influence of incubation water content on oxygen uptake in embryos of the Burmese python (*Python molurus bivittatus*). Pages 137–145. *In*: Respiration and Metabolism of Embryonic Vertebrates, R. S. Seymour (ed.). Dordrecht: Dr. W. Junk Publishers.

Blasiola, G. C., P. Morales, and J. Simmons. 1982. Intestinal obstruction in an anaconda, *Eunectes murinus,* caused by the ingestion of plastic plants. Drum and Croaker 20(2):10–14.

Blomberg, R. 1956. Giant snake hunt. Nat. Hist. 65:92–97.

Boos, H. E. A. 1979. Some breeding records of Australian pythons. Internatl. Zoo Yrbk., 19:87–89.

Bosman, W. 1705. A New and Accurate Description of the Coast of Guinea Divided into the Gold, the Slave, and the Ivory Coasts. London: Ballantyne and Co., Ltd., Pages 368–385.

Boulenger, E. G. (n.d.) Reptiles and Batrachians. New York: E. P. Dutton.

Bourke, J. G. 1884 [1984 reprint]. The Snake-Dance of the Moquis of Arizona. Tucson: The University of Arizona Press.

Branch, W. R. 1984. Pythons and people: predators and prey. African Wildlife, 38(6):236–237, 240–241.

Branch, W. R. 1988a. Field Guide to the Snakes and Other Reptiles of Southern Africa. Sanibel Island: Ralph Curtus Books. 328 pp.

Branch, W. R. 1988b. South African Red Data Book - Reptiles and Amphibians. South African Natl. Sci. Prog., Report No. 151.

Branch, W. R. and H. Erasmus. 1984. Captive breeding of pythons in South Africa, including details of an interspecific hybrid (*Python sebae natalensis* x *Python molurus bivittatus*). J. Herpetol. Assoc. Africa, 1984 (30):1–10.

Branch, W. R. and W. D. Hacke. 1980. A fatal attack on a young boy by an African rock python, *Python sebae*. J. Herpetol. 14(3):305–307.

Branch, B. and R. Patterson. 1974. Notes on the development of embryos of the African rock python, *Python sebae*, (Serpentes: Boidae). J. Herpetol. Assoc. Africa. (12):26–30.

Broadley, D. G. 1959. The herpetology of southern Rhodesia. Part 1. Snakes. Bull. Mus. Comp. Zool., 120(1):1–100.

Broadley, D. G. 1983. FitzSimons' Snakes of Southern Africa. Johannesburg: Delta Books. pp 376.

Broadley, D. G. 1984. A review of geographical variation in the African python, *Python sebae* (Gmelin). British J. Herpetol., 6(10):359–367.

Broderip, W. J. 1826. Some account of the mode in which the Boa constrictor takes its prey, and of the adaptation of its organization to its habits. Zool. J. London, 2:215–221.

Brown, C. B. 1876. Canoe and Camp Life in British Guiana. London: Edward Stanford.

Bruton, M. N. and W. D. Haacke. 1980. The reptiles of Maputaland. Pages 251–285. *In*: Studies on the Ecology of Maputaland (eds. M. N. Bruton and K. H. Cooper) Rhodes Univ. and The Natal Branch of the Wildl. Soc. of Southern Africa, Grahamstown and Durbin.

Buck, F. 1932. Wild Cargo. New York: Simon & Schuster.

Buck, F. 1935. Fang and Claw. New York: Simon & Schuster.

Buck, F. 1939. Animals are Like That. New York: R. M. McBride and Co.

Bullock, T. H. and R. Barrett. 1968. Radiant heat reception in snakes. Commun. Behav. Biol., Pt. A, 1:19–29.

Burdett, A. F. 1971. Observations of captive pythons (*P. sebae*) in Malawi over a three year period. J. Herpetol. Assoc. Africa, 1971(8):11–15.

Burton, R. F. 1864. A Mission to Gelele, King of Dohome. London: Tinsley Brothers.

Burton, R. F. 1869. The Highlands of Brazil. London: Tinsley Brothers.

Campbell, J. 1988. The Power of Myth with Bill Moyers. New York: Doubleday.

Campden-Main, S. M. 1970. A field guide to the snakes of South Vietnam. Div.

Amphib. Rept., U. S. Nat'l. Mus., Smithsonian Inst., Washington, DC.

Cansdale, G. S. 1961. West African Snakes. West African Nature Handbooks. Longmans.

Cantor, T. 1847. Catalogue of Reptiles Inhabiting the Malayan Peninsula and Islands, Collected or Observed. Calcutta: J. Thomas at the Baptist Mission Press.

Caras, R. A. 1975. Dangerous to Man. London: Barrie and Jenkins. Chilton Books.

Cardinall, A. W. 1927. In Ashanti and Beyond. London: Seeley, Service and Company, Ltd.

Castiglioni, A. 1942. The serpent as a healing god in antiquity. Ciba Symposia 3(12):1158–1167.

Cesaresco, E. M. 1909. The Place of Animals in Human Thought. London, 376 pp.

Channer, O. 1895. The food by *Python molurus*. J. Bombay Nat. Hist. Soc. 9:491

Charles, N., R. Field and R. Shine. 1985. Notes on the reproductive biology of Australian pythons, genera *Aspidites, Liasis* and *Morelia*. Herpetol. Rev. 16(2):45–47.

Chiszar, D., H. M. Smith, A. Petkus and J. Dougherty. 1993. A fatal attack on a teenage boy by a captive Burmese python (*Python molurus bivittatus*) in Colorado. Bull. Chicago Herpetol. Soc. 28(12):261–262.

Clark, B. 1996. Python color and pattern morphs. Reptiles, Guide to Keeping Reptiles and Amphibians 4(3):56–67.

Clark, L. 1953. The Rivers Ran East. New York: Funk and Wagnalls. 366 pages.

Coborn, J. 1975. Report on the reproduction of captive Indian pythons (*Python molurus bivittatus*). British J. Herpetol. 5(4):471–472.

Cogger, H. 1975. Reptiles and Amphibians of Australia. Sydney: A. H. & A. W. Reed. 584 pp.

Comrie-Greig, J. 1984. How the rock python became protected in Natal. African Wildl., 38(6):237.

Conant, R. 1975. A Field Guide to Reptiles and Amphibians of Eastern and Central North America. Boston: Houghton Mifflin. 429 pp.

Cox, M. J. 1991. The Snakes of Thailand and Their Husbandry. Malabar, Florida: Krieger Publishing. 526 pp.

D'Abreu, E. A. 1917. Pythons breeding in captivity. J. Bombay Nat. Hist. Soc. 25: 509–510.

Dammerman, K. W. 1948. The fauna of Krakatau, 1883–1933. Verhand. der Koninkijke Nederland. Akad. Van Wetenschappen, Afd. 44:212, 348–9.

Davis, R. 1974. Not quite striking distance. The Evansville Courier (Indiana) Oct. 3, 1974.

Deoras, P. J. 1965. Snakes of India. New Delhi: National Book Trust. pages 97–99.

Deraniyagala, P. E. P. 1955. A Colored Atlas of Some Vertebrates From Ceylon. Volume 3. Serpentoid Reptilia. Colombo: Government Press. 121 pp.

de Rooij, N. 1917. The Reptiles of the Indo-Australian Archipelago. II. Ophidia. Leiden: E. J. Brill.

Deschanel, J. P. 1978. Reproduction of anacondas, *Eunectes murinus* at Lyons Zoo. Internatl. Zoo Yrbk. 18:98–99.

de Silva, A. 1990. Colour Guide to the Snakes of Sri Lanka. Avon, Portishead: R & A Publ.

de Vega, G. la. 1966. Royal Commentaries of the Incas and General History of Peru. Part 1. Translated by H. V. Livermore. Austin: Univ. of Texas Press.

de Vosjoli, P. 1993. In support of the keeping of boas and pythons by the private sector. Vivarium, 4(4):34–45

Deyang, L. 1986. *Python molurus bivittatus* occurred in Qingchuan County of Sichuan Province. Acta Herpetol. Sinica, 5(3):198.

Dhungel, S. K. 1983. Ordeal with a rock python. Tiger Paper, 10(2):7–8.

Diamond, J. 1987. Did Komodo dragons evolve to eat pygmy elephants? Nature 326:832.

Diamond, J. 1994. Dining with the snakes. Discover (April):50–59.

Dickey, H. S. 1932. My Jungle Book. Boston: Little Brown.

Diefenbach, C. O. and S. G. Emslie. 1971. Cues influencing the direction of prey ingestion of the Japanese snake, *Elaphe climacophora* (Colubridae, Serpentes). Herpetologica 27(4):461–466.

Dinardo, J. R. 1993. Letter to Editors: The Tympanum. Bull. Chicago Herpetol. Soc. 28(12):275–276.

Ditmars, R. L. 1931. Snakes of the World. New York: Macmillian. 208 pp.

Ditmars, R. L. and W. Bridges. 1935. Snake-hunters Holiday. New York: D. Appelton Century Co. 309 pp.

Doucet, J. 1963. Les serpentes de la République de Côte d'Ivoire. Acta Tropica, 20 (3–4):225–228.

Dowling, H. 1960. Thermistors, air conditioners, and insecticides. Animal Kingdom 63:202–207.

Duncan, J. 1847. Travels in Western Africa in 1845 and 1846. Comprising a journey from Whydah, through the kingdom of Dahomey to Adofoodia in the interior. London: Richard Bentley. 2 Vols.

Dunn, E. R. 1944. Los generos de anfibios y reptiles de Colombia, III Tercera Parte: Reptiles; orden de las serpientes, Caldasia, 3(12):155–224.

Dunn R. W. 1979. Breeding African pythons, *Python sebae*, at Melbourne Zoo. Internat. Zoo Yearbk 19:91–92.

Dyott, D. M. 1929. Man Hunting in the Jungle. New York: Blue Ribbon Books.

Eig, J. 1990. Python attacks worker. The Dallas Morning News, July 24:21A-2A.

Ellis, A. B. 1890. The Ewe-speaking Peoples of the Slave Coast of West Africa. London: Chapman and Hall.

Emmanuel, T. and R. Sittamparam. 1995. Tapper killed and partly swallowed by giant python. New Straits Times, September 6, 1995.

Emmons, L. H. and F. Feer. 1990. Neotropical Rainforest Mammals, A Field Guide. Chicago: Univ. Chicago Press.

Fawcett, P. H. 1953. Exploration Fawcett. London: Hutchinson.

Fife-Cookson, J. C. 1887. Tiger-shooting in the Doon and Ulwar with Life in India. London: Chapman and Hall.

FitzSimons, F. W. 1930. Pythons and Their Ways. London: George G. Harrap, & Co. Ltd. 155 pages.

FitzSimons, F. W. 1932. The Snakes of South Africa: Their Venom, and the Treatment of Snake Bite. Cape Town: T. Maskew Miller.

Fitzsimons, V. 1953. Length of anacondas. African Wildl. 7:346–347.

Flower, S. S. 1899. Notes on a second collection of reptiles made in the Malay Peninsula and Siam, from November 1896 to September 1898, with a list of the species recorded from those countries. Proc. Zool. Soc. London, 1899: 600–697.

Forbes, W. A. 1881. Observations on the incubation of the Indian python (*Python molurus*), with special regard to the alleged increase of temperature during this process. Proc. Zool. Soc. London, 1881: 960–967.

Forsyth, W. 1911. Habits of the python, *Python molurus*. J. Bombay Nat. Hist. Soc. 21:277–278.

Fountain, P. 1904. The Great Mountains and Forests of South America. London: Longmans, Green, and Co. 306 pp.

Fountain, P. 1914. The River Amazon From its Sources to the Sea. London: Constable and Co.

Frost, D. R. and D. M. Hillis. 1990. Species in concept and practice: herpetological applications. Herpetologica 46:87–104.

Frye, F. L. 1981. Biomedical and Surgical Aspects of Captive Reptile Husbandry. Edwardsville, Kansas: Veterinary Medicine Publishing Company.

Fuchs, K. 1975. Chemistry and Technology of Novelty Leather. Rome: FAO. 201 pp.

Gardner, G. 1849. Travels in the Interior of Brazil. London: Reeve, Benham and Reeve.

Gasc, J.-P. and M. T. Rodrigues. 1980. Liste préliminaire des serpents de la Guyana française. Bull. Mus. Natl. d'Hist. Nat., Paris, 4e Série, (Zoologie) 2(2):559–598.

Gibbons, W. 1993. Keeping All the Pieces, Perspectives on Natural History and the Environment. Washington, D.C.: Smithsonian Institution Press.

Gilmore, R. M. and J. C. Murphy. 1993. On large anacondas, *Eunectes murinus*

(Serpentes: Boidae), with special reference to the Dunn-Lamon record. Bull. Chicago Herpetol. Soc. 28(9):185–188.

Gilmore, S. H. 1925. Jungle terror: a human struggle in which a boa of the French Guiana bush yields his skin. Asia (April): 296–300, 332–335.

Goodrich, S. G. 1870. Johnson's Natural History, Comprehensive, Scientific, and Popular, Illustrating and Describing The Animal Kingdom With Its Wonders and Curiosities, From Man, Through All The Divisions, Classes, And Orders, To The Animalculae In A Drop Of Water; Showing The Habits, Structure, And Classification Of Animals, With Their Relations To Agriculture, Manufactures, Commerce, And The Arts. Volume 2. New York: A. J. Johnson, Publisher.

Goodyear, N. C. 1994. *Python molurus bivittatus* (Burmese Python). Movements. Herpetol. Rev. 25(2):71–72.

Gosse, P. H. 1850. Natural History, Reptiles. London: Soc. Promoting Christian Knowledge.

Gould, C. 1884 (1992 reprint). Mythical Monsters, Fact or Fiction. London: Studio Editions.

Gow, G. F. 1977. A new species of python from Arnhem Land. Australian Zool., 19(2):133–139.

Gow, G. F. 1989. Graeme Gow's Complete Guide to Australian Snakes. North Ryde: Angus & Robertson Publishers. 171 pp.

Greene, H. W. 1992. The ecological and behavioral context for pitviper evolution. Pages 107–118. In: Biology of the Pitvipers, J. A. Campbell and E. D. Brodie, Jr (eds). Tyler, TX: Selva.

Greene, H. W. and M. A. Santana. 1983. Field studies of hunting behavior by bushmasters. Amer. Zool., 23:879.

Greenwell, R. 1993. Big snake stories. BBC Wildlife, April, pp. 63–64.

Groombridge, B. and R. Luxmoore. 1991. Pythons in South-East Asia: A Review of Distribution, Status and Trade in Three Selected Species. Lausanne: Secretariat of CITES. 127 pp.

Groves, J. D. 1980 (1981). Observations and comments on the post-parturtient

behaviour of some tropical boas of the genus *Epicrates*. British J. Herpetol. 6:89–91.

Grow, D., S. Wheeler, and B. Clark. 1988. Reproduction of the amethystine python, *Python amethistinus kinghorni,* at the Oklahoma City Zoo. Internatl. Zoo Yrbk. 27:241–244.

Haacke, W. D. 1981. A possible further incident of a human as prey of the African rock python (*Python sebae*). J. Herpetol. Assoc. Africa (25):15–16.

Haacke, W. D. 1982. 'Boy bites attacking python to death.' J. Herp. Assoc. Africa 1982(28):9–10.

Haacke, W. D. and N. G. H. Jacobsen. 1990. Geographical distribution: *Python sebae natalensis.* J. Herp. Assoc. Africa 1990 (37):56.

Haagner. G. W. 1991. Life history: *Python sebae natalensis,* aquatic behaviour. J. Herp. Assoc. Africa 1991 (39):23–24.

Haagner, G. W. 1992–93. The husbandry and captive propagation of the southern rock python, *Python sebae natalensis.* British Herpetol. Soc. Bull. (42):30–40.

Hagenbeck, C. 1910. Beasts and Men. (an abridged translation by H. S. R. Elliot and A. G. Thacker). London: Longmans, Green, and Co.

Halliday, T. R. and K. Adler (eds.). 1986. The Encyclopedia of Reptiles and Amphibians. New York: Facts on File.

Hambly, W. D. 1931. Serpent worship in Africa. Anthropology Series, Field Museum of Nat. Hist., Publ. 289, Vol. 21(1):1–85.

Hardy, D. L., Sr. 1993. Constricting snakes do not kill prey by suffocation. (Abstract) Program and Abstracts, Combined Meetings of AISH, HL, Annual larval fish Conference, and The American Elasmobranch Society. 27 May-2 June, 1993. Univ. Texas at Austin. Pages 161–162.

Hardy, D. L., Sr. 1994. A re-evaluation of suffocation as the cause of death during constriction by snakes. Herpetol. Rev. 25(2):45–47.

Hartline, P. H. 1971. Physiological basis for detection of sound and vibration in snakes. J. Experimental Biol. 54(2):349–371.

Hartwig, G. 1873? The Tropical World. London. 556 pp. (we have seen a photocopy of pages 616–634 only).

Hay, P. W. and R. W. Martin. 1966. Python predation on Uganda Kob. East African Wildl. J. 4:151–152

Henderson, R. W. 1994. A splendid quintet: the widespread boas of South America. Lore (Milwaukee Public Museum) 44(4):2–9.

Henderson, R. W., T. Waller, P. Micucci, G. Puorto, and R. W. Bourgeois. 1995. Ecological correlates and patterns in the distribution of neotropical boines (Serpentes: Boidae): a preliminary assessment. Herpetol. Nat. Hist. 3(1):15–27.

Heuvelmans, B. 1958. On the Track of Unknown Animals. New York: Hill and Wang.

Hickey, G. C. 1982. Sons of the Mountains: Ethnohistory of the Vietnamese Central Highlands to 1954. New Haven: Yale University Press.

Hoffstetter, R. 1959. Un dentaire de *Madtsonia* (Serpent géant de Paléocène de Patagonie). Bull. Mus Natn. Hist. Nat. Paris (2ᵉ ser.) 31:379–386.

Holmstrom, W. F. [misspelled Holstrom on publication] 1980. Observations on the reproduction of the common anaconda, *Eunectes murinus* at the New York Zoological Park. Herpetol. Rev. 11(2):32–33

Holmstrom, W. F. and J. L. Behler. 1981. Post-parturient behavior of the common anaconda, *Eunectes murinus*. Zool. Garten, NF 51:353–356.

Hoogerwerf, A. 1970. Udjung Kulon: The Land of the Last Javan Rhinoceros. Leiden: E. J. Brill. 512 pp.

Hopley, C. 1882. Snakes: Curiosities and Wonders of Serpent Life. London: Griffith and Farran

Humboldt, A. von 1885. Personal Narrative of Travels to the Equinoctial Regions of America. During the Years 1799–1804. Translated by T. Ross. Vol. 2.

Hutchison, V. H., H. G. Dowling and A. Vinegar. 1966. Thermoregulation in a brooding female Indian python, *Python molurus bivittatus*. Science 151(3711):694–696.

Irvine, F. R. 1954. Snakes as food for man. Brit. J. Herpetol. 1:183–187.

Isemonger, R. M. 1956. Snakes and Snake Catching in Southern Africa. Cape Town: Howard Timmins.

Jennings, H. 1889 (1980 reprint). Serpent Worship. Toronto: Tutor Press. 131 pages.

Jensen, N. 1980. Python killed after swallowing pointer and her pups. Custos 9(7):18–19, 20, 23.

Joshi, P. N. 1967. Reproduction of *Python sebae*. British J. Herpetol. 3(7):310–311.

Juan, G. and A. de Ulloa. 1758. A Voyage to South America. London: John Stockdale [Translated 1807 by John Adams.]

Karsten, R. 1926. The Civilization of the South American Indians. New York: Alfred Knopf.

Keays, R. W. 1930. An unpleasant experience with a python. J. Bombay Nat. Hist. Soc. 33:721–722.

Kingsley, C. 1890. At Last: a Christmas in the West Indies. New York: Macmillan, 334 pp.

Kingsley, M. H. 1897. Travels in West Africa. New York: Macmillan.

Kluge, A. G. 1990. Species as historical individuals. Biology and Philosophy 5:49–63

Kluge, A. G. 1991. Boine snake phylogeny and research cycles. Misc. Publ. Mus. Zool., Univ. Michigan (178):1–58.

Kluge, A. G. 1993. *Aspidites* and the phylogeny of pythonine snakes. Records of the Australian Mus., Supplement 19:1–77.

Kopstein, F. 1927. Over het verslinden van menschen door *Python reticulatus*. Overdruk uit De Trop. Natuur 1927(4):65–67.

Kopstein, F. 1938. Ein Beitrag zur Eierkunde und zur Fortpflanzung der Malaiischen Reptilien. Bulletin of the Raffles Museum, Singapore, Straits Settlements, 14:81–167. [English summary].

LaBarre, W. 1969. They Shall Take Up Serpents. New York: Schocken Books.

La Gironiere, P. P. De. 1853? Twenty Years in the Philippines. London: James Vizetelly and Henry Vizetelly.

Lange, A. 1912. In the Amazon Jungle. New York: G. P. Putnam's Sons.

Lange, A. 1914. The Lower Amazon. New York: G. P. Putnam's Sons.

Laurent, R. F. 1956. Contribution a l'Herpetologie da la region des Grands lacs de l'Afrique centrale. III. Ophidiens. Ann. Mus. Royal Congo Belge, Tervuren (Belgique) Ser. 8, Vol. 48:85.

Lederer, G. 1942. Fortpflanzung und Entwicklung von *Eunectes notaeus* Cope (Boidae). Zool. Anz. 139(9–10):162–176.

Lederer, G. 1944. Nahrungserwerb, Entwicklung, Paarung und Brutfurosorge von *Python reticulatus* (Schneider). Zool. Jahrbuch. (Anatomie) (Jena), 68: 363–398.

Leigh, C. 1951. Egg-laying by a python in captivity. J. Bombay Nat. Hist. Soc. 50:183.

Lillywhite, H. B. 1988. Snakes, blood circulation, and gravity. Sci. Amer. (Dec.): 92–98.

Lim, K. K. P. and F. L. K. Lim. 1992. A Guide to the Amphibians and Reptiles of Singapore. Singapore: Singapore Sci. Centre. 160 pp.

Lloyd, D. J., A. F. R. Cotton, H. W. Parker, and D. Prain. 1933. The Collection of Reptile Skins for Commercial Purposes With Respect to the Possibilities in Empire Countries. London: Imperial Institute.

Loop, M. S. and L. G. Bailey. 1972. The effect of relative prey size on the ingestion behavior of rodent-eating snakes. Psychon. Sci. 28:167–169.

Lopez C., G. 1984. Fauna Legendaria. Caracas: Editorial Arte.

Loveridge, A. 1929. Blind snakes and pythons of East Africa. Bull. Antivenin Inst. America 3(1):14–19.

Loveridge. 1931. On two amphibious snakes of the Central African lake region. Bull. Antivenin Inst. America 5(1):7–12.

Loveridge, A. 1947. Tomorrow's a Holiday. New York: Harper & Bros.

Loveridge, A. 1953. I Drank the Zambezi. New York: Harper & Bros.

Low, T. 1989. Python on the prowl. Australian Nat. Hist. 23(1):61–65.

Luxmoore, R., B. Groombridge and S. Broad. 1988. Significant Trade in Wildlife: a Review of Selected Species in CITES Appendix II. Volume 2: Reptiles and Invertebrates. IUCN, Gland, Switzerland. 306 pp.

Madsen, T. and R. Shine. 1996. Seasonal migration of predators and prey—a study of pythons and rats in tropical Australia. Ecology 77(1):149–156.

Martin, R. W. 1995. Field observation of predation on Bennett's tree-kangaroo (*Dendrolagus bennettianus*) by an amethystine python (*Morelia amethistina*). Herpetol. Rev. 26(2):74–76.

Mash, P. 1945. Indian python (*Python molurus*) preying on monitor lizard (*Varanus monitor*). J. Bombay Nat. Hist. Soc. 45:249–250.

Mattison, C. 1995. The Encyclopedia of Snakes. New York: Facts On File. 256 pp.

Mayer, C. 1920. Recruiting for the menagerie. Asia 1920:849–854.

McArthur, A. G. 1922. A python's long fast. J. Bombay Nat. Hist. Soc. 28: 1142–1143.

McCarty, V. O., R. A. Cox, and B. Haglund. 1989. Death caused by a constricting snake-an infant death. J. Forensic Sci. 34(1):239–243.

McDowell, S. B. 1975. A catalogue of the snakes of New Guinea and the Solomons, with special reference to those in the Bernice P. Bishop Museum. Part 2. Anilioidae and Pythoninae. J. Herpetol. 9(1):1–80.

McFalran, D. (ed.) 1991. The Guiness Book of World Records 1991. New York: Bantam Books.

McLees, F. 1928. Killing by constriction. Bull. Antivenein Inst. America, 1(4):105.

Medem, F. 1981. Los Crocodylia de Sur America. Vol. 1. Los Crocodylia de Colombia. Minstero de Educat. Nac., Bogota. 354 pp.

Mell, R. 1922. Beiträge zur Fauna Sinica. 1. Die Vertrbraten Südchinas: Feldisten und Feldnoten der Säuger, Vögel, Reptilien, Batrachier. Arch. Naturgesch, Berlin. ser. A, 88(1):1–134.

Michaels, S. 1970. Anacondas. Bull. Chicago Herpetol. Soc. 5(2):31–33.

Miller, T. and H. M. Smith. 1979. The lesser African rock python. Bull. Maryland Herp. Society 15:70–84.

Minton, S. A. 1966. A contribution to the herpetology of West Pakistan. Bulletin of the American Museum of Natural History 134:29–184.

Minton, S. A. and M. R. Minton. 1973. Giant Reptiles. New York: Charles Scribner's Sons, 345 pp.

Mitchell, P. C. and R. I. Pocock, 1907. On the feeding of reptiles in captivity. With observations on the fears of snakes by other vertebrates. Proc. Zool. Soc. of London 1907: 758–794.

Mjöberg, E. 1930. Forest Life and Adventures in the Malay Archipelago. London: George Allen & Unwin Ltd. [Translated by A. Barwell.]

M'Leod, J. 1818. Voyage of His Majesty's Ship Alceste, Along the Coast of Corea to the Island of Lewchew; Account of Her Subsequent Shipwreck. London: John Murray.

Mole, R. R. 1924. The Trinidad snakes. Proc. Zool. Soc. London, 1924:235–278.

Mole, R. R. and F. W. Urich. 1894. Biological notes upon some of the ophidia of Trinidad, B. W. I., with a preliminary list of the species recorded from the island. Proc. Zool. Soc. London, 1894:499–518.

Montgomery, G. G. and A. S. Rand. 1978. Movements, body temperature and hunting strategy of a boa constrictor. Copeia 1978:532–533.

Mookerjee, S. 1946. Mango-fruit - on the menu of the common python (*Python molurus*). J. Bombay Nat. Hist. Soc. 46:733.

Morris, R. and D. Morris. 1965. Men and Snakes. New York: McGraw-Hill. 223 pp.

Mozans, H. J. 1910. Up the Orinoco and Down the Magdalena. New York: D. Appelton and Co.

Mthembu, P. 1982. I killed a huge, deadly snake - with my teeth. Natl. Enquirer, 1982.

Murphy, J. C., H. K. Voris, and D. R. Karns. 1994. A field guide and key to the snakes of the Danum Valley, a Bornean tropical forest ecosystem. Bull. Chicago Herpetol. Soc. 29(7):133–151.

Muthusamy, E. and P. Gopalakrishnakone. 1990. Python bites—case reports. The Snake 22:113–119.

Neill, W. T. and R. Allen. 1956. Secondarily ingested food items in snakes. Herpetologica 12(3):172–174.

Neill, W. T. and E. R. Allen. 1962. Parturient anaconda, *Eunectes gigas* Latreille, eating own abortive eggs and foetal membranes. Florida Academy Sciences Quarterly Journal 25:73–75.

Newman, A. C. 1963. Some African folklore regarding snakes. J. Herpetol. Assoc. Rhodesia 1963 (20):11–13.

Oliver, J. A. 1958. Snakes in fact and fiction. New York: The Macmillan.

O'Shea, M. T. 1994. *Eunectes murinus gigas*. (Northern Green Anaconda). Cannibalism. Herp. Rev. 25(3):124.

O'Shea, M. T. 1996. A Guide to the Snakes of Papua New Guinea. Port Moresby: Independent Publ.

Parker, H. W. and A. G. C. Grandison. 1977. Snakes—A Natural History. London/Ithaca: British Museum (Natural History) and Cornell University Press.

Patterson, R. W. 1974. Hatching the African Python, *Python sebae*, in captivity. Internat. Zoo Yearbk. 14:81–82.

Perry, R. 1970. The World of the Jaguar. New York: Taplinger Publishing Co. 168 pp.

Petzold, H. G. 1983. Die Anakondas. A. Ziemsen Verlag, Wittenberg Lutherstadt. 142 pp.

Phipson, H. M. 1887. Observations on the feeding et cetera, of the Indian rock snake (*Python molurus*) kept in the Society's rooms. J. Bombay Nat. Hist. Soc. 2:165–167.

Pienaar, U. de V. 1966. The reptile fauna of the Kruger National Park. Koedoe (1):1–223.

Pitman, C. R. S. 1938. A Guide to the Snakes of Uganda. Kampala: Uganda Society. 1.

Pitman, C. R. S. 1974. A Guide to the Snakes of Uganda. Revised Edition. Codicote: Wheldon and Wesley, Ltd.

Pliny, The Elder. The Antipathy of the elephant and the serpent. Page 73, In: Treasury of Snake Lore, B. Aymar (ed.), 1956. New York: Greenberg Publ.

Pope, C. H. 1935. Natural History of Central Asia. Vol. X. The Reptiles of China. New York: Amer. Mus. Nat. Hist.

Pope, C. H. 1955. The Reptile World. New York: Alfred Knopf. 325 pp.

Pope, C. H. 1961. The Giant Snakes. New York: Alfred Knopf. 290 pp.

Porter, B. W. 1988. Life history notes: *Python sebae natalensis*, African rock python, reproduction. J. Herp. Assoc. Africa 34:44.

Pritchard, P. C. H. 1994. Letter to Editors: The Tympanum. Bull. Chicago Herpetol. Soc. 29(2):37–39.

Pritchard, P. C. H. and P. Trebbau. 1984. The Turtles of Venezuela. Soc. Study Amphib. Rept., Ithaca, New York. Contrib. Herpetol. 2.

Pycraft, W. P. 1905. The Story of Reptile Life. London: George Newnes, Ltd.

Quelch, J. J. 1898. The boa constrictors of British Guiana. Ann. Mag. Nat. Hist. Series 7, 1:296–308.

Rattray, R. S. 1923. Ashanti. Oxford: At the Claredon Press.

Raven, H. C. 1946. Adventures in python country. Natural History 55:38–41

Reitinger, F. 1978. Common Snakes of South East Asia and Hong Kong. Hong Kong: Heinemann. 114 pp.

Richardson, M. 1972. The Fascination of Reptiles. New York: Hill and Wang.

Riches, F. C. 1930. Capturing monitor lizards and pythons. J. Bombay Nat. Hist. Soc. 34:828–829.

Ridley, H. N. 1899. The habits of Malay reptiles. Journal of the Straits Branch of the Royal Asiatic Soc. 32:185–210.

Roosevelt, K. 1923. Foreward. pp. xiv–xv, In: F. W. Up de Graff, 1923. Head Hunters of the Amazon. Garden City, New York: Garden City Publishers.

Roosevelt, T. 1914. Through the Brazilian Wilderness. New York: Charles Scribner's Sons. 409 pages.

Root, J and A. Root. 1971. Mzima, Kenya's spring of life. Natl. Geog., 140(3):350–373.

Rose, W. 1955. Snakes, Mainly South African. Cape Town: Maskew Miller Limited.

Rose, W. 1962. The Reptiles and Amphibians of Southern Africa. Cape Town: Maskew Miller. 494 pp.

Ross, R. A. and G. Marzec. 1990. The Reproductive Husbandry of Pythons and Boas. Instit. Herpetol. Res., Stanford, CA. 270 pp.

Roth, W. E. 1915. An inquiry into the animism and folk-lore of the Guiana Indians. 30th Annual Report of the Bureau of the American Ethnology 1908–1909 (1915):143–144.

Saint Girons, H. 1972. Les serpents du Cambodge. Mém. Mus. Nat. d'Hist. Nat., Paris. Nouv. Ser., Ser. A. Zool. 74:1–170.

Savage, T. S. 1842. Observations on the habits of the *Python natalensis*. Boston J. Nat. Hist. 4:242–246.

Savage-Landor, A. H. 1913. Across Unknown South America. Boston: Little Brown and Co. Vol. II.

Schenkel, R. 1990. Rhinoceroses. In: Grizimek's Encyclopedia of Mammals, S. P. Parker (ed.) 4:610–617. New York: McGraw-Hill.

Schmidt, K. P. 1924. Herpetology of the Belgium Congo. Bull. American Mus. Nat. Hist. 49:1–444.

Schomburgk, R. H. 1922. Travels in British Guiana, 1840–1844. Translated and edited by W. E. Roth. Georgetown Daily Chronical Office. Vol. 1.

Schomburgk, R. H. 1931. Robert Hermann Schomburgk's Travels in Guiana and on the Orinoco. During the years 1835–1839. Edited by O. A. Schomburgk. Georgetown, British Guiana: The Argosy Co., Ltd. 202 pages.

Sclater, P. L. 1862. Notes on the incubation of *Python sebae*, as observed in the Society's gardens. Proc. Zool. Soc. London 1862:365–368.

Shelford, R. W. 1917 (1985 reprint). A Naturalist in Borneo. Singapore: Oxford University Press.

Shine, R. 1988. Parental care in reptiles. Pages 275–329. In: Biology of the Reptilia Vol. 16, Ecology B, Defense and Life History, C. Gans and R. B. Huey (eds.) New York: Alan R. Liss.

Shine, R. 1991. Australian Snakes, A Natural History. Ithaca, New York: Cornell Univ. Press. 223 pp.

Shine, R. 1993. Sexual dimorphism in snakes, pp. 49–86. In R. A. Seigel and J. T. Collins (eds.), Snakes: Ecology and Behavior. New York: McGraw-Hill.

Shine, R. and D. Slip. 1990. Biological aspects of the adaptive radiation of Australasian pythons (Serpentes: Boidae). Herpetologica 46(3):283–290.

Singh, A. N. 1983. A study of diverse prey species of python (Python molurus) with special reference to its interaction with jackal (Canis aurius). Tiger Paper 10(3):31–32.

Skeat, W. W. 1900. Malayan Magic. New York: Macmillian.

Slip, D. J. and R. Shine. 1988. Feeding habits of the Diamond Python, Morelia s. spilota: ambush predation by a boid snake. J. Herpetol. 22(3):323–330.

Smith, L. A. 1981. A revision of the Liasis olivaceus species-group (Serpetnes: Boidae) in Western Australia. Records of the Western Australian Museum 9(2):227–233.

Smith, M. A. 1914. The snakes of Bangkok. Jour. Natural History Soc. of Siam 1(1):5–18.

Smith, M. A. 1943. The Fauna of British India, Ceylon and Burma Including the Whole Indo-Chinese Sub-Region. Reptilia and Amphibia. Vol. III. Serpentes. London: Taylor and Francis. 583 pp.

Smith, M. J. 1985. Wonambi naracoortensis The Giant Australian Python. Pages 156–159. In: Kadimakara Extinct Vertebrates of Australia P. V. Rich and G. F. van Tets (eds.). Princeton: Princeton University Press.

Somander, S. V. O. 1941. The Ceylon Python. Loris, 2(5):283–285.

Spawls, S. and B. Branch. 1995. The Dangerous Snakes of Africa. Sanibel Island, FL: Ralph Curtis Books.

Staedeli, J. H. 1961. Raising a giant snake. Zoonooz, 34(10):4–7.

Starin, E. D. and G. M. Burghardt. 1992. African rock pythons (Python sebae) in The Gambia: observations on natural history and interactions with primates. The Snake, 24(1):50–62.

Steadman, J. G. 1796. Narrative of a Five Year's Expedition Against the Revolted Negroes of Surinam in Guiana on the Wild Coast of South America; From the Years 1772 to 1777. Vol. 1, pages 170–177.

Stemmler-Morath, C. 1956. Beitrag zur Gefangenschafts-und Fortpflanzungsbiologie von Python molurus L. Der Zoologica Garten (Leipzig) 21:347–364.

Stevenson-Hamilton, J. 1947. Animal Life in Africa. New York: E. P. Dutton.

St. John, S. 1863. Life in the Forests of the Far East; Or Travels in Northern Borneo. London: Smith, Elder and Co.

Strimple, P. D. 1993. Overview of the natural history of the green anaconda (Eunectes murinus). Herpetol. Nat. Hist., 1(1):25–35.

Stucki-Stirn, M. 1979. The Snake Report, 721.Teuffenthal, Switzerland: Herpto-Verlag.

Swan, L. W. and A. E. Leviton. 1962. The herpetology of Nepal: a history, check list, and zoogeographical analysis of the herpetofauna. Proc. California Acad. of Sci. Fourth Series. 32(6):103–147.

Sweeney, R. C. H. 1961. Snakes of Nyasaland. The Nyasaland Soc. and the Nyasaland Gov't.

Talbot, P. A. 1967. Some Nigerian Fertility Cults. London: Frank Cass and Company.

Taylor, E. H. 1965. The serpents of Thailand and adjacent waters. University of Kansas Science Bulletin 45(9):609–1096.

Tennent, E. 1861. Sketches of the Natural History of Ceylon . . . London: Longman and Roberts.

Thomas, I. 1985. . . . And a rock python kills a green-spotted dove. African Wildl. 39(6):229.

Thorbjarnarson, J. 1995. Trailing the mythical anaconda. Américas (July/August):38–45.

Tweedie, M. W. F. 1957. The Snakes of Malaya. Singapore: Singapore National Printers.

Up de Graff, F. W. 1923. Head Hunters of the Amazon. Duffield & Co., NY.

Ussher, C. 1979. Brunei's largest snake. The Brunei Museum Journal 4(3):180–181.

Valenciennes, M. 1841. Observations faites

pendant l'incubation d'une femelle du Python a deux raies (*Python bivittatus,* Kuhl) pendant les mois de mai et de juin 1841. Compendus Rendus Acad. Sci. Paris, 13:126–133

Van Mierop, L. H. S. and S. M. Barnard. 1976a. Thermoregulation in a brooding female *Python molurus bivittatus* (Serpentes: Boidae). Copeia, 1976(2):398–401.

Van Mierop, L. H. S. and S. M. Barnard. 1976b. Observations on the reproduction of *Python molurus bivittatus* (Reptilia, Serpentes, Boidae). J. Herpetol. 10(4):333–340.

Van Mierop, L. H. S. and S. M. Barnard. 1978. Further observations on thermoregulation in the brooding female *Python molurus bivittatus* (Serpentes: Boidae). Copeia, 1978(4):615–621.

Van Rompaey, H. 1985. A rock python with a taste for veal. (letter to editor) African Wildl., 39(6):85.

Vettel, P. 1986. Just when you thought it was safe, a toliet snake! Chicago Tribune, November 16, 1986.

Vinegar, A. 1973. The effects of temperature on the growth and development of embryos of the Indian python, *Python molurus* (Reptilia, Serpentes, Boidae). Copeia, 1973(1):171–173.

Vinegar, A., V. H. Hutchison and H. G. Dowling. 1970. Metabolism, energetics and thermoregulation during brooding of snakes of the genus *Python* (Reptila, Boidae). Zoologica, 55(2):19–48.

Wagner, E. P. 1973. Breeding *Python molurus bivittatus.* HISS News J. 1:112.

Walker, E. P. 1975. Mammals Of The World, third ed., 2 Volumes, Baltimore: Johns Hopkins Univ. Press.

Wall, F. 1912. A popular treatise on the common Indian snakes. Part 17:447–476.

Wall, F. 1921. Snakes of Ceylon. H. R. Cottle, Gov't. Printer, Colombo, Ceylon.

Wall, F. 1926. The reticulated python, *Python reticulatus.* J. Bombay Nat. Hist. Soc. 31:84–90.

Wall, F. and G. H. Evans. 1900. Occurrence of *Python molurus* in Burma. J. Bombay Nat. Hist. Soc. 13:190–191.

Wallace, A. R. 1853. A Narrative of Travels on the Amazon and Rio Negro. London: Reeve & Co.

Wallace, A. R. 1869. The Malay Archipelago, The Land of the Orang-Utan and the Bird of Paradise, A Narative of Travel with Studies of Man and Nature. London: Macmillan.

Walsh, J. 1967. Time is Short and the Water Rises. New York: E. P. Dutton & Co.

Waterton, C. 1909. Wanderings in South America. New York: Sturgis & Walton Co.

Wehekind, L. 1955. Notes on the food of the Trinidad snakes. British J. Herpetol. 2(1955):9–13.

Wells, C. 1923. Six Years in the Malay Jungle. Garden City: Garden City Publishers. 261 pp

Whitaker, R. 1978. Common Indian Snakes, a Field Guide. Bangalore: Macmillan India Ltd. 154 pp.

Whitaker, R. 1993. Population status of the Indian python (*Python molurus*) on the Indian subcontinent. Herpet. Nat. Hist., 1(1):87–89.

Worcester, D. C. 1898. The Philippine Islands and Their People. New York: Macmillian.

Worrell, E. 1963. Reptiles of Australia. Sydney: Angus and Robertson.

Wray, G. O. 1862. Extract of letter communicated to the secretary of the Zoological Society. Proc. Zool. Soc. London. 1862(19):107.

Wucherer, O. 1861. On the ophidians of the Province of Bahia, Brazil. Proc. Zool. Soc. (London), 8:113–114.

Yadav, R. N. 1967. A note on the breeding of Indian pythons, *Python molurus,* at Jaipur Zoo. Int. Zoo Yrbk. 7:182–183.

Zhao, E. and K. Adler. 1993. Herpetology of China. Soc. Study Amphib. Rept., Ithaca, New York. Contrib. to Herpetol. 10.

INDEX

Boldface type designates an illustration.